Be, Become, Bless
Jewish Spirituality between East and West

Yeshivat Otniel

MAGGID

Yakov Nagen

BE,
BECOME,
BLESS

Jewish Spirituality between East and West

Translated by Elie Leshem

Yeshivat Otniel
Maggid Books

Be, Become, Bless
Jewish Spirituality between East and West

First English Edition, 2019

Maggid Books
An imprint of Koren Publishers Jerusalem Ltd.

POB 8531, New Milford, CT 06776-8531,
USA & POB 4044, Jerusalem 9104001, Israel
www.maggidbooks.com

Original Hebrew Edition © Yakov Nagen, 2013

English Edition © Yakov Nagen, 2019

Cover Photo © Lesley Onstott

The publication of this book was made possible
through the generous support of *Torah Education in Israel*.

The publisher apologizes for any errors or omissions in copyright
acknowledgments and permissions referenced in this book and
would be grateful to be notified of any corrections or permissions
that should be incorporated in future reprints or editions.

ISBN 978-1-59264-527-5, *softcover*

A CIP catalogue record for this title is
available from the British Library

Printed and bound in Israel

Lovingly Dedicated to

Hillel and Shira
Noa
Michael
Yonatan
Naama
Yinon
Ayala
Sheva Berakhot each day

Contents

Acknowledgments

Were our mouth as full of song as the sea, and our tongue as full of joyous song as its multitude of waves… we still could not thank You sufficiently, the Lord our God and God of our forefathers.

– Nishmat Kol Ḥai

The roots of this book were instilled in me by my parents, Azriel and Ahuva Genack, including love for all human beings, and a fusion of Torah and faith with intellectual breadth, openness, and curiosity.

A constant partner in this book, as in all of my life, was my wife, Michal. Thanks to her powers of renewal, each and every day together is a new world.

I want to thank my students at Otniel Yeshiva for the ideas that came up during our studies together and enriched this book. Special thanks go to Amichai Chasson, Yedidya Ish Shalom, Netzach Sapir, Yaakov Berger, and Erica Haffetz, to the yeshiva heads, Rabbis Benny Kalmanson and Re'em HaCohen, and to our director Rabbi Ronen Katz, for a beit midrash steeped in the light of Torah and an atmosphere of creativity and freedom.

Be, Become, Bless

I am grateful to the team of talented people at Maggid Books. At every step they gave their input with warmth and dedication, professionalism, and marvelous advice. In particular I thank the publisher Matthew Miller; my dear friend and chairman of the editorial board Rabbi Reuven Ziegler; marketing director Yehudit Singer; managing editor Ita Olesker; assistant editor Shira Finson; and copy editor Nechama Unterman. Elie Leshem, the translator, managed to project exactly the voice for which I had hoped. All of you together turned the process of putting out a book from merely a means to an end, to a partnership of joint creativity and vision.

I am grateful to my dear friends, Shimon and Rachel Laufer and Simon and Rachel Grunbaum, who together with the Targum Shlishi foundation and its director, Aryeh Rubin, supported the publication. Finally, I thank my uncle and aunt, Gary and Ayala Barnett. The support of their foundation has freed me to have the time to write.

This book is an attempt to learn about life, and thus I dedicate it to my children, who are life itself.

Yakov Nagen

Introduction

One of the defining characteristics of our time is the ever-expanding search for spirituality. The more accessible material wealth becomes, the stronger the longing for meaning in life. At the root of the search for spirituality is the sense that there is more to life than what is visible and familiar – a secret that, once discovered, can facilitate a deeper understanding and light up our lives. This search encompasses many sections of society: men and women, religious and secular, young and old. It seems as though the rising thirst for spirituality is part of a broader societal shift, one that emphasizes experience, feeling, and imagination.

Those searching for answers to existential questions within the world of Judaism tend to gravitate toward the esoteric, taking up Kabbala studies in various centers, perusing books on the inner meaning of the Torah, or adopting modern-day Israeli incarnations of Breslov and other hasidic traditions. For me, the search for the secret of life and the face of God is part of a life-long journey, revealing meanings that have become my guiding lights. My contemplation of life draws on the Jewish canon in its broadest sense: Bible and Talmud, Hasidism and Kabbala. I am also greatly indebted to the people I have met along the way, who have enriched my spiritual world in immeasurable ways. Secular sources, Jewish and otherwise – including poetry and literature, music and film – have also informed my studies, along with academic methods. This book is the story of my meeting with these sources. The main challenge in writing it was to strike a balance between an enriching breadth and a depth of focus.

The World Is Within God

When my children were four and six years old, we had a conversation at home about the relationship between God and humanity. Noa returned from daycare and declared that God is in heaven. Hillel replied, "God is everywhere – in the mountains and in the sea and in heaven too. I will explain it to you: Do you see how our house surrounds us and we are inside it? God is like our house." In his succinct and astonishing explanation, my son echoed a profound kabbalistic insight: the world is within God.

Later I discovered that the simile my son chose appears in the ancient kabbalistic work *The Bahir* (1:14): "Why is the letter *bet* closed on all sides and open in the front? This teaches us that it is the house (*bayit*) of the world. God is the place of the world, and the world is not His place."[1]

Kabbala teaches us that God is present in everything: in life, in humanity, and in humanity's relationship with the world and all living creatures. We can begin to approach the realization that our lives are guided by the Great Spirit – the awesome secret of the meaning of God in our lives – through the experience of living. If we open ourselves up to this way of thinking, it will change the basic consciousness mediating our experience of reality. This is true of every human encounter, every vagary of life. It is an insight that teaches us to open our eyes and hearts to the light and goodness in the world and in humanity, to love life and

---

1. Aryeh Kaplan, trans., *The Bahir* (York Beach, MA: Weiser Books, 1979), 6.

consider it a blessing, to understand that there is a principle that unifies everything.

God, in encompassing all, is the source of life for all: God sustains me and you, predator and prey, enemy nations. The primary idea in a growing awareness of God is that He encompasses all and sustains all. We consider black and white to be opposites, but at their source they are one. While this idea appears in many spiritual systems that emphasize the unifying principle of life, Kabbala introduced the idea of encompassment. Even though there are principles that unify all life forms in the world, they do not erode the uniqueness of the expressions that life takes in each and every individual. The "I" is not devalued; it is significant, as is the "you," and as is the entire world with its staggering wealth of variegated life forms. There is significance to every unique expression, and we must find a way to encompass it.

A good example of this principle can be found in the Zohar (*Vayikra* 12b), which notes that the Hebrew word for "peace," "*shalom*," begins with the letter *shin* and ends with the letter *mem*. The *shin*, it explains, represents fire (*esh*), while the *mem* represents water (*mayim*). Peace is the capacity to encompass those binary opposites. Similarly, the Talmud (Yerushalmi Sanhedrin 1a) points out that the word "*emet*," "truth," is composed of three letters: *alef*, the first letter of the Hebrew alphabet; *mem*, which is in the middle; and *tav*, which is last. This observation reflects the idea that truth is not a specific point of view but rather a complex gaze that encompasses everything.

This complexity is readily apparent in the question of Jewish national identity. Judaism is connected to the world, to humanity as a whole, and yet it retains a distinct identity. Its vision of the end of days does not efface national identity and convert all of humanity to Judaism; rather, it establishes a reality in which all peoples coexist in solidarity. The same is true in the life of the individual: my private existence has meaning; I do not efface myself in relation to the world or to God, but rather come to understand them from within my own uniqueness.

Light or Darkness?

One's conception of reality, the manner in which one experiences it, is no less important than reality itself. A reader of my blog once said to me, "What a beautiful world you live in!" His intention, as I understand it, was not to comment on my biography or geographic location. Rather, he understood that a beautiful conception of reality can generate a beautiful life. Put in contemporary terms: our point of view shapes our attitude toward our experiences, eventually becoming an indivisible aspect of reality itself. Everything is in the eye of the beholder. "Everywhere you look, you see nothing but light, while I only see darkness," the author Yosef Haim Brenner was reported to have said to Rabbi Abraham Isaac Kook. One's conception of reality radiates on one's life and experience. My intention with this book is to set out a progression of ideas, a conception of reality, that everyone can embrace. In that regard, this book is a manual for spiritual practice, a volume that, beyond presenting readings of Jewish sources and beautiful ideas, teaches renewal – the capacity to create an ever-regenerating reading of the Torah and of life.

The Weekly *Parasha*: A Renewing Reading

I chose as a structure for this book the *parasha*, the weekly Torah portion, read each week in synagogue. I chose it for two reasons: First, musings on the weekly portion have always served as foundations for new Torah literature, from Midrash to Kabbala, to Hasidism and contemporary thought. In each and every generation, people recognize themselves and their stories in the *parasha*. This is due to the fact that the Torah relates stories taken from life: relationships between men and women, between parents and their children, among friends, and between humanity and God. The *parashot* grapple with the fundamental values of society – morality and justice – and the basic problems facing the individual: injustice and evil, internal and external enemies, and the difficulties of day-to-day life. A second reason is that reading from the Torah is an activity that unites the entire Jewish people, from the believer, who studies it as the word of God, to the secular Jew, who sees the Bible as our origin story. No matter their approach, the meanings unearthed in the *parasha* become embedded in their identities.

This book is a summation of my insights about life, along with a perception of reality and an approach to it. Consequently, it is less a *parasha* book with insights about life and more a book about life that follows the course of the *parashot*.

While writing the book I was surprised to find that the passing weeks revealed hidden threads linking my commentaries, which took on the shape of a spiritual journey of sorts, beginning in the Genesis stories, continuing through slavery in Egypt, the Exodus, and the years in the desert, and culminating at the gates of the Land of Israel. May the fruits of my journey through the *parashot* introduce many readers to miraculous and fascinating paths in their own lives.

Bereshit

To Be or to Do?

It was 1954, decades before hordes of Israelis would flood the Indian subcontinent, when Ezriel Carlebach, the legendary editor of *Maariv*, traveled to India. In a book about his experiences, *India: Account of a Voyage*, Carlebach sums up well the difference between the Western and Eastern mindsets. He quotes a conversation he had with the prime minister of India at the time, Jawaharlal Nehru, who described the cultural divide:

> We mentioned the diplomatic complications, which seem difficult to overcome, and I remarked, "Well, the question is what to do." He gazed at me for a while, and said, "You see? That is a typical question for a European." "How so?" I asked. "Well," he replied, "an Indian would have asked, 'What to be?'"[1]

---

1. Ezriel Carlebach, *India: Account of a Voyage* [Hebrew] (Tel Aviv: Sifriyat Maariv, 1986), 266.

The difference between "doing" and "being," in this intercultural comparison, is the difference between wanting to change reality through action and the capacity to accept reality as is, between orientation toward the future and a recognition of the present. Existentially speaking, it is the difference between defining oneself in relation to the question "What do I do?" and the question "Who am I?"

The Land of Israel is at the crossroads of East and West, a geographical-historical fact that carries profound spiritual implications. Judaism contains ideas that are generally identified with Eastern religions, along with ideas that underpin Western thinking. Judaism's grand spiritual message is, to my mind, the synthesis of these disparate elements, an outlook that unifies "being" and "doing."

Was the World Created Twice?

The distinction between "being" and "doing," and their synthesis, is foreshadowed already in the Creation story. The Torah relates the creation of the world twice: chapter 1 of Genesis divides it into seven days, while the telling in chapter 2 focuses on Man in the Garden. Torah commentators have sought to explain the repetition and the differences between the stories (preeminent among them in recent generations were Rabbi Joseph Soloveitchik in his essay *The Lonely Man of Faith*, and Rabbi Mordechai Breuer in various writings). Some see the dual telling as an expression of the complexity and multifariousness of reality; others as an expression of varying attributes of God's sovereignty over humanity and the world.

I wish to suggest an alternative reading that considers the difference between the stories as an expression of the gap between a life approach of "doing" and a life approach of "being." The terms "being" and "doing" are not extraneous to the Torah – they appear in the text itself. The two principles are among the foundation stones of *Parashat Bereshit*, and the interplay between them is a motif throughout the Torah.

In the first description of Creation, the Torah relates a story of action. Humanity is made in God's image, and its purpose is to rule over the world: "Be fruitful, and multiply, and replenish the earth and subdue it; and have dominion over the fish of the sea, and over the fowl of the air, and over every living thing that creeps upon the earth" (Gen. 1:28). In describing the purpose of Creation, the Torah uses the word "*laasot*," meaning "to *do*" (2:3).

The second story, in contrast, describes an existential experience of "being": humankind is portrayed as living in harmony with nature in the Garden of Eden, and the purpose of its creation is given as "It is not good that the man should *be* alone" (2:18). In the first description, the relationship between Adam and his wife is outward-facing – they are charged with changing reality by being fruitful and multiplying, enjoined to procreate so as to dominate the world. But in the second narrative, the relationship faces inward, and rather than multiply, the male and the female coalesce: "...and [he] shall cleave to his wife, and they shall be one flesh" (2:24). Together, a man and a woman are the answer to human solitude, and being in union is the pinnacle of their relationship.

Reflecting the twin narratives of Creation, expressions of "being" and "doing" pervade Judaism. The Jewish week is divided into six days of "doing" – "Six days shall you labor, and do all your work" (Ex. 20:9) – and a day of rest: "But the seventh day is a Sabbath to the Lord your God, in it you shall not do any manner of work" (20:10). The obvious question is whether "being" and "doing" are inherently contradictory, thus entailing the admission that life is fundamentally dualistic. Must we choose between a life of "being" and a life of "doing"? Are these two aspects of our lives irreconcilable?

The Torah casts these two principles in separate Creation stories in order to elucidate each on its own. Yet, ultimately, they are not separate, but rather two sides of the same coin. In our lives, too, there is need to separate the various principles, but the goal is nevertheless to lead a dynamic lifestyle that enables interplay between their expressions – a harmony of "being" and "doing."

The Taste of the Fruit and the Taste of the Tree: Rav Kook and Tom Sawyer

The opportunity to examine God's intention, His blueprint for the world, is fascinating. In chapter 1, God commands the earth to sprout "fruit-tree bearing fruit," but instead it brings forth "tree bearing fruit" (Gen. 1:11–12). Rashi, based on a midrash in Genesis Rabba, writes, "Fruit trees: That the taste of the tree should be like the taste of the fruit. It [the earth] did not do so, however." Midrashic literature refers to this act of disobedience as "the sin of the earth." What is the import of this sin, and why is it so important that the tree have flavor? Rav Kook (*Orot HaTeshuva* 6:7) explains the relation between the tree and the fruit as an allegory for the relations between means and ends: the fruit is the end and the tree is the means. God intended for the tree itself, and not only its fruits, to have flavor. It follows that actions – beyond being means to an end – should have intrinsic value.

This idea can be taken in other directions and applied to the question of the relation between form and content. The original purpose of Creation, according to Rav Kook's cosmology, was to construct a world in which the forms that life takes are perfect likenesses of their content: the body would describe the soul, the external would reflect the internal, and we would be capable of expressing ourselves externally just as we experience ourselves internally. And like us the trees, the animals – all of creation. But the earth sinned in separating form from content. Thus, the tree became a means to the fruit, its treeness utterly devoid of the flavor of the fruit. The earth, as Rav Kook puts it, "betrayed its essence." Instead of daring to be itself, as the Lord had intended, it chose to actualize itself only partially. Thenceforth, all of our actions in the world have been mere stages en route to some future goal, bereft of inherent existential meaning.

Mark Twain's classic novel *Tom Sawyer* can help elucidate Rav Kook's idea. In one of the chapters, Tom's Aunt Polly punishes him by ordering him to paint the fence in the yard. The aunt signifies a reality in which the tree does not taste like the fruit. In it, only the "fruit," meaning the painted fence, has value, while the act of painting – the means – is punishment. But Tom – perhaps thanks to his tender age – gleans a competing intuition about the ideal life, and shares the secret with his friends: the path is not merely a curse, or even a means; it is a bountiful blessing. Tom's friends are so enamored of his insight that by the end of the story they are handing Tom their treasures merely for the privilege of helping to paint the fence.

We can extract a profound secret about life from the midrash quoted by Rav Kook. An "awakening" is generally the goal of spiritual outlooks, the basic assumption being that people's lives are passing them by while they sleep. The contrasting of "sleep" and "wakefulness" refers to one's awareness and the manner in which people lead their life. Generally speaking, an absence of awareness of life stems from the mind wandering either backward to thoughts of past experiences, or forward, anticipating what is yet to come. Thus the individual is absent from the one place where life occurs: the present. As John Lennon said, "Life is what happens while you're busy making other plans." A sleeping person is not present, while one who is "awakened" can concentrate and truly exist in the moment.

This ties into the question we raised earlier: whether the world of "doing" can be connected to the world of "being." When action is entirely expedient, relating only to purpose, it is cut off from its nature. It is an expression of the "sin of the earth," where the world of doing (*assiya*) exists separately, cut off from our inner essence. When, however, we succeed in experiencing action as a value, as an essence in itself, it becomes an actualization of our nature. We find that "doing" can become our "being."

The Tree of Knowledge and the Tree of Life

Now we can better understand the sin for which humanity is expelled from the Garden of Eden. Eating from the Tree of Knowledge causes a fundamental shift in Adam and Eve's consciousness.

Their eyes are opened to good and evil, so that everything in the reality of their lives becomes either positive or negative. It is not reality that changes; it is their consciousness, their relation to it. This opening of the eyes, which enables a more adult perspective on life, is also a punishment: "In the sweat of your face shall you eat bread" (3:19), God says, dooming humankind to a life of struggle. At first glance, the statement indeed appears to describe the curse of Man. But is it perhaps possible to transform the curse – the immense effort we invest in surviving and living – into a blessing, a connection to the very essence and flavor of life? Rabbi Nahman of Breslov, in a refreshing reading (*Likutei Moharan, Tanina* 6), teaches that the Hebrew word for "sweat," "*ze'ah*," can be read in the acrostic of the verse "This (*Zeh*) is the day which the Lord (*Hashem*) has made (*asa*); we will rejoice and be glad in it" (Ps. 118:24). In the very sweat with which man has been cursed, Rabbi Nahman finds a blessing, and happiness.

"The sweat of your face" is only a curse if one sees it as such. As soon as one realizes, however, that the very same sweat can be a key to finding existential meaning, it turns into a blessing. The connection to the Tree of Life, denied us with the expulsion of Adam and Eve from the Garden, is attainable as an act of mind. Should we succeed in deconstructing the curse of "In the sweat of your face shall you eat bread" and translating it into the blessing of "This is the day which the Lord has made," perhaps we can restore a modicum of wholeness to our splintered life experience, bringing it a step closer to a unified existential reality. The Jewish message is the sustainment of both forces – being and doing – within life itself.

Noaḥ

John Lennon and the Tower of Babel

Imagine there's no countries
It isn't hard to do
Nothing to kill or die for
And no religion, too
Imagine all the people living life in peace
Living life in peace
You may say I'm a dreamer
But I'm not the only one
I hope someday you'll join us
And the world will be as one.

– John Lennon, "Imagine"

Many of us are moved by this song. After all, who would not want to see a united humanity with nothing to fight over, a situation where wars were a thing of the past, where people had far more in common – including a shared language – and where peace reigned? The power of the song comes from the power of the dream, and the depth of our yearning to return to the beginning of the world, to a natural, pristine reality that precedes all mistakes and strife. For we all share a common father, and were birthed by a common mother. This idea can be found in the Mishna (Sanhedrin 4:5): "Therefore man was created alone … for the sake of peace among people – that one might not say to his fellow, 'My father was greater than yours.'" The fact that the Torah opens with the story of the creation of humanity undermines the basis for assertions of racial or national superiority. Yet, John Lennon's song, which is rooted in the imaginary, is evidence of how far we have strayed from the awareness that all human beings are brothers and sisters. The world is engulfed in war and strife, separatism and hate. An examination of the Tower of Babel story can, perhaps, help us come to grips with the divided reality of humanity, and its consequences.

The Tower of Babel: Megalomania or Fear?

> And the whole earth was of one language and of one speech …. And they said, "Come, let us build us a city, and a tower, with its top in heaven, and let us make us a name; lest we be scattered abroad upon the face of the whole earth." (Gen. 11:1, 4)

The above verses describe the first adolescent rebellion in history: all of humanity gathers and decides to devote itself to the construction of a tower. But why a tower, and what do they intend to do with it?

Rashi describes the defiant energy as an expression of megalomania: "They came with one scheme and said, '…Let us ascend to the sky and wage war with Him'" (11:1). The people understand that the power of the individual is dwarfed by that of the Creator, and that they can only become powerful collectively, through teamwork. The purpose of the tower is to overrun the supernal world: "We will go up there and show Him who we are!" the people think. God, in response, scatters humanity to the four corners of the earth and muddles their language. Thus, the builders of the tower are prevented from realizing their scheme.

Rashbam (11:4) has a different take on this adolescent rebellion. He interprets the construction of the tower as an expression of humanity's fear of its own power; not a no-holds-barred amplification of that power: "On the face of it, what was the sin of the generation of [the Tower of Babel]?...because the Lord enjoined them, 'Be fruitful, and multiply, and replenish the earth, and subdue it,' and instead they chose a place to settle and said, 'Lest we be scattered abroad upon the face of the whole earth,' He decreed that they be scattered." God has big plans for humanity. He commands them to spread to all corners of the earth, to evolve national identities, cultures, and languages: from the Inuit who would learn to live in extreme cold to the desert dwellers and the farmers. Yet, people are afraid to fulfill their destiny; they refuse to accept their role. Instead, they assemble in one location, communicate in the same language, and focus their energy on building a single tower. In response, God puts them back on track: "So the Lord scattered them abroad from there upon the face of all the earth.... Therefore was the name of it called Babel; because the Lord did there confound the language of all the earth; and from there did the Lord scatter them abroad upon the face of all the earth" (11:8–9).

Rashbam's reading of the story is diametrically opposed to Rashi's. While Rashi posits a narrative in which God promotes human unity and people are to blame for discord, Rashbam offers an interpretation that is surprising, radical, and relevant to our day: the construction of the tower is frustrated not by man's naked ambition and desire to conquer the heavens, but by human passivity and dread at the prospect of going out into the world and subduing the earth.

It emerges that demographic and geographic dispersal is not a punishment but rather a means for actualizing humanity's potential, for generating a wealth of cultures and languages. The tower is called "Babel," a word whose root denotes mixing and confusion, due to the cultural distance generated by the fragmentation of language – "that they may not understand one another's speech" (11:7). The purpose of the confounding is to shatter national and cultural homogeneity: "And the Lord said, 'Behold, they are one people, and they have all one language; and this is what they begin to do; and now nothing will be withheld from them, which they purpose to do'" (11:6). Human beings try to live together, but God wants to divide them and scatter them throughout the earth. If history is any indication, there are profound disadvantages to the divisions between cultures and nations, including the hatred, strife, and suspicion that have often led to war. So what did God find so attractive in the prospect?

Down with Big Brother

A myth of Lurianic Kabbala can provide a fresh perspective on the story of the Tower of Babel. In the beginning, it says, the cosmos was whole – unified and harmonious – and the vessels, meaning the physical world, received the divine influx and were permeated by it. However, there came a stage where the vessels could no longer withstand the power of that light, and they shattered, scattering the divine light that indwelled within them. That light has remained embedded in reality in the form of sparks.

The myth of the raising of the sparks is a foundation of Kabbala and Hasidism. It says that every thing, and every action, in the reality of our lives contains a spark of holiness. Our mission is to uncover those sparks and redeem them from the husks that enclose them, thus raising them up. People's purpose in the world is to repair the vessels, gather all of the scattered sparks and, by fusing them together, manifest unity in reality. The parallels to the Tower of Babel are clear: the initial unity of the nations corresponds to the primordial reality of the light-filled vessels, and the splintering of that unity – and subsequent dispersal of humanity throughout the land – recalls the shattering of the vessels. History, populated as it is with a rich cast of peoples, cultures, and languages, is like the sparks scattered throughout the cosmos in the aftermath of the shattering. The astonishing conclusion is that within every nation and culture is embedded a unique spark of holiness, waiting to be revealed and raised up, thus rectifying reality and restoring it to a state of oneness.

A century ago, this fundamental kabbalistic idea figured in Rav Kook's characterization (*Orot HaKodesh*, pt. 2, 539–40) of social changes in the modern world as evidence of a major shift. He recognized the evolving consciousnesses of many nations as to their histories and their place in the world as part of a broader, pan-human story. In the past, he writes, "each group and community was secluded in its own setting, individuals were overtly influenced only by their immediate surroundings, and, in their innocence, both individuals and communities thought the world did not extend beyond their own spiritual and physical environs." In contrast, "the elect, who possess an expansive consciousness, always knew the secret of spiritual oneness; they knew that the human spirit is universal." In the modern era, "the social consciousness has shifted and broadened; every individual feels that he is not alone, not sequestered in an utterly separate setting; that he acts upon and is in turn shaped by a profusion of groups, by a variety of often-alien settings."

If that is the case, why did humanity have to endure the ordeal of the splintering and scattering of reality? What was the point of thousands of years of bloodshed among nations? What, indeed, was the purpose of the shattering of the vessels?

We can conclude, based on Rav Kook, that before the shattering, the world was not only unified, but uniform. It was only thanks to the dispersion and distance afforded by the shattering that each group could evolve in its unique way, ultimately yielding the immense cultural and human diversity that we see today. The shattering is the source of all variety in reality. The terror of a sameness devoid of all individuality is largely associated with totalitarian regimes. In his classic novel *1984*, George Orwell describes in nightmarish terms the uniformity that Big Brother seeks to impose. The Netziv (*Haamek Davar*, Genesis 11:7) offers a similar reading of the story of the Tower of Babel. The verse, "And the whole earth was of one language and of one speech" (11:1), he writes, describes an attempt to build a watchtower, a Big Brother of sorts, that enforces uniformity of thought. From it, the tower's builders can be surveilled and prevented from migrating to a land where they are free to think differently.

The deeper meaning of the Tower of Babel story is the understanding that God does not desire a world where everyone is alike. Rather, God expects us to reveal our inimitable selves, and revel in our unique identities as individuals and as communities. The grand challenge is to retain our individuality within the communal setting, to safeguard the self in a variegated society.[1]

The Rabbi and the Swami

In his book *The Soul of the Story*, Rabbi David Zeller describes his personal journey through various worldviews, Jewish and otherwise, and the interfaith meetings that he approached with a new and significant Jewish message that helped clarify their purpose:

---

1. Rabbi Jonathan Sacks, in his book *The Dignity of Difference: How to Avoid the Clash of Civilizations* (London: Bloomsbury Academic, 2003), deals at length with the challenge of preserving the individuality of every culture in the global era, based on the Tower of Babel story.

When I was on stage singing and teaching about Jewish mysticism and meditation, Swami Vishnu chimed in, "Oh, Rabbi, this is just like we teach in yoga philosophy. You see, we really are all one, and all the teachings are here in yoga!"...

[I replied,] "No Swamiji, we are not all one. We are all different. We are all part of one greater whole, but that whole depends on each part fulfilling its separate function: unity in diversity. In Kabbala, we learn that the human body is a metaphor for the world. My body is whole and healthy *because* each separate organ and system is doing its task in harmony with all the others...

"Each religion, each people, each culture is like an organ in the body of humankind. But for all humanity to be truly whole and harmonious, each part must fulfill its mission while recognizing the essential importance of all the others. Each people is chosen to be the organ that it is, with its particular purpose, for the good of the whole world. Today, we suffer a lot from religions that say, 'This is the only way, and everyone must be like us and accept our way.' We must accept and nurture our differences for the good of the whole."...

If we explore the language of no boundaries and all being one in the medical journals, we will find it is the description of cancer. There are no distinctions, no boundaries, no borders – all is one – but it is cancer, and the system will die from that oneness.[2]

---

2. David Zeller, *The Soul of the Story: Meetings with Remarkable People* (Woodstock: Jewish Lights Publishing, 2006), 193–194, used with permission of the copyright holder.

Interfaith dialogue carries a risk of effacing uniqueness. New Age attitudes rely on the implicit assumption that all spiritual traditions are fundamentally alike, and can come together as an eclectic, universal religion. Zeller's Orthodox practice did not prevent him from maintaining dialogue and a respectful relationship with the spiritual world he grew up in and the people who populated it. His observation is a powerful message for our generation: an individual's uniqueness is not revealed through denial of the other, and an authentic Judaism, clearly demarcated by boundaries of practice and belief, has something to offer to the entire world, but also something to learn from it.

Accepting the Other Without Losing the Self

In the beginning of the *parasha*, there is an interesting parallel between the attitude of the generation of the Flood and that of the following generation, which builds the Tower of Babel. According to Professor Benjamin Ish-Shalom, the generation of the Flood seeks to escape the categories that divide it and attain a new commonality, but in so doing, it effectively causes the world to regress. It corrupts its morals, especially sexually – there is no more "mine" and "yours," only depravity – and the natural world reacts in the same vein: the upper waters (the sky) and the lower waters (the ocean) merge for the first time since Creation, to flood the earth. Rabbi Tzadok HaKohen of Lublin writes extensively of the wasted potential and missed opportunity of the generation of the Flood. It has the potential to usher in the redemption, because it grasps that everything has a single source, that all is equal. But a unity that obscures and denies difference will not only fail to redeem the world, it will bring about its destruction.

The people of the Tower of Babel try to reconstruct the goal of the Flood, to access perfect oneness by effacing difference – "one language and one speech." Hence the desire to build a tower that erases the division between heaven and earth. The existence of the world depends on *tzimtzum* (constriction and limitation), on definitions, which cannot but differentiate.

"Who is wise?" the Mishna (Avot 4:1) asks, and replies, "One who learns from every man." Still, there is an ever-present tension between one's drive to safeguard a unique self and one's capacity to give to and learn from the other. It is a tension we must balance. All individuals must be capable of defining their boundaries, of stating clearly who they are and what they believe in, for when the answers are nebulous, they run the risk of losing their identity – without which there can be no encounter with the other. One must focus on one's own place and ask, "Who am I?" Honest answers to that question are a prerequisite for receiving from others. The same applies to societies and nations: it is only when we gain a thorough understanding of ourselves that we can be at peace with our neighbors.

A Pure Language

"… And how to preserve, without debasement, all the abundance of the [Jewish] spiritual world in the wake of the revolutions wrought by external influence, and how to draw from them only what is good and true, righteous and fair" (*Orot HaKodesh*, pt. 2, 540). In this passage, Rav Kook addresses Judaism's place in the global village as an incontrovertible given. That status is reinforced in the era of the internet, which has brought awareness of other cultures and their beliefs into everyone's home. I believe that the intercultural encounter is not only necessary but supremely important, and that both Judaism and the nations of the world will be enriched through profound dialogue. Every religion and people expresses its unique qualities, as does Judaism. The onus is on us to open our hearts, and learn from one another how to break free of the husks and receive the light.

According to the vision in the book of Zephaniah, at the end of days people will go back to speaking a "pure language." Perhaps it is not a literal single language, but rather a universal state of being where everyone understands and accepts one another, and helps one another. As the prophet says, "For then will I turn to the peoples a pure language, that they may all call upon the name of the Lord, to serve Him of one accord" (Zeph. 3:9).

Lekh Lekha

Go to Yourself

I learned from my teachers that the first four *parashot* in Genesis lay down the path to spiritual enlightenment. In the beginning (*Bereshit*), one must be at rest (*Noaḥ*, a state of repose), in peace and tranquility. Only then can one move on to walking (*Lekh lekha*). The redundancy in the phrase "*Lekh lekha*," which can be read literally as "go to you," teaches us that the voyage that one must undertake is inward – a voyage to oneself. It is a process that culminates in enlightenment (the Hebrew word for which, *he'ara*, comes from the same root as *Vayera*): "And the Lord appeared (*Vayera*) to him" (Gen. 18:1).

The Voyage to the Self

In the beginning of the *parasha*, God told Abraham to go: "Get yourself (*Lekh lekha*) out of your country, and from your kindred, and from your father's house" (Gen. 12:1). The Zohar interprets the apparent redundancy as an imperative to embark on a voyage to the self: "Get (*Lekh*) to yourself (*lekha*)...to know and to rectify yourself" (Zohar, *Lekh Lekha* 77b–78a). Rav Kook, in a sublime passage, teaches us that to arrive at one's self is to discover God:

"I was in exile" (Ezek. 1:1): The inner, essential I.... We have sinned with our fathers – the sin of Adam, who spurned his essence, who was drawn to the perspective of the snake and lost himself, and was unable to provide a clear answer to the question "Where are you?" (Gen. 3:9), for he did not know his own soul, for his true I-ness had been lost to him.... Thus the world continues to decline with the loss of everyone's I.... "The breath of our nostrils, the anointed of the Lord" (Lam. 4:20)... it is not external to us; it is the breath of our nostrils.... The Lord our God... we will seek... our own I we will seek; we will seek ourselves and we will find.... I am the Lord. (*Orot HaKodesh*, pt. 3, 140–41)

Rav Kook reads Ezekiel's biographical pronouncement "I was in exile" as an existential statement. The "I," the true identity, is exiled, outside of the self. Humanity's primal sin is alienation from the self – our society may be rife with alienation between people, but the primary schism, according to Rav Kook, lies within the individual. Thus we are incapable of answering God's question, "Where are you?" Rav Kook goes on to draw a bold, astonishing conclusion: When we seek and find ourselves, our essential "I," we discover that "I am the Lord," that God dwells within us. When I am true to myself, I find that transcendence, holiness, and the wellspring of life are all manifested in me. God exists within me, and I within Him.[1]

---

1. Rav Kook's insight is hinted at in Psalms (27:8): "Of you, my heart said, 'Seek My face'; Your face, Lord, will I seek." The verse opens with the psalmist's heart enjoining him to seek its face, but ultimately he learns that to seek the face of one's heart is to seek the face of God.

The spiritual teacher Eckhart Tolle (author of *The Power of Now*) tells of an epiphany he arrived at through the frustration expressed by the sentence "I can't live with myself." He suddenly realized that there is an "I" and there is a "self," and that the distinction between the two was not merely semantic; rather, they relate to two layers of the psyche that clash with each other. He claims that one is the true self and the other is the self that the individual seeks to break free of.

Rav Kook presents a similar dichotomy, albeit from a religious point of view, in which he identifies the inner, authentic self with God. In this, Rav Kook is influenced by the story of Creation in Genesis, according to which humanity was created "in the image of God" (1:26–27).[2] His desire to bring to light a true self that is identified with God is also the supreme wish of the Upanishads, the ancient Hindu scripture. According to the Upanishads, the purpose of humanity is to realize that Atman, the inner self, and Brahman, the infinite, are one and the same.

This similarity between Judaism and the Upanishadic religions also highlights the difference, a gap that, to my mind, lies in the meaning each assigns to humanity's presence in the material world. The Upanishads imply that people can break free of materiality – which is *maya*, an illusion – through self-knowledge. Those who are not "liberated" from illusion during their lifetimes are reincarnated and given another shot. Souls come into the world in order to escape it. Judaism, on the other hand, sees the soul's descent into the world as a mission: humanity is saddled with the grave responsibility of rectifying and improving reality. Three times a day, Jews vow in their prayers to try to perfect that world under the sovereignty of the Almighty. This imperative emerges from another of the Zohar's readings of the phrase *"Lekh lekha"*

2. Rav Kook opens his book *LiNevukhei HaDor* with the assertion, "That man is created in the image of God is the basis of the Torah."

(Gen. 12:1) – as God's injunction to the soul, which is called upon to set out from its supernal seat and descend into earthly reality. The Lord equips each soul with the means to carry out its defined mission – to work, to maintain, and to repair – and promises it a blessing. And indeed, the next verse affirms, "And I will make of you a great nation, and I will bless you, and make your name great; and you will be a blessing."

The two readings of the phrase "*Lekh lekha*" recall the question of the relation between inward-facing "being" and outward-facing "doing." The answer, to my mind, lies in the realization that doing generates existence and an encounter with reality. One could think that giving is only outward-facing, but it is always a two-way street. You are what you do: people discover and improve themselves by encountering and interacting with life and reality – not by disconnecting from them. They discover themselves in their daily toil to provide for their families, by raising children, by doing good works, and endeavoring to rectify society. Yet, it is clear that doing does not always enhance one's awareness of oneself. By nature, it turns one's gaze upon the outer world, the world of doing. In order to draw conclusions from one's actions and internalize them in the world of the soul, one must cultivate self-awareness. My friend Erez Nir once explained that the Garden of Eden features a Tree of Life and a Tree of Knowledge because Judaism aspires to completeness through the union of knowledge, meaning awareness, and life.

When Abraham Met Brahma

During one of my trips to India, I traveled to the northern city of Haridwar, where Anandamayi Ma, one of the great gurus of the previous century, had her ashram. The head of the ashram at the time was Swami Vijayananda, a ninety-two-year-old guru. But Vijayananda was not always his name; his mother and father, a rabbi in southern France, had named him Abraham Jacob

Weintraub. Like his biblical namesake in the beginning of our *parasha*, Abraham-Vijayananda came to a crossroads. Before traveling to India he had planned to immigrate to Israel. During the 1948 War of Independence, he tried to volunteer for the Haganah paramilitary organization but was rejected (it turns out that a relative of his was in charge of recruitment in France and was afraid to put him in harm's way). Although Abraham had been raised in a religious home, he was an atheist.

One day, he stumbled upon a volume of Indian philosophy that described the capacity to "find God within oneself." Captivated by the idea, he decided to travel to India and learn more. Abraham eventually arrived at the ashram of Anandamayi Ma, who immediately sensed that he was special: even before he could apply, and despite a policy of turning away Westerners, she took him on as a student. Years later, she named him as her successor. When I arrived at the ashram, he had already been there fifty-five years, during which he had never left India. He had faced two options at the outset of his journey: "*lekh lekha*," or "get yourself," literally, to the Land of Israel, to fight for his people; or "go to yourself," to search his inner world.

I entered his austere room, and noticed a few Jewish tomes on the shelf – a Bible, a *Tanya*, the *Sefat Emet*, Simcha Raz's *Tales of the Righteous*, and a biography of Ariel Sharon. Vijayananda felt that he had never stopped being Jewish, and found that there was no contradiction between Judaism and the Indian Vedic philosophy he was drawn to. One of Vijayananda's students told me that he was once asked whether it was true that he used to be Jewish. Vijayananda straightened his back proudly and exclaimed, "I *am* Jewish!" Though he had never visited Israel, he felt a deep connection to events in the country. He had a subscription to the *Jerusalem Post*, and several of his students who resided in Israel would call him once in a while to keep him abreast of the latest news. When I visited him, he sang Naomi Shemer's "Jerusalem of Gold" with deep feeling. I asked Vijayananda for advice about spiritual seeking, and he replied, "There are many paths to the top of the mountain, but those who change paths on the way up will never make it to the top. One must remain utterly committed to a single path, based on one's tradition." There is value to taking interest in a variety of paths – it enables one to see the good in others and respect them. One can also gain valuable knowledge about one's own path by becoming acquainted with other ways. But one must remain committed to walking a single path; otherwise, even copious information about alternative routes will yield little wisdom.

After our meeting, I pondered Vijayananda's advice. As someone who had remained in the ashram for fifty-five years, he almost certainly qualified as having stuck to a single path. But what of his assertion that the path should adhere to "one's own tradition"? Was he expressing sorrow over the loss of the road he had chosen not to take? Was it possible that, had he known earlier that the spiritual outlooks that drew him to India also existed in Judaism, he would have chosen differently? Suddenly, I imagined what could have been: a Rebbe Abraham Jacob, thronged by grandchildren and students, and tens of thousands of Jews animated by the light of his Torah. I felt sad, both for the old man whom I instantly adored, and for the Jewish people, which was denied the spiritual bounty of this large soul. I felt compelled to return and speak to him again. During my second visit my cab got stuck in traffic and I only had a few minutes to see him before I had to catch a train to Delhi. When we parted we both gazed at each other, both realizing that it would be our final meeting. As I left, Vijayananda said, "Next time you go to the Western Wall, pray for me." During the following Sukkot festival, I made the pilgrimage to Jerusalem, and when I came to the Western Wall I carried out Abraham's wish and prayed for him.

Four years later he passed away, but not before requesting, in a departure from the Indian custom – especially as it applies to saints such as himself – that his body be buried rather than cremated. Vijayananda's followers at the ashram respected the unusual request, which stemmed, no doubt, from his desire to be interred in keeping with the Jewish tradition. His body was thus flown to France to be buried in the presence of his Jewish family, who recited the Kaddish at his graveside.

Vayera

God Is Other People

The Zohar, or the Book of Splendor, is named for the inner dimension of reality, which Kabbala identifies with the divine. The book instructs its readers to encounter this hidden splendor and recognize God in it, a meeting that leads to enlightenment. One of the great contributions of the Zohar is the perception that the divine interpenetrates life itself, including individual people, in their relationships with the world and with others. Contrary to mystical modes of consciousness that seek to break with the world and transcend it, the Zohar proposes a relationship with the divine that connects the earthly and supernal realities. The journey to God, according to the Zohar, passes through interpersonal relationships: from a couple's intimate bond to the mundane interactions between the individual and the community. Much of the book consists of conversations between friends, who encounter the Torah through studying, traveling, and generally spending time together. Quietist outlooks, by which one walls oneself off from the world, are foreign to Judaism – and particularly to the Zohar. The crucial point is that transcendence lies within life, not beyond it.

Shattered Vessels, Broken People

At the end of the *parasha* is the story of the *Akeda* (the binding of Isaac). The Torah does not say why God decides to test Abraham, and both the Midrash and the Zohar attempt to explain what transpired beforehand. The difference between the Midrash's straightforward explanation and the Zohar's esoteric approach can help elucidate the novel message of Kabbala. Both interpretations explain the test of the *Akeda*, which ultimately brought Abraham closer to God, as a reaction to Abraham refraining from giving something to God and thus damaging his relationship with Him. Consequently, Abraham is tested with the ultimate demand – to give his only son. Let us look over the sources to see how they characterize Abraham's earlier sin and the thing that he refrained from giving.

Here is the Midrash, as quoted by Rashi:

> "After these things" (Gen. 22:1): Some of our sages say (Sanhedrin 89b) [that it happened] after the words of Satan, who was accusing and saying, "Of every feast that Abraham made, he did not sacrifice before You one bull or one ram!" [God] said to him, "Does he do anything but for his son? Yet, if I were to say to him, 'Sacrifice him before Me,' he would not withhold [him]."

According to the Midrash, Abraham celebrates Isaac's weaning, but does not offer God a sacrifice of thanks. Abraham's sin is forgetting to show gratitude to God. Satan seizes the opportunity and describes the error as the symptom of a rift between Abraham and God, who thus decides to test Abraham with the *Akeda*.

The Zohar has a different interpretation:

Rabbi Shimon opened, saying: Whoever rejoices on the festivals without giving the blessed Holy One His share – that evil-eyed Satan hates him and accuses him and removes him from this world.... The share of the blessed Holy One consists in gladdening the poor as best as one can. For on these days the blessed Holy One comes to see those broken vessels of His. Entering their company and seeing they have nothing to celebrate, He weeps over them – and then ascends to destroy the world! Many members of the Academy come before Him and plead: "Master of the universe! You are called Compassionate and Gracious. May Your compassion be aroused for Your children!" He answers them, "Do not the inhabitants of the world realize that I based the world solely on love? As it is written: I said, 'The world shall be built on love (Ps. 89:3).' By this the world endures." (Zohar, *Hakdamot* 10b)

Later, according to the Zohar, Satan arrives at Abraham's celebratory banquet disguised as a pauper. No one notices him, and he comes before the Lord to denounce Abraham: "Master of the universe, You called Abraham 'My beloved' (Is. 41:8)? He held a feast and gave me nothing, and nothing to the poor." Abraham's is a social transgression: he disregards the poor. Unlike the Midrash, which focuses on the direct dialogue between Abraham and his Maker, the Zohar takes in the entire human vista, where the encounter with the infinite God takes place.

Here, the idea of "shattered vessels," which we discussed in relation to *Parashat Noah*, takes on a slightly different aspect. The shattering is described as the cause of all privation. Prior to it, everything was harmonious, and the vessels received direct divine light; however, a fault in the process of Creation caused the vessels to shatter, and their sparks to be strewn throughout the cosmos (thus turning the entire cosmos into a divine space).

Humanity's purpose is to repair the vessels, and to reveal and raise up the sparks. The shattered vessels are people; each contains a lost divine spark. The individual is repaired through contending with human want, which is in fact divine want. The Zohar explains that in giving to the poor one is not merely fulfilling an interpersonal mitzva, but rather giving to God Himself. The human realm and its privations are part and parcel of the divine realm, and Abraham's status as God's beloved thus depends on his treatment of the other, of the poor.

The social implications of the myth of the shattering of the vessels are further elucidated in the thought of one of the preeminent kabbalists of the twentieth century, Rabbi Yehuda Ashlag. To him, the shattering of the vessels is an expression of the damage wrought by an unjust distribution of wealth, a reality that corrupts the world, including the rich. In 1958, then-prime minister David Ben-Gurion wrote to Yehuda Tzvi Brandwein, a close disciple of the rabbi: "[Rabbi Ashlag] asked me on many occasions after the establishment of the state whether we would institute a communist regime." Later, when he learned of the atrocities perpetrated in the Soviet Union, he became disillusioned with communism and renounced his vision of a just distribution that could be effected through politics.[1]

Happiness and Wealth

It is relatively simple to give alms to the poor, but the Zohar's demand extends further: one must bring them joy as well. According to the Zohar's broader definition of social justice, social responsibility is not merely economic; it has to do with human interaction. As Douglas Adams put it in the foreword to *The Hitchhiker's Guide to the Galaxy*:

---

1. Micha Odenheimer, "Latter-day Luminary," *Haaretz*, December 16, 2004, https://www.haaretz.com/latter-day-luminary-1.144149.

Most of the people living on [the planet] were unhappy for pretty much all of the time. Many solutions were suggested for this problem, but most of these were largely concerned with the movement of small green pieces of paper, which was odd because on the whole it was not the small green pieces of paper that were unhappy.[2]

A similar attitude emerges from the story of Satan disguising himself as a pauper who is ignored at Abraham's party. In addition to railing at the food that he is denied, he fumes at the experience of alienation. The Talmud (Bava Batra 9b) says that it is preferable to comfort the poor with words than to give them alms.

Sadly, discussions of social justice, even when they stem from good intentions, tend to be reduced to questions of money and budgets, and end with the usual sigh over poverty reports. The question of happiness is missing from the economic equations, seemingly highlighting one of the great gaps in the communist idea: that in addition to a redistributing of wealth, there must be a redistribution of happiness. Even some immensely wealthy people are profoundly unhappy, shattered vessels that must be repaired. To paraphrase the popular Israeli singer Muki, "Everybody talks about money, nobody talks about happiness." A correct social outlook should seek a way to make all human resources, physical and spiritual alike, available throughout society. Spiritual resources in this context are intimacy with other people, inclusion of the other, happiness, responsibility, giving, and spiritual aspirations.

The key to happiness lies not only with heaven; we must not forget that we are responsible for the world. The verse "The world shall be built on love" is generally interpreted as a request that we make of God, but the Zohar interprets it as a statement

---

2. Douglas Adams, *The Hitchhiker's Guide to the Galaxy* (London: Pan Macmillan, 2009), 8.

about human responsibility. The existence of the world depends on us, on the kindness and compassion that we show to one another. Divine reality, the Zohar reminds us, is constructed by man.

Hospitality and God

Before the Torah tells of the destruction of Sodom and Gomorrah, it relates the following:

> Abraham shall surely become a great and mighty nation, and all the nations of the earth shall be blessed in him. For I have known him, to the end that he may command his children and his household after him, that they may keep the way of the Lord, to do righteousness and justice. (Gen. 18:18–19)

God chooses Abraham because he believes in his ability to raise his progeny in the way of the Lord, the way of righteousness and justice. But Abraham's message to the world is that the benefits of righteousness and justice should extend to the other as well – not only to one's family and friends. The novelty of that message is driven home by the context: the verse appears just before the destruction of Sodom and Gomorrah, and serves as an introduction of sorts to that episode. True to form, Abraham tries to convince God to commute the sentence (18:23–25): "And Abraham drew near, and said: 'Will You indeed sweep away the righteous with the wicked?...shall not the judge of all the earth do justly?'" In his outcry, Abraham emphasizes that righteousness and justice are God's paths, in which he, Abraham, treads and which he perpetuates in the world.

Abraham's conception of the other stands in stark contrast to the prevailing attitudes in Sodom. In an earlier episode (14:21), the king of Sodom makes a proposal to Abraham that at first blush seems admirable: "And the king of Sodom said to Abram: 'Give me the people, and take the goods for yourself.'" Ostensibly, he is a wonderful leader, ceding the money because people are more important. But his true meaning is deeply sinister: he does not consider himself responsible for non-citizens of Sodom, who, like Lot's guests, are fair game for unthinkable savagery. The *Beit HaLevi* contrasts Lot's hospitality with that practiced by Abraham. Lot, he writes, is prepared to forfeit his life for his guests, but only because he knows they are messengers of God. But Abraham is unaware of their identity; he is under the impression that they are wayfarers, and yet his tent remains open to them. Food is served, water is proffered to the parched vagabonds to drink and to wash their feet, and a true encounter ensues.

The Talmud (Shabbat 127a) makes the astounding assertion that "hospitality to wayfarers is greater than welcoming the presence of the *Shekhina*" – the human is placed above the divine. The Zohar teaches us that hospitality is itself a welcoming of the *Shekhina*.

Abraham's turn toward the radically other resonates in the modern philosophies of Martin Buber and Emmanuel Levinas. Buber's dialogic approach is founded on "I-thou," rather than "I-it," relations. I-thou relations facilitate a genuine connection between people based on the understanding that it is only through the other that one is constructed as a spiritual personality. Buber's insight was sown by tragedy. At the turn of the twentieth century, he was engaged in the study – both academic and practical – of Eastern religions. One day, while Buber was meditating, one of his students approached and asked to speak to him. Buber ignored the student. On the next day, he learned that the man had taken his own life. Buber, who blamed the student's death on his own aloofness and excessive pursuit of detachment from the world, decided to change, and began to develop his dialogic philosophy.

Levinas, a French-Jewish philosopher, sought to gaze into the face of the other and through it find himself. According to him, God is the "ultimate other," that which is diametrically opposed to myself. The individual's task is to open up to the human infinity before him.

The philosophy of Levinas is especially germane to the Israeli experience. The Israeli "other" is anyone who is not "us," who does not look like "us" or speak "our" language. A glance at those who reside in Israel's "backyard" is enough to drive home the extent of the country's tribalism and social alienation. Our approach to other religions and nations outside Israel is equally lacking. The true challenge of our time is to look kindly upon those others who are lost in the Israeli public space.

Ramadan, According to the Zohar

I wish to end with a poignant event that I was privileged to participate in. On an Iftar, the traditional meal at the end of each day's fast during the month of Ramadan, a group of Jews, Muslims, Christians, and Druze came together in the Galilee to promote coexistence and a shared life of peace and mutual appreciation. Asked to address the assembly as a representative of Judaism, I decided to honor my hosts by opening with a relevant Quranic precept that highlights the connection between the human and the divine. According to the Quran, one who is unable to fast on Ramadan can instead fulfill the obligation by giving food to the poor. I was struck by the manner in which the Quran equated divine worship with human-social action. I went on to acquaint the audience with parallels in Jewish sources, including the passage in the Zohar on *Vayera* that enjoins us to open our hearts to the other. At the end of the study session, we all came together and prayed that both the shared and disparate elements of our religions would assist us, children of Abraham all, in fostering mutual appreciation and peace.

The God of Abraham – Heavenly Father or the Infinite?

Abraham's life journey culminates in *Parashat Ḥayei Sara*. Embedded in the Hebrew meaning of his name is the divine promise that he will become "father of a multitude of nations" (Gen. 17:5). That promise was indeed fulfilled, and today most people – Jews, Muslims, and Christians – consider him a patriarch, emulate him, and name their children after him.

His defining features are the pioneering of the belief in a single God – he is traditionally thought to have been the first monotheist – and his close relationship with that God (the Muslims gave him the title *Khalilullah*, or "friend of Allah"). In Judaism, too, Abraham is more emblematic of a spiritual legacy than of an ethnic heritage. According to Jewish law, converts are required in praying to recite the line "which the

Lord swore to our fathers to give us," despite not having been born Jews. Maimonides (*Mishneh Torah, Hilkhot Bikurim* 4:3) explains: "…for [Gen. 17:5] states with regard to Abraham: 'I have made you a father to a multitude of nations.' Implied is that he is the father of all those who enter under the shelter of the Divine Presence." Abraham was the progenitor of the Western religions, in whose wake idolatry was eradicated from the West and monotheism was instilled.

It was in India that I realized the extent to which we should not take that reality for granted. When I arrived at the Sivananda ashram in Rishikesh, I asked Swami Nirliptananda, the vice president of the ashram, whether Hinduism would ever be able to function without idols. He said no, explaining that without them, the masses would be incapable of approaching the divine.

Although there is a significant gap between Eastern and Western religions on the question of idol worship, there are Jewish sources that point to similarities between Jewish and Eastern ideas. In fact, they specifically indicate that those traditions were inspired by the legacy of Abraham, based on Genesis 25:6, which tells of the "gifts" that he bestowed upon the sons of his concubines who migrated to "the east country." The Zohar (*Vayera* 100b) says he gave them gifts of wisdom, and relates a story about Rabbi Abba, who comes upon an Eastern book and finds its contents similar to the Torah. Still, Rabbi Abba warns of idolatrous elements in those books, even expressing concern that they could turn readers away from worshiping God.

Let us examine the similarities and differences between conceptions of the divine in Judaism and some Eastern religions.

The Dalai Lama and the Prayer for Rain

The Western religions are based mostly on dualism, meaning a clear differentiation between the divine and the earthly. Creator and creation exist independently of one another – a distinctness that enables dialogue. God created the world, He steers it and acts upon it; man talks and prays to Him, and examines His ways in an effort to learn from Him and obey Him. The individual can maintain a real relationship with God, with room for feelings such as love and hate, fear and anger. These religions cast God in human terms, as Father, Lover, and Brother.

The Eastern religions, on the other hand, are non-dualistic. They consider God and the world to be one, and their religious experience is an awakening to the oneness underlying everything (Brahman, or "infinite expansion," in Hinduism, and "emptiness" in Buddhism).

My friend the late Rabbi Menachem Froman used to relate an anecdote that illustrates the difference between the two outlooks. During his first visit to Israel, the Dalai Lama took part in an interfaith conference by the Sea of Galilee. It was a drought year, and Rabbi Froman, who also attended the conference, convinced the other religious leaders to join him in a prayer for rain. They all stood together – rabbis, sheiks, and priests – and begged for rain. But the Dalai Lama whispered to Rabbi Froman that he did not believe "in this kind of thing." When everything is one, he said, there is no room for such supplications. It is only when God is a separate entity that He can be approached with prayers and entreaties.

The difference between the two approaches recalls the fundamental gap between "being" and "doing." In a world where everything is one, humanity's purpose is to reveal the unity underlying reality, which to the naked eye seemingly comprises endless disparate elements. However, when God is conceived as being outside the cosmos and acting upon it, the individual's challenge is to act and strive to rectify reality.

Two Aspects of the Divine

Rav Kook addresses this apparent dichotomy in his *Shemona Kevatzim* (1:65), and explains that the Jewish conception of the divine is composed of two aspects: on the overt level of reality, God is distinct from the world and maintains a relationship with it, but on a deeper, more concealed level, all is one; everything is divine. The sources of "overt" Judaism, including the Bible, Talmud, and halakha, deal mostly with a personal God, while Jewish mysticism – Kabbala and Hasidism – is concerned with the inner Torah, with uncovering the divine in all of reality.

The complex relationship between God and the world can be likened to the love between a man and a woman: In order for there to be a loving relationship, each must reserve a place in their lives and their personalities that is separate from the other. It is only from such a place that they can emerge, love, and carry on a relationship. At the same time, each aspires to feel, even within that separate space, a sense of unity and shared experience with the other. A great example of this ideal is Rabbi Aryeh Levin, who – as the famous story goes – went with his wife to the doctor and complained, "My wife's leg hurts us."

Love, it emerges, can be described as the fertile tension between being two and being one. On the overt level, the man and the woman are separate beings, each aware of the existence of the other. But inside they are one – "bone of my bones, and flesh of my flesh" (Gen. 2:23), as Adam says in Eden. That is also the relation between God and the world.

The same tension is apparent in the Jewish Creation myth: at first, man was created as a single creature with two aspects – male and female – locked in a state that kabbalists refer to as *aḥor be'aḥor*, or "back to back," in which neither was aware of the existence of the other. It was only afterward that God severed them into separate male and female entities, so that they could ultimately reunite: "And [he] shall cleave to his wife, and they shall be one flesh" (2:24). Their renewed connection was what kabbalists call *panim befanim*, or "face to face." Each saw the other, each loved the other.

Om and *Shalom*

The word "yoga" means "to unite." Among practitioners, there is a custom to end each session by chanting "*Om*," a sacred Indian mantra that connotes an infinitely expanding, ultimate unity. I had a Jewish yoga teacher who would conclude each lesson with "*shalom*," the Hebrew word for "peace." Unwittingly, he touched upon a profound idea: that "*Om*" and "*shalom*" rhyme is no accident,[1] and the relation between the two words reflects both the similarities and the differences between Judaism and Eastern spiritual traditions.

For one, both "*Om*" and "*shalom*" refer to the divine: "*Om*," as noted above, connotes infinity, and according to the Zohar (*Vayera* 108b) is one of God's names. "*Shalom*," too, the Midrash says, is among God's names (Leviticus Rabba 9:9).

Another similarity is the manner in which both words are used to summarize and conclude: "*Om*" often appears at the end of sacred texts, such as in Hinduism's Upanishads. The word "*shalom*," too, concludes many prayers, including the Grace after Meals ("The Lord will bless His people with peace"), *Amida* ("Who blesses His people Israel with peace"), and the Priestly Blessing ("and give you peace"). In talmudic and mishnaic literature, many tractates are concluded with peace.

Both "*Om*" and "*shalom*" connote oneness and harmony. At the heart of *Sefer Yetzira* (The Book of Creation), one of the most ancient treatises on Jewish mysticism, lies the belief that language has the power not only to describe reality, but to act upon it, shape it, and create within it. At the root of language are three "mother" letters – *alef*, *mem*, and *shin* – each of which represents a different element of creation: *mem* stands for water, *shin* for fire,

---

1. As the English transcriptions show, the difference between *Om* and *shalom* is not merely phonetic; indeed, one is contained within the other. Some have also pointed out a visual similarity between the *Om* symbol, ॐ – which looks like the Hebrew letters *shin* and *mem*, topped by the letter *vav* – and the Hebrew spelling of "*shalom*."

and *alef* for air (*Yetzira* 3:4). The three elements reflect the dialectic between fire and water, with air symbolizing the synthesis between them (2:1).

The book also describes the sounds those letters make: "Three Mothers – *alef mem shin*. *Mem* hums (*domemet*), *shin* hisses, and *alef* is the breath of air deciding between them" (ibid.). Rabbi Abraham ben David, in his commentary on *Sefer Yetzira*, divulges a secret: "*Mem* hums, meaning a still small voice." The term "still (*demama*) small voice" refers to what Elijah the Prophet hears at Horeb, the Mount of God, where he shelters from his pursuers (I Kings 19). The still hum of the *mem* is especially reminiscent of the "*Om*," the sound of stillness thought to reflect the spiritual oneness of all being.[2] As we saw in the above quote from *Sefer Yetzira*, the humming *mem* symbolizes water. In Eastern culture as well, we find a potent association of the "*Om*" with water. One well-known expression of that connection is a scene in Hermann Hesse's novel *Siddhartha*, in which Siddhartha, the future Buddha, hears the "*Om*" in the river's voice.

Eastern Water, Western Fire

Eastern culture and Western culture can be compared to water and fire, respectively. In the foundational text of Taoism, the *Tao Te Ching*, water is likened to the Tao itself (the indefinable, infinite principle that underlies and sustains all of creation). The book praises water and its attributes – nothing is as soft and yielding as water, which is yet strong enough to overcome and wear away that which is hard. Consequently, the Tao advocates inaction (*Wu wei*), a passive approach to reality. Many other Eastern traditions also teach that enlightenment is attained by accepting reality and

---

2. In his commentary on *Sefer Yetzira*, Rabbi Aryeh Kaplan asserts, "The resemblance between [the hum of the *mem*] and the 'Om' chant is certainly more than coincidental" (*Sefer Yetzirah: The Book of Creation* [Boston: Weiser Books, 1997], 97).

"flowing" into it, a process that takes place mostly in one's psyche, irrespective of action. The sound of the *"Om"* rises up from the water.

Western culture, on the other hand, seems to be founded on fire. The calendar is derived from the solar year, and the Christian Sabbath is Sunday, the day of the sun. Greek mythology, which, in many respects, remains to this day the foundational mythology of the West, associates the dawn of civilization – the very possibility of creation and progress – with Prometheus, who stole fire from the Gods and gave it to humanity. Fire symbolizes the active principle, that which imposes its will upon reality. Dynamism, the will to effect change in the world, and the desire for progress – these are the foundations of Western society.

Shalom: A Fusion of Fire and Water

The word *"shalom"* contains, alongside the *"Om,"* the letter *shin*, which is associated with fire. Rabbi Nahman, based on the Zohar, likens peace to a connection between the two elements:

> What is peace? It is what links opposites. As our sages of blessed memory elucidated (Zohar, *Vayikra* 12b) regarding the verse "He makes peace in His high places" (Job 25:2): There is one angel of fire, and one of water – they are opposites, for water quenches fire – and the Lord, blessed be He, makes peace and binds them together. (*Likutei Moharan*, 80)

Informing the Zohar's interpretation is the common root shared by *"shalom"* and *"shalem,"* or "whole." In a complicated and multifaceted reality, only peace can provide wholeness by accommodating even those elements that seem to contradict and oppose one another. Indeed, *Sefer Yetzira* implies that the root *shin-lamed-mem* itself contains the opposites – both the water of *mem* and the fire of *shin*.

Jews, as we know, are Semites, descendants of Shem, whose name is spelled *shin mem*. The manner in which Jewish tradition encompasses the elements of fire and water lends new meaning to the term Semite, and could perhaps shed a new light on the ubiquity of anti-Semitism throughout the ages. There are those who attack us for the element of water that we possess; others assail us for our fire. And then there are those who set upon us for the audacity to fuse the two.

City of Brotherly Friendship

Ḥayei Sara evokes questions not only about the correct attitude toward distant nations, but also about the correct way to approach those that are closer to us. The *parasha* describes the transaction by which Abraham purchases the property that will come to be known as the Cave of the Patriarchs in Hebron, and Sarah's burial there. Every year on Shabbat *Ḥayei Sara*, tens of thousands of Jews gather at the Cave in Hebron to pray and visit the tombs of the Patriarchs. The site has come to epitomize the Jewish-Arab conflict. Among the many atrocities committed in the city was the massacre of 1929, in which Arabs slaughtered their Jewish neighbors, effectively annihilating the community. Many were also deeply shaken when, in 1994, a Jewish man mowed down dozens of Muslim worshipers while they prayed in the Cave.

In Israeli discourse, the question of the right to Hebron has become extremely contentious. Yet, our *parasha* shows that there is another way. Despite the tension between Abraham's sons, Isaac and Ishmael, both come to the Cave after Abraham's death and bury him together: "And Abraham expired, and died in a good old age, an old man, and full of years; and was gathered to his people. And Isaac and Ishmael his sons buried him in the cave of Machpelah, in the field of Ephron the son of Zohar the Hittite, which is before Mamre" (Gen. 25:8–9).

In employing the phrase "gathered to his people" to describe Abraham's death, it seems that the Bible is hinting at a moment of reconciliation in his family. The following verse further takes pains to emphasize that both Isaac and Ishmael are Abraham's sons, seemingly superfluously. Yet, it is possible the Bible reiterates their kinship in order to signal that it is not merely a biographical fact, but also an intrinsic connection. There is no reason why my affinity for the graves of my ancestors should preclude the affinity of their other descendants. It is a great honor to Abraham for all of his sons to visit his grave and pray to his God, the God of Abraham.

It was in that spirit that my friend Rabbi Froman would organize joint Jewish-Muslim prayers at the Cave of the Patriarchs. The city, he would say, is named *Al-Khalil* in Arabic, meaning "the friend," and there is a midrash that ties its Hebrew name, Hebron, to *ḥaver*, which also means "friend." May we merit to witness Hebron becoming once more a city of friendship, and may the heritage we share with our neighbors bring us closer together and engender peace.

Toledot

Does the End Justify the Means?

The infamous Machiavellian phrase, "The end justifies the means," denotes an approach that is responsible for much of the evil the world has known. It was evident, for instance, in the attitude of many Western intellectuals toward communism during the twentieth century. Many of those intellectuals, who considered themselves humanists, chose to support the Soviet Union even after they learned of the atrocities Joseph Stalin had committed against his own people. They chose to turn a blind eye to flagrant injustice in the belief that it was a necessary evil along humanity's path to a better, more just future.

The question is: can it be any other way? All good in reality is tinctured with evil and all evil contains traces of good, and to defer all action until unadulterated, unequivocal conditions arise would mean to never act at all. Very rarely do we encounter opportunities to act in ways that do not exact a price from anyone around us. Unfortunately, the question is most acutely felt in complex situations, when human lives are at risk. Here in Israel, the most salient example is the discourse surrounding the need to defend ourselves even at the cost of harming innocents (Israeli or others). How do we decide what is permissible and what is not? And, once we do act, how are we to relate to the price exacted and the pain inflicted by our action?

To Deceive or Not to Deceive

The same moral conundrum emerges in *Parashat Toledot*. Rebecca learns that Isaac has resolved to bestow his blessings on their eldest, Esau. She encourages her younger son, Jacob, to disguise himself as his brother, fool his father, and take the blessings for himself. How should we relate to Rebecca's problematic ruse? And does Jacob do the right thing in following her instructions? Might it have been preferable for him to forgo the blessings despite their immense importance to the Jewish people?

The Zohar (*Vayeshev* 185b) takes a unique approach to the problem, suggesting that much of Jacob's suffering throughout his life is punishment for stealing Isaac's blessings. Just as Jacob puts goatskins on his arms and neck to deceive his father, who feels him and mistakes him for his brother (Gen. 27:16, 22–23), so Jacob's own sons pull the wool over his eyes by dipping Joseph's coat in goat's blood (37:31). Jacob's punishment is measure-for-measure – the subterfuge he employs in appropriating the blessings is punished, seemingly proving that his actions were wrong. It is surprising, then, that the Zohar nevertheless insists Jacob did the right thing, and that even God Himself approved of his actions. Yet, he had to be punished, "even though the blessed Holy One approved those blessings" (Zohar, *Toledot* 144b).

It follows that, even in doing the right thing, one should bear responsibility for one's deeds, and heed their consequences. We must immerse ourselves in the complexities of reality, remaining responsible for our actions and ever-aware of the price we pay for them. Cognizance of consequences may deter an individual from action, but a mature outlook on life will accept the price without shirking responsibility. We can at once recognize the fact that our very presence on this crowded planet, and our very nature as consumers of resources, harms the Earth, and understand that such is the nature of life and choose to live. It is only the cynic, Oscar Wilde once said, who knows the price of everything and the value of nothing.

What Goes Around Comes Around

Still, the question remains: why would the Torah see fit to play up to such an extent the punishment Jacob receives for his just actions? Perhaps the Torah is seeking to drive home the fact that we are expected to pay a price for our moral choices, even when they are virtuous. When we are confronted with the consequences of every action, there is reason to assume we will not go above and beyond what is strictly necessary. We will seek alternatives, and even when we conclude that an action is inescapable, we will invest thought and resources into reducing the damage as much as possible, and even redressing it. On a deeper level, an awareness of cost can make us more open to other opinions. Were various groups more cognizant of the price of their ideologies – and not only their benefit – the public sphere would be far less toxic.

Psychologically speaking, in our *parasha*, Jacob's measure-for-measure punishment can be seen as a direct consequence of his behavior. Subterfuge within the familial context is a potential double-edged sword. It is a well-known principle that "the actions of the forefathers set an example for their children." A younger generation that learns from its elders that it is acceptable to lie and cheat will end up lying and cheating. Another indication that deception is endemic to Jacob's family is the fact that he acts on the instructions of his mother, whose brother Laban is not exactly a paragon of truth either. Indeed, while Rebecca uses her tendency to deceive for good, the trait remains in the family, and is passed on to the next generations, Laban and Rebecca's grandchildren. The atmosphere of duplicity breeds a suspicion and ambiguity that are only amplified among Jacob's sons.

God Is in the Sensitivity

The Zohar's interpretation is also novel in the explanation it gives for Jacob's punishment. In its telling, Jacob is punished not for lying or stealing – "Your brother came with guile, and has taken away your blessing" (27:35) – but for the emotional wound he inflicts on his father: "And Isaac trembled very exceedingly" (27:33). The Zohar writes, "For having terrified his father Isaac with trembling, Jacob was inflicted with the punishment of Joseph, trembling similarly when [his sons] told him [brandishing Joseph's bloody coat], 'This we have found' (37:32)" (Zohar, *Toledot* 144b).

The Zohar interprets Rachel's death in a similar vein. When Jacob flees Laban with his family, Rachel steals her father's teraphim (apparently, idols of some sort). Laban pursues and overtakes the fugitives, and demands that the teraphim be returned to him. Jacob, who does not know Rachel has pilfered them and is sure of his party's innocence, tells Laban that any member of his household found to be the culprit "shall not live" (31:32). On the face of it, Rachel's death is poetic justice, a direct consequence of Jacob's curse. Yet, the Zohar says that she is punished for hurting her father emotionally:

> Rachel, even though she acted to uproot her father from idolatry, was punished; for she never raised Benjamin nor existed with him for even an hour – all on account of her father's suffering, despite her good intentions. (Zohar, *Vayetzeh* 164b)

The Zohar is consistent in its approach: even when an idolater is on the receiving end, there is a price to be paid for inflicting emotional wounds on another. Rachel, like Jacob, is punished despite her good intentions.[1] The ensuing generation is also enjoined to show sensitivity to the suffering of the other: the Zohar (*Vayeshev* 189b), like the Midrash before it, explains that Joseph's troubles in the home of Potiphar in Egypt stem from him having "curled his hair" while his father mourned for him.

In ascribing paramount importance to consideration for others' feelings, the Zohar was a harbinger of contemporary trends. Today, ever more people are coming to terms with the fact that a purely intellectual outlook on life is incomplete, and that emotion must also be given proper consideration. That is the power of the Zohar, which relates many stories of rabbis who, in response to a question, "sat for a while and wept" (*Pinhas* 218b et al.). In contrast with the popular Israeli song about the men who "weep at night," the protagonists of the Zohar shed their tears in the daytime as well. The Jewish man, as opposed to the stereotypically macho Western male, is meant to be sensitive.

---

1. I will not deny that I am disquieted by the lingering sense that Rachel's punishment was disproportionate to her sin. Further along, the Zohar writes that God is particular with saints even in matters as light as a single hair (Zohar, *Vayishlah* 175a). Still, it is implied that her death was not itself punishment for how she treated her father, only its timing. Rachel hurt her father and therefore died while giving birth to Benjamin, with whom she never got to form a relationship.

Vayetzeh

I Do Not Get Along with Myself

One night during his voyage to Haran, Jacob dreams of a ladder into heaven by which angels of God ascend and descend. The dream brings enlightenment to Jacob: "And Jacob awakened from his sleep, and he said: 'Surely the Lord is in this place, and I knew it not'" (Gen. 28:16). For us, his descendants toiling along the paths to our own awakening, the verses may contain models for spiritual work. In one of his books, Rabbi Lawrence Kushner gives an impressive presentation of the powerful ways in which various readings of that verse represent different approaches to spirituality. In this chapter I will endeavor to emulate his approach.[1]

---

1. *God Was in This Place and I, i Did Not Know: Finding Self, Spirituality and Ultimate Meaning* (Woodstock: Jewish Lights Publishing, 1993). The quotes and discussion about Rashi, Rabbi Menahem Mendel of Kotzk, and Rabbi Pinchas Horowitz, among others, draw from Kushner's analysis.

The Unaware Life Is Not Worth Living

In Rashi's reading, when Jacob says "and I knew it not," he is implying that "had [he] known, [he] would not have slept in such a holy place." As is his wont, Rashi is searching for the most straightforward interpretation of the verse: Jacob was unaware of God's presence in that place; otherwise, how could he have slept? Informing Rashi's reading is an idea that relates to every one of us – that just as God was present along the road to Haran without Jacob's knowledge, so He can dwell, undetected by us, in other places. The challenge is to develop the capacity for awareness of our own lives, and God's presence in them. First, we must become aware of our actions and stop coasting through our lives on "auto-pilot"; listen to the life that surrounds us and pick up on the small details, reacting to them with joy and a sense of gratitude; and learn to appreciate our health, and cherish our families and the people we come into contact with. Gradually, we will come to discern hidden depths in everything we encounter. Divine presence and providence are perceptible in our lives not only in moments of prayer or special spiritual elation, but also in the mundane.

The discernment of God's presence, which we think of as spiritual "awakening," is conveyed in the case of Jacob through a literal awakening. One can whittle away all of one's life in sleep before rousing and recognizing the spiritual dimension that lay dormant in that life. Rabbi Nahman is quoted as saying, "There are those who tell stories to put others to sleep, while I tell stories to wake them up." Stories have the power to stimulate a new awareness of life, as can an inspiring interpretation of a verse in Torah, but the gateway to spiritual awareness is always our capacity to be present in the moment. Rabbi Menahem Mendel of Kotzk – in discussing the verse "And the Lord said to Moses, 'Come up to Me to the mount and be there'" (Ex. 24:12) – says that it is not enough to traverse the path to one's destination; one must be present en route as well.

When the "I" Is Too Big, God Can't Come In

Rabbi Pinchas Horowitz, a student of the Rabbi Dov Ber of Mezeritch, has a different take on the verse. He brings our attention to the "I" in "and I knew it not." The ego, he says, is what stands in the way of recognizing God's presence in our lives. It is so hard for us to comprehend that there is something beyond ourselves, a larger story that we are a part of; the fact that what guides reality is not "[our] power and the might of [our] hand" (Deut. 8:17), but rather the Master of the universe. The source of this difficulty is our powerful sense of self. We experience ourselves not only as separate from our surroundings, but, fallaciously, as the center of the universe. In truth, we are merely parts of a massive human tapestry, of biological, historical, and even cosmic fabrics. It is only through opening ourselves up to that insight that we can facilitate a life abounding with love, giving, and receiving. There is meaning to be found in doing for others and not only for ourselves.

This idea is encapsulated in our verse: we arrive at "this place," where God is, by diminishing our sense of ourselves as the center. "And I knew not" is the key containing both the problem and its solution. The "I" initially prevents us from comprehending what lies beyond us, but if we learn to moderate the outsize impact of the self on our outlook, we can come to know that God is in "this place."

When Moses recounts the Giving of the Torah, he tells the people of Israel, "The Lord spoke with you face to face in the mount out of the midst of the fire. I stood between the Lord and you at that time, to declare to you the word of the Lord" (Deut. 5:4–5). Moses is the medium communicating the awesome divine revelation to the people standing at the foot of Mount Sinai. The Baal Shem Tov, embodying the spirit of Hasidism, reads Moses' description as a template for spiritual work: the verse "I stood between the Lord and you," he says, implies that the "I," the ego, is what stands between us and the Lord. An overdeveloped ego tends to worship itself; it is only by practicing humility and meekness, and making room for the other, that we can draw closer to God.

And I Knew Not Myself

So far we have seen that it is the ego that obstructs our path to God. But there is another way to read the statement "Surely the Lord is in this place, and I knew it not." In Hebrew, the verse can be taken to imply that Jacob cannot detect God's presence[2] because he does not know "I," meaning himself. Ardent existential awareness of God's presence can only emanate from a profound connection to my own life: my inner world, narrative, family, talents, disappointments, joys, and loves. Only in a room of my own can I access the key to the meaning of my life and God's presence therein. When I succeed in truly knowing myself, connecting to myself, *being* myself fully, I will also find my connection to God. My deep inner identity is my place within the fabric of reality and the universe, and my journey is toward myself, the love of my life, my children, the world, life, and God. When I fail to reach myself, it is generally because I am being held back by something: fear of others' opinions, an insufficient capacity for self-awareness, and other hang-ups and anxieties. By constantly striving toward a purer, more precise and more authentic inner space, eventually I will reach Him.

Consequently, we can propose an interpretation that, on the face of it at least, seems diametrically opposed to the one posited by Rabbi Horowitz. "And I knew it not," in this reading, would imply not that annulling the ego is the path to God, but the inverse – that an inability to recognize God's presence could stem from people's failure to know themselves. People who do not know themselves cannot perceive the divine within themselves; nor, Rav Kook adds,

---

2. See Rav Kook as quoted above in the chapter on *Lekh Lekha*.

can they see the other: "And as there is no 'I,' there can be no 'him,' much less a 'you'" (*Orot HaKodesh*, pt. 3, 140).[3]

The Ego and I

Yet I believe that, ultimately, there is no contradiction between the interpretation we posited and the one put forth by Rabbi Horowitz, for identity can be said to have two layers: the "I" and the "self." The first, true identity must be cultivated, while the false self should be sloughed off and left behind. When one is engaged in spiritual work, the great challenge is to distinguish between the two identities and learn when to annihilate the ego and when to listen to an inner voice and nurture it.

There is grave danger in that path. People can come to deceive themselves and intensify the negative sides of their personalities, bringing the ego to the fore rather than nullifying it. Statements to the effect that one does or does not do something due to some inner truth can, rather than reflect the voice of the soul, express base desires cloaked in spiritual jargon. In such cases, instead of helping to propel one forward, insights regarding the existence of an inner self can hold one back.

Paradoxically, it is those very spiritual seekers who are most at risk. To strive spirituality is to grapple with the self, and putting oneself in the center generally entails a bias in favor of the ego.

---

3. I once presented the three interpretations of the verse in a class I gave, and one of my students suggested a tripartite interpretation of the following famous mishna in Tractate Avot (1:14): "He [Rabbi Hillel] used to say: If I am not for me, who will be for me? And when I am for myself alone, what am I? And if not now, then when?" "If I am not for me, who will be for me?" the student suggested, implied that one must cultivate one's inner self and remain true to it (in the spirit of Rav Kook). "And when I am for myself alone, what am I?" he continued, tells us that the "I," or the ego, must be annulled (in the spirit of Rabbi Horowitz's reading). "And if not now, then when?" the student concluded, refers to the need for one to live in the moment (as in Rashi's take).

The Ego Barrier

First, we must acknowledge that the journey to the self is long. In fact, it lasts a lifetime, and it relies on the understanding that one must never fixate on a specific spot and sanctify it, but rather constantly travel inward, moving slowly.

Second, the order of the inner work must follow the stages delineated in the statement "Depart from evil, and do good" (Ps. 34:15). At first, the focus of the movement is on shedding the unwanted identity, whittling away ego and base desires. Only through this can one come to the second stage – bringing to light, cultivating, and empowering an inner voice that is pure and righteous. It is a process that Rav Kook describes as follows: "Morality is the hallway, and holiness is the drawing room" (*Shemona Kevatzim* 1:133). A rectified morality frees one of character flaws in preparation for the holy.

Third, in order to counter the danger of inner work that only magnifies the ego, one must complement inward spiritual efforts with practical work that focuses on the other.

Finally, one must come to terms with the attributes of one's true and false identities, so as not to confuse them.

The belief that God is inherent in my soul signifies that within me is a connection with the transcendent. And my link to this root of my soul is what enables me to recognize that selfsame spark in the other. Only when my singularity resonates with God, the Torah, and the other, when I recognize that my unique branch grows out of a broad trunk that forks into countless other branches, will I know that I have come into contact with my inner self.

The ego, conversely, is the barrier between me and reality, and between me and transcendence. When I am angry, jealous, or arrogant, I am faced with the extent to which that barrier is yet present within me, the degree to which my ego still controls me.

Spiritual progress does not depend on freeing oneself of those negative traits so much as on recognizing them, when they arise, as expressions of the ego. Self-awareness, which enables one to observe those qualities from an external vantage, cuts us off from negative emotions: I see my anger, but I do not identify with it. The perspective from which I observe these emotions is itself an expression of the deep, positive place that I strive for within myself.

Love or Children?

Another theme in *Vayetzeh* is couplehood. Jacob's relationships with Rachel and Leah differ fundamentally from one another. Rachel is Jacob's beloved, Leah the mother of his children. The tragedy of the story is that each wife wants what her sister has; Rachel yearns for children, while Leah pines for Jacob's love: "And when Rachel saw that she bore Jacob no children, Rachel envied her sister; and she said to Jacob, 'Give me children, or else I die'" (30:1). But even when Rachel gives birth to a son, she does not feel fulfilled. Instead, as Joseph's name signifies, she can only gaze into the future, hoping for a second son: "And she called his name Joseph, saying, 'The Lord add to me another son'" (30:24). The fulfillment of that wish comes at the price of her life: "And it came to pass, as her soul was departing – for she died – that she called his name Ben-oni" (35:18).

Leah's story is a mirror image of Rachel's, a fact evident in the names she gives her own children:

> And Leah conceived and bore a son, and she called his name Reuben, for she said, "Because the Lord has looked upon my affliction; for now my husband will love me." ... And she conceived again and bore a son, and said, "Now this time will my husband be joined to me, because I have borne him three sons." Therefore his name was called Levi.... And Leah said, "God has endowed me with a good dowry; now will my husband dwell with me, because I have borne him six sons." And she called his name Zebulun. (29:32, 34; 30:20)

Ultimately, Rachel and Leah attain only in death the things they yearn for in life: Leah is buried alongside Jacob in the Cave of the Patriarchs, while Rachel is considered the mother of Israel, buried on the way to Ephrath so that when her children go into exile she can pray for them (Genesis Rabba 82:10):

> So says the Lord: A voice is heard in Ramah, lamentation, and bitter weeping, Rachel weeping for her children; she refuses to be comforted for her children, because they are not. So says the Lord: Refrain your voice from weeping and your eyes from tears; for your work shall be rewarded, says the Lord; and they shall come back from the land of the enemy. And there is hope for your future, says the Lord; and the children shall return to their own border. (Jer. 31:14–16)

Self-Actualization Through Couplehood

The twin expressions of couplehood – the loving relationship and the child-rearing partnership – highlight two human aspects that relate to the essence of the connection between a man and a woman. The first Creation story describes a relationship whose purpose is procreation: "Be fruitful, and multiply, and replenish the earth" (Gen. 1:28), while the second portrays the intimate relationship as a value in itself: "It is not good that the man should be alone … and [he] shall cleave to his wife, and they shall be one flesh" (2:18, 24).[4]

The stories of Rachel and Leah are a testament to the tragedy inherent in relationships that only contain one of the two elements. This explains the blessing given to Ruth and Boaz by the crowd at their wedding: "May the Lord make the woman that is coming

---

4. Rabbi Soloveitchik discusses the two models of couplehood at length in his book *Family Redeemed: Essays on Family Relationships* (New York: Ktav Publishing House, 2000).

into your house like Rachel and like Leah, both of whom built the house of Israel" (Ruth 4:11). The community wishes upon the couple a relationship that combines both aspects. As my students have pointed out to me, the blessing is indeed fulfilled in Ruth: she is loved by Boaz and her offspring includes King David (her great-grandson). A relationship encompassing both elements generates a state of oneness, in which each element deepens the other and fuses with it: on one hand, the outward-facing, creative life partnership – birthing and raising children – generates a profound intimacy between the partners; on the other, just as children enrich the love between the partners, so the parents' love contributes to their children. There is no greater gift for a child than to grow up with parents who love each other.

Couplehood: Traveling an Inner World

Aspirations for a life of meaning are challenged more than anything else by the difficulty of maintaining a loving, growing relationship. We all long for a relationship in which we can experience our love as a power that unites us as one flesh, as one vision. Love is the key to go beyond ourselves. The yearning, in a romantic relationship, is for two to become one. Physical intimacy fulfills one aspect of the yearning; a second is actualized through having and raising children. Yet, many couples are plagued by the feeling that they are emotionally incapable of attaining the significant intimacy that they aspire to.

Hedy Schleifer, a couples' therapist and expert in the Imago method, highlights a misconception underlying the power struggles that prevent couples from deepening their relationships: both partners know that, as a couple, "We are one," but sometimes each partner mistakenly thinks, "That one is me." Just as ego can form a barrier between the individual and God, a false model of couplehood can drive a wedge between two partners in a relationship. The capacity to maintain a relationship that is supportive, respectful, and conducive of growth depends on recognition of the fact that, as a couple, "We are two." If I am to grow in the relationship, I must accept and learn my partner's language and visit their inner world, thus building our "one" out of the meeting of our two worlds. Schleifer teaches us that in order to create a common space that facilitates a true encounter, both partners must learn to diminish themselves and recognize the existence of the other: an other whose purpose is not to serve or enlighten me; an other who exists independently; an other who is whole. A couple that experiences such a complete relationship, where ego does not come between the partners, can transpose that model to the relationship with God. When we make room, the focus is no longer on us alone or on God alone, but rather on the meeting between us; we open ourselves fully to the recognition that "surely the Lord is in this place, and I knew."

Vayishlaḥ

The Blessing of Pain

As a doctor in a major public hospital in the United States, Rachel Remen treated many patients who suffered from serious illnesses. She herself had been grappling, from a young age, with a range of incurable conditions. Her intimate acquaintance with both sides of the medical world endowed her with profound insights into the human soul. For one thing, she realized that patients' physical hardship, excruciating as it may be, paled in relation to their emotional suffering. A comprehensive medical approach, Remen contended, would treat not only physical symptoms but also maladies of the soul – fear of death, difficulties dealing with loss and accepting disabilities, and more. Thus she sought to implement the spiritual teachings of her grandfather, a kabbalist rabbi who died when she was only seven years old. Her book *My Grandfather's Blessings* describes her interactions with patients. A recurrent theme in the book is the idea that life in its entirety, including pain, is a blessing. It is a message she learns from the following story in *Parashat Vayishlaḥ*:

And Jacob was left alone, and a man wrestled with him until the breaking of the day. And when he saw that he could not prevail against him, he touched the hollow of his thigh; and the hollow of Jacob's thigh was strained as he wrestled with him. And he said: "Let me go, for the day breaks." And he said: "I will not let you go, except if you bless me." (Gen. 32:25–27)

Jacob wrestles with a man who later turns out to be an angel of God. During the struggle, the man inflicts a serious wound upon Jacob that, to this day, serves as his progeny's basis for not eating the sciatic nerve (32:31–32). Eventually, Jacob succeeds in overpowering the angel, at which point, surprisingly, he asks him for a blessing.

A sick person experiences life as a struggle. Yet, in health too our lives are fraught with moments of pain, injury, and loss. The story of Jacob's struggle with the angel shows us how pivotal those moments can be for us: they encourage us to ask fundamental questions about life, and to try and contain the difficult realities that are forced upon us. Jacob's story teaches us that there is a latent blessing in hardship, a power to foster newfound strength and insight.[1]

We find a similar idea in Genesis Rabba (10:10), where the midrash relates that every single blade of grass is paired with an angel that strikes it and tells it to grow. At times, blows lead to growth and – as in the case of the angels and the grass – can themselves be seen as a blessing.

Jacob-Israel, the Striving Man

At first it seems as though Esau, the hunter and outdoorsman who lives by the sword (27:40), is the stronger of the twins, while Jacob,

---

1. Rachel Naomi Remen, *My Grandfather's Blessings: Stories of Strength, Refuge, and Belonging* (New York: Riverhead Books, 2001), 25–27.

the quiet tent-dweller (25:27), is passive and weak, a "mama's boy" (25:28). However, the struggle with the angel paints an entirely different picture and sheds new light on the character of Jacob. We already know Jacob has tremendous physical strength (when he arrives in Haran, he rolls the stone off the well on his own, a feat generally requiring the efforts of three men [29:8–10]), but the encounter with the angel reveals a powerful capacity to confront and overcome obstacles. Indeed, after wrestling with the angel, Jacob is given a new name that symbolizes those abilities: "And he said, 'Your name shall be called no more Jacob, but Israel; for you have striven with God and with men, and have prevailed'" (32:29). Jacob's strength is no longer merely physical – it is a power of will and spirit.

In truth, Jacob's original name, given him due to his prenatal strivings, also denotes a propensity for struggle – in that case, an attempt to overcome fate and supersede his brother: "And after that came forth his brother, and his hand was holding on to Esau's heel; and his name was called Jacob" (25:26).

Jacob's two names allude to the progression of his life, a life of struggle. It seems as though the cards are perpetually stacked against Jacob, who time and again is forced to fight for his survival. Having been born second, he is forced to buy his twin's birthright, and since his father prefers Esau to him, he has no choice but to pilfer the blessings underhandedly. Thus he is forced into a twenty-year exile in Haran. But there, too, his life is ridden with adversity and strife. He is forced to work fourteen years for Rachel's hand, rather than seven, and in order to win his bread finds he must wrangle with his father-in-law and employer. "These twenty years have I been with you," he tells Laban, "in the day the drought consumed me, and the frost by night; and my sleep fled from my eyes. These twenty years have I been in your house: I served you fourteen years for your two daughters, and six years for your flock; and you have changed my wages ten times" (31:38, 40–41). Even when he finally sets off for Canaan after twenty years in exile, he discovers that his brother still wants to murder him, and is coming to greet him with an army of four hundred.

Nevertheless, Jacob not only succeeds in surviving, but also raises twelve sons, the progenitors of the tribes of Israel. But he pays a heavy price – his life is steeped in pain. "Few and evil have been the days of the years of my life," he tells Pharaoh (47:9). Needless to say, his wish to "dwell in tranquility" (Rashi on Genesis 37:2) is never fulfilled.

Esau: The Here and Now

Esau's story is the opposite of Jacob's. Everything comes to him effortlessly: he is his father's favorite and the intended recipient of his blessings. Esau is good-looking (the Torah describes him as "ruddy," a reference to physical beauty)[2] and – as opposed to solitary Jacob (the verse "And Jacob was left alone" [32:25] can be taken as a metaphor for his entire life) – he has charisma and leadership qualities and an entourage of four hundred men. But for him it is easy come, easy go. His effortlessly obtained birthright he scorns and sells off for pottage, practically as an afterthought (25:34), and is ultimately divested of his blessings as well. It is only after he loses those things that he recognizes their value, and weeps and "crie[s] with an exceeding great and bitter cry" (27:34, 38). Later, too, when the land can no longer sustain both Jacob and Esau, it is Esau who relinquishes Canaan and leaves (36:6–8).

Put in terms of "doing" and "being" – changing or accepting reality – one would think the outdoorsman is the man of action and the tent-dweller is resigned to the way things are. However, the Torah paints the opposite picture: Jacob is the one who engages with reality and changes it, while Esau is pliant, his fate determined by others.

---

2. See the description of David in I Samuel 16:12.

Both brothers ultimately suffer bitter fates. Jacob achieves success, but at a heavy personal price, while Esau departs Canaan bereft of both birthright and blessing. Yet, the stories of both men continue, and in the ensuing *parashot* we learn that their two characters are not mutually exclusive.

What Comes Easily to Rachel

Rachel and Leah are drawn as foils to Esau and Jacob. They, too, grow up together but diverge in their qualities – differences corresponding to those that set the brothers apart. I have no intention of drawing a moral comparison between Rachel and a killer like Esau; yet she, like him, is depicted as one to whom things come effortlessly.

Rachel is the pretty sister, beloved of Jacob and intended to him. As the Bible scholar Robert Alter notes, the first statement attributed to Rachel recalls words uttered by Esau. "Give me children, or else I die," she tells Jacob (30:1), echoing Esau, who says, "'Let me swallow, please, some of this red, red pottage; for I am faint'.... And Esau said, 'Behold, I am going to die" (25:30–32).

Leah, on the other hand, like Jacob, wages war with reality: on his wedding night she poses as Rachel to steal the marriage, just as Jacob poses as Esau to steal the blessings. Later, Rachel, like Esau, who forfeits his birthright for pottage, barters relations with Jacob for mandrakes (30:15). According to Rashi (ibid.), it is due to that transaction that she is not buried alongside her husband.

Love is important to both Jacob and Leah. The Torah says Leah wanted to be loved, while Jacob is described as a lover. The word is not used to describe Esau and Rachel.

Rather than have identical qualities, couples should complete each other. The Midrash says Leah was Esau's intended, and Rachel was promised to Jacob (*Tanḥuma Vayetzeh* 12), meaning, in light of the above, that each was meant to complement the other.

Israel: Striving with God and Men

We, Jacob's progeny, carry to this day the name given him by the angel. Indeed, the apple did not fall far from the tree, and the story of the Jewish people shares many of the motifs of Jacob's life. There is a curse attributed to Chinese sources that says, "Have an interesting life." That curse, I am afraid, seems to epitomize the history of the Jewish people, who were forced, throughout two thousand years of exile, to fight for their right to retain their faith and heritage, only rarely winning respite and peace. Even now, having finally returned to our land, we find, like Jacob, that here, too, the existential struggle continues, and we are consigned to ceaseless strife. Still, despite all of the blows we have sustained throughout our history, we have not faded. On the contrary, we have given rise to a rich and diverse spiritual tradition, and lots of life, joy, and love.

Esau Loves Jacob

Esau's feelings toward Jacob are not one-dimensional, and are composed of more than just hate. They show us that not only can love curdle into hate, but hate can become love. Still, it is a long process. Rebecca advises Jacob to flee to escape Esau (27:41–43), convinced that time will mollify her eldest: "Until your brother's anger turns away from you, and he forgets that which you have done to him" (27:45). But her hope proves unfounded – even twenty years later, Esau neither forgives nor forgets. Jacob realizes that his brother and the four hundred men marching at his side are not coming to greet him, but rather to carry out his threat. He prays to God: "Deliver me, please, from the hand of my brother, from the hand of Esau; for I fear him, lest he come and smite me, the mother with the children" (32:12).

It seems, at first, that Jacob will share Abel's fate. But Jacob ultimately succeeds in appeasing his brother, who, in a dramatic twist, abandons his plan to murder him. Even more, his hatred gives way to love: "And Esau ran to meet him, and embraced him, and fell on his neck, and kissed him; and they wept" (33:4). In Torah scrolls, unusually, the word for "and kissed him," "*vayishako*," is adorned with a series of dots, which one midrash says signifies that "he kissed him wholeheartedly" (Genesis Rabba 78:9).

Here, too, the Torah comes full circle. Jacob returns to his father (35:27), and when Isaac dies and the time comes for Esau to carry out his plan to kill him for stealing the blessings (27:41), we find the two siblings cooperating: "And Isaac expired, and died, and was gathered to his people, old and full of days; and his sons, Esau and Jacob, buried him" (35:29).

The Generations of Esau

Ultimately, Jacob and Esau part amicably. Their reason for parting, as in the case of Abraham and Lot, is their burgeoning assets: "For their substance was too great for them to dwell together; and the land of their sojournings could not bear them because of their cattle" (36:7).

The *parasha* ends with Esau's genealogy, which takes up a seemingly incongruous forty-three verses – even more than the space devoted to the Creation story.

The detailed treatment of the dynasty of Edom teaches us that there is no winner and loser in the story of Jacob and Esau – each receives his due. The Edomite ends up in Edom, and the Torah warns Jacob's descendants from infringing on his progeny's rights: "Contend not with them; for I will not give you of their land…because I have given Mount Seir to Esau for a possession" (Deut. 2:5). Jacob, who places great value on his family's heritage, is awarded residence in Canaan, the land of his father, as the Torah emphasizes after delineating Esau's genealogy: "And Jacob dwelt in the land of his father's sojournings, in the land of Canaan" (Gen. 37:1).

Yet, there seems to be something more at play here: the Torah takes pains to name the kings of Edom, and even notes that their reigns preceded those of the first king of Israel. In that, too, we see a contrast between Jacob, who encounters adversity at every turn, and Esau, whose success is effortless. The Israelites, Isaac's blessing notwithstanding, must endure a long and tortuous process before they can anoint a king. Esau, meanwhile, gives rise to an entire dynasty of monarchs "that reigned in the land of Edom, before there reigned any king over the children of Israel" (36:31).

Throwing Away the Strange Gods

Still, it would be an exaggeration to say the story has a happy ending. The struggle between Jacob and Esau yet endures, branded in our very flesh. The Torah seems to imply that there was a missed opportunity to arrive at a deeper rapprochement between the two sides. Esau seeks out Jacob's company on several occasions, and is rebuffed. After they are reunited, for example, when Esau embraces Jacob and kisses him, he asks to escort the latter's caravan, but Jacob refuses: "And he said, 'Let us take our journey, and let us go, and I will go before you.' And he said to him, 'My lord knows that the children are tender, and that the flocks and herds giving suck are in my care; and if they overdrive them one day, all the flocks will die'" (33:12–13).

Moreover, when the Torah lists Jacob's children who forded the Jabbok River, it omits Dinah. Rashi, based on the Midrash, criticizes Jacob: "But where was Dinah? He put her into a chest and locked her in, so that Esau should not set eyes on her. Therefore, Jacob was punished for withholding her from his brother – perhaps she would have caused him to improve his ways" (Rashi on Genesis 32:23).

By the end of the brothers' reunion, Esau opens up more than Jacob. It is understandable, considering Jacob's life in exile and struggle for survival under a constant fear of violent death at the hand of his brother. In a similar vein, the suffering endured by the children of all nations holds them back from opening up to the other; a victim has a harder time changing his attitude than his aggressor does. Clearly, the Jewish people's hardship-steeped history is that of a "people that shall dwell alone" (Num. 23:9), and yet we must open up to other nations' genuine attempts to forge friendly relationships. At times, suffering idealizes alienation. Jacob entreats his family to "put away the strange gods that are among [them]" (Gen. 35:2), which Rav Kook reads, in a play on words, as a demand that they renounce alienation (*Orot HaKodesh*, pt. 3, 140).

In his commentary on the Torah, the Netziv, one of Rav Kook's teachers, notes that while the hug and kiss that Esau and Jacob share is singular, indicating that Esau is the sole active party, the weeping is mutual:

> And they wept, meaning they both wept. This teaches us that Jacob, too, was then kindled with love for Esau. Consequently, in ensuing generations, at times when Esau's offspring are stirred by a spirit of purity to perceive the offspring of Israel and their virtue, we, too, are stirred by a spirit of purity to recognize that Esau is our brother. This is reminiscent of Rabbi [Yehuda HaNasi, redactor of the Mishna], who was genuinely fond of [the Roman emperor] Antoninus, and many others. (*Haamek Davar*, Genesis 33:4)

Vayeshev

Meeting with an Angel

Every Person Is an Angel

Parashat Vayeshev relates the story of Joseph, whom Jacob sends to check in on his brothers, a task that will completely change the boy's life. At first, he has trouble finding them, but he does meet a mysterious figure who sets him on the right path:

> And a certain man found him, and, behold, he was wandering in the field. And the man asked him, saying, "What do you seek?" And he said, "I seek my brothers. Tell me, please, where they are feeding the flock." And the man said, "They are departed hence; for I heard them say: Let us go to Dothan." And Joseph went after his brothers, and found them in Dothan. (Gen. 37:15–17)

Why does the Torah linger on this anecdote? What is it about an encounter with a nameless passerby that merits mention? The Torah could have omitted the episode and proceeded directly to Joseph's meeting with his brothers in Dothan. On the face of it, the point is to show that Joseph is making an effort to carry out his father's instructions. He could easily have given up and gone home without having found his brothers.

The Midrash (Genesis Rabba 84:14) says that the man was an angel of God. At crucial crossroads in our lives, the Midrash teaches us, God intervenes to actualize His plans. Thus, Joseph's meeting with the man is no chance encounter; it changes the course of history. He goes on to find his brothers, who sell him off, paving the way for Jacob's children to descend into Egypt. That, the Midrash says, is the will of God, realized through His messenger, whom He placed on Joseph's path.

Nahmanides (on 37:15) posits a sublime existential interpretation of the Midrash: "The blessed Holy One furnished [Joseph] with an unwitting guide to deliver him into [his brothers'] hands.... The story was not for nothing; its purpose was to inform us that the counsel of the Lord shall stand." Here, the figure Joseph meets is an ordinary man. Nahmanides agrees with the Midrash as to providence's impact on our lives, but asserts that the angels we meet are flesh and blood rather than holy seraphs. You can be a divine messenger in my life, and I in yours.

The realization that it is the hand of providence, not chance, that steers reality has the power to permeate our lives with meaning. The idea that everything is left to the vagaries of chance can cause us to slide into doubt and depressing thoughts: "If only I would have done that" and "What if things were different?" On the other hand, the feeling that God is watching and listening – and directing our experiences so as to maximize the actualization of our abilities, talents, and purpose – can help us contain and accept life's difficulties.

Such an outlook also entails reading life as a story, whose meaning we must unearth and which we can challenge with penetrating questions. And it can bring us to wonder how many times in our own lives *we* have met an angel. On a personal level, I feel that I was privileged to meet many guiding "angels" at the important crossroads of my life, from my immigration to Israel, through meeting my wife and finding a job, to the internal shifts that have come to define me.

Miracle and Deed

But does the realization that our lives are not governed by the caprices of chance undermine our sense of personal responsibility? Would not giving God a larger place in the world necessarily come at the expense of man's place? Indeed, if so many things in my life are entirely beyond my control, who and what am I?

Professor Uriel Simon deals with these questions in an especially impressive chapter of his book *Seek Peace and Pursue It*. He demonstrates in great detail how, in the stories of Joseph and his brothers, "not only is providence not at odds with divine recompense, but, miraculously, they complement one another."[1] From his daughter Michal, my wife, I learned a similar idea, though in different terms. She taught me the conception of "miracle and deed," according to which there are "miracles" in life – meaning times of grace, when a person receives divine direction – that remain meaningless if they are divorced from human action. For example, two people may meet by way of a highly improbable coincidence, a "miracle"; yet, the meeting's meaning will derive from what preceded it, from the work that the two did to become who they are.

I was told of one such encounter by Dalia Emmanuel-off, whose son Dvir was the first Israeli soldier killed in Operation Cast Lead, the 2008–9 war in Gaza. A few months after her son's death, Dalia was at a Meir Banai concert, and a young boy approached her and began to play with her. The boy's parents called him, urging him, "Come back to Ima, Abba, and Dvir." Dalia noticed that the parents had a several-months-old baby,

---

1. *Seek Peace and Pursue It* [Hebrew] (Tel Aviv: Yediot Books, 2002), 58.

and concluded that the baby was named Dvir. She approached the parents and asked them how old the baby was, deducing from their answer that he was born shortly after her son's death. "Why did you choose the name Dvir?" she pressed, and the parents replied that they had been so moved by the life story of Dvir Emmanueloff that they had decided to name their son after him. When she told them who she was, the parents were shocked. On the following day, Shiri, baby Dvir's mother, sent a text message to Dalia: "God does not bring people together for nothing," it said. Although it was the "miracle" that brought them together, it was the parents' choice to honor Dvir's memory that imbued the meeting with meaning.

At times, as in the story of Joseph and his brothers, the order is reversed, meaning the divine action, or "miracle," precedes the human deed. God challenges us and sends us to a certain crossroads, but it is up to us to choose our way. God and humanity are partners in directing the course of reality. To me, the sense that God is a partner in the emergence of my own life story only enhances the meaning of my choices and actions, rather than diminishing it.

In Jacob's life, too, there is evidence of a tension between chance and providence, between human deeds and divine direction. Many of Jacob's tribulations seem to stem from an entirely arbitrary occurrence: his emergence from the womb several minutes too late. Thus he is forced to buy the birthright, finagle the blessings, and spend twenty years in exile. As in the proverb "For want of a nail," which attributes catastrophic military loss to the absence of a seemingly inconsequential item, things seem to happen to Jacob merely due to a minor biographical fact. Yet, as we see in the story of the struggle between Jacob and the angel in *Parashat Vayishlaḥ*, the confrontation is not chance; it is tied to Jacob's very nature, and it is from it that his new name, Israel, is derived: "For you have striven with God and with men, and have prevailed" (32:29).

Descent in Order to Ascend

Ultimately, despite Jacob's efforts to give his son an easier life, Joseph is forced to contend with ordeals that echo those of his father – hatred and threats from his brothers, and a decades-long exile. Joseph inherits not only Jacob's genes but also his life story, laden as it is with harsh trials and choices that eventually bring him to where he belongs.

The Torah interrupts its account of Joseph's life mid-act in order to relate the story of Judah. Jacob's fourth son is the one to propose Joseph's sale into slavery, and the Midrash – commenting on the verse "And it came to pass at that time, that Judah went down from his brothers" (38:1) – says that Judah loses his standing among his brothers because they blame him for it (Rashi ibid.). It seems as though Judah's descent corresponds to Joseph's descent into Egypt, and that both foreshadow the climactic confrontation between the two men in *Parashat Vayigash* – hence the interjection of Judah's story. As in Joseph's case, Judah's descent ultimately turns out to have been part of a larger trajectory of growth.

Judah descends not only in terms of his status but also in his personal life. His two eldest sons, Er and Onan, die, and his grief is compounded by embarrassment when – flying in the face of the levirate marriage custom, by which a man whose brother dies must marry his widow and have offspring by her – he refuses to wed their widow, Tamar, to his third son, Shelah. Tamar then dresses as a prostitute and seduces Judah in order to become pregnant.[2]

Judah deposits his cord, signet, and staff with her as collateral (38:18), and when the "prostitute" absconds with them, he fears news of his iniquity will come out and he will be "put to shame" (38:23). The cord, signet, and staff are symbols of a man's status, and their loss would signify the loss of that status. When he

---

2. Apparently, before the Giving of the Torah, the duty of levirate marriage also extended to a dead man's father.

learns that his daughter-in-law is pregnant, he swiftly condemns her to death by fire. Judah hits rock bottom, but it turns out to be his turning point, and he begins to ascend anew. When Tamar produces Judah's signet, cord, and staff, proving that she is carrying his offspring, she essentially establishes her innocence. Judah admits his error and says, "She is more righteous than I" (38:26). Thus, Judah's descent becomes an opportunity for growth, building up to his dramatic meeting with Joseph, which affords him the chance to truly change.

Perez and Zerah

The importance of the story of Judah and Tamar lies not only in its meaning for the process of Judah's personal development; it has, on its own, far-reaching consequences: Tamar births twins, Perez and Zerah, the former of whom is the progenitor of the House of David. Indeed, the genealogy at the end of the Book of Ruth opens with "Now these are the generations of Perez" (Ruth 4:18). The story of the twins' birth is itself freighted with significance, whose purpose, we learn, is not merely to build the future but also to rectify the past:

> And it came to pass in the time of her travail, that, behold, twins were in her womb. And it came to pass, when she travailed, that one put out a hand; and the midwife took and bound upon his hand a scarlet thread, saying, "This came out first." And it came to pass, as he drew back his hand, that, behold his brother came out; and she said, "Why have you made a breach for yourself?" Therefore his name was called Perez. And afterward came out his brother, that had the scarlet thread upon his hand; and his name was called Zerah. (Gen. 38:27–30)

Kabbala teaches us that a levirate marriage facilitates the reincarnation of the deceased (the transmigration of the soul is given in-depth treatment in the Zohar on *Parashat Mishpatim* and in Rabbi Isaac Luria's *Gate of Reincarnations*). Clearly, the two boys born to Tamar correspond to Er and Onan, Judah's dead sons.

Yet, to me it seems there is a more basic rectification inherent in the story of the birth of Perez and Zerah, one that relates to an event that preceded the deaths of their brothers. When I studied the story with my son Yonatan, he noted its thematic similarity to the birth of Jacob and Esau. Both pregnancies are fraught with difficulty – Rebecca's infertility, Tamar's widowhood – and both births feature a struggle over which twin will be the first to emerge. The names also echo one another: Zerah, whose name connotes the sunrise, is named for the red thread the midwife ties on his hand, while Esau is named "Edom" (36:1), which is Hebrew for "red." Zerah is also the name of Esau's grandson (36:17) and of one of the ancestors of Edom's kings (36:33). Perez, meanwhile, is associated with Jacob, who is blessed, "and you shall spread (*ufaratzta*, from the same root as 'Perez') abroad to the west, and to the east" (28:14), and about whom it is said, "And the man increased (*vayifrotz*) exceedingly" (30:43).

Yet, although the stories share major similarities, they end differently. Like Esau, Zerah begins to emerge first, but Perez – unlike Jacob, who only manages to grab his brother's heel – succeeds in thrusting through first, winning the birthright. That difference is embedded in the names of both men: "Jacob" connotes struggle, clutching at the heel, while "Perez" implies propagation and success.

We realize what Jacob's fate would have been had he succeeded, like his grandson Perez, in overtaking his twin and emerging first from the womb. So what is the point, then, of the first version, in which Jacob emerges second, when that not only causes him difficulties but also, presumably, contributes to Esau's debasement?

It seems that it is only through the first story that we can arrive at the second one. As we have seen, Jacob must pass through a very specific crucible in order to become himself. His sons Joseph and Judah must also endure difficult and complicated ordeals. The story of Perez and Zerah is a source of hope. Perhaps things do not always have to start at square one, and processes initiated by earlier generations can be built upon by their descendants. Thus, Jacob's hopes for Joseph – that he will not have to suffer through the same tribulations – are finally realized a generation on, in Perez and Zerah.

Miketz

Joseph's Portrait

Blessed Memory

In the previous *parasha*, Joseph hit rock bottom. His brothers cast him into a pit and sold him into slavery, and even after apparently rising up, he again lost everything when he was thrown in prison on trumped-up fornication charges. In *Parashat Miketz*, however, his fortunes turn, and he swiftly advances to become the strongest man in Egypt aside from Pharaoh. He marries a "high-born" woman, daughter of the priest of On, who bears him two sons. The names Joseph gives them are a telling indication of his attitude toward his previous life. The eldest he names Menashe, "for God has made me forget (*nashani*) all my toil, and all my father's house" (Gen. 41:51). Joseph thanks God for making him forget his "toil," meaning the tribulations he endured, as well as his "father's house." Joseph seemingly puts it all behind him – good and bad alike. Repression enables a traumatized individual to begin a new life. We can find similar behavior among the Holocaust survivors who chose not to tell their children about their past in Europe, both in the camps and before the war. For them, all memory threatened to reopen old wounds.

With the birth of Joseph's second son, there is a shift in his approach to the past: "And the name of the second he called Ephraim, 'for God has made me fruitful (*hefrani*) in the land of my affliction'" (41:52). Joseph chooses not only to remember his suffering, but also to acknowledge the good that is his lot in "the land of his affliction." Thus he attains the spiritual stature of his father, who, in wrestling with the angel, sought blessing in pain. We can now understand why Jacob, in his twilight years, chooses to bless Ephraim first, despite the fact that Menashe is the elder.

The Midrash (*Tanḥuma Vayeḥi* 17) relates a story that elucidates the nature of Joseph's special power. It tells of Jacob's funeral procession, which passes by the very pit into which Joseph's brothers cast him so many years earlier. When the brothers see the pit, they are filled with fear: will the sight of the "scene of the crime" cause Joseph to succumb to his desire for revenge? Yet Joseph, bucking their expectations, instead stands next to the pit and recites a benediction: "Blessed be He who performed a miracle for me in this place." The story, which culminates the *Tanḥuma* on Genesis, is an expression of the psychological and spiritual stature that Joseph attains. After all those years, he is able to contemplate pain and see the seed of blessing contained within. Like other midrashim, this one, too, is based on an idea that is explicated in the biblical source text. The verses describe the brothers' fear of reprisal by Joseph after Jacob's death (50:15), and Joseph's reassurance that everything that passed between them was part of a divine plan: "And as for you, you meant evil against me; but God meant it for good, to bring to pass, as it is this day, to save a great number of people alive" (50:20).

It Is Lonely at the Top

It would be glib to say that the story of Joseph and his brothers has a happy ending. The irony is that while Joseph learns that what initially seems bad can turn out to be good, he also learns the inverse – that the appearance of good can be deceiving. As a boy, he dreamed that he is above it all. He enthusiastically told his father and brothers about dreams in which everyone is bowing to him. But when those dreams come true and Joseph ascends to power, he finds that it is cold and lonely at the top. After their father dies, Joseph's brothers beg that he forgive them; they fall before him and offer themselves up as slaves. Yet Joseph, rather than feeling vindicated in the moment when his dream is realized, can only weep (50:17). He attains everything he dreamed of as a boy but, now, all he truly wants is to break down the walls alienating him from his brothers, to be welcomed back into the family.

They say that when Rav Kook's mother died, he cried bitterly and was inconsolable. When the people around him tried to mollify him with platitudes, he responded, "You do not understand. There was one person in the world who called me Avreimeleh. Now there are none."

We need leaders capable of grasping what Joseph grasped – that the purpose of leadership must not be ascendancy over others, that power is no more than a necessary evil. We need leaders who are driven by a sense of mission rather than egotism.

Jacob and Rachel's Son

By grasping the ways in which Joseph is a reflection of his parents, Jacob and Rachel, we can understand his unique attributes. Already as a child, Joseph is blessed with the beauty and grace of his mother. But it is only after a long and arduous path that he finds within himself the qualities of his father as well. The turning point is in the home of Potiphar, where he valiantly passes a test posed by his master's wife. Rashi quotes an aggada that says Joseph only withstands temptation after "his father's image appeared" before him (Rashi on Genesis 39:11). The ability to wrestle with the evil inclination and best it is Jacob's heritage, and when Joseph exercises it we learn that he is spiritually equipped to walk in his father's footsteps. Furthermore, thanks to the rare convergence of Rachel's and Jacob's traits, Joseph succeeds in surpassing his father. The ability to wrestle and withstand adversity, combined with his beauty and grace, makes him a natural leader.

The power that emerges from the mingling of those two sets of traits is prefigured in Noah's blessings to his sons: "God enlarge Japheth, and he shall dwell in the tents of Shem" (Gen. 9:27). The blessing seeks to join Japheth's beauty (the name Japheth is from the same root as "beautiful") with Shem. Though the verse does not divulge Shem's character, we see him as a spiritual antecedent of Jacob, whom the Torah also describes as a tent dweller. Indeed, the union of Jacob and Rachel fulfills that blessing in the body of Joseph.

Esau and David

As we have noted above, Rachel's positive qualities complement Jacob and correspond to Esau's character, while Joseph is portrayed as an amalgamation of the traits of both his parents. But there is another biblical hero who seems to partake of Esau's attributes, the only other character whose ruddiness is emphasized – David.

The foundational story of David's election includes the following: "And he sent, and brought him in. Now he was ruddy, with beautiful eyes, and good to look upon (*tov ro'i*). And the Lord said, 'Arise, anoint him; for this is he'" (I Sam. 16:12). Early commentators noted the parallel. The thirteenth-century kabbalist Rabbi Joseph Gikatilla, in his book *Shaarei Orah* (gate 2), identifies some of Esau's traits in David; for instance, his pugnacity. Meanwhile, the description of David as "*tov ro'i*," which in Hebrew can also be taken to mean "good looking," he associates with Jacob.

I wish to invert the correlation and propose that David's beauty is linked to his ruddiness ("And when the Philistine looked about, and saw David, he disdained him; for he was but a youth, and ruddy, with a fair countenance" [I Sam. 17:42]). Like Esau, David has both beauty and charisma, and is beloved of Michal, Jonathan, and all of Israel.[1] Conversely, like Jacob, David has the strength and ability to fight for things that matter to him, and he too was pursued (as he fled from Saul). This combination makes him the ideal leader for the people of Israel, and to this day we, too, await the arrival of the Messiah, son of David, a leader bearing this same singular blend of traits.

---

1. There is another parallel between Esau and David, in addition to ruddiness: Esau marches on Jacob with an entourage of four hundred (Gen. 32:7), the same number of men who accompany David when he chases down Amalek, Esau's descendants (I Sam. 30:10).

Vayigash

Nation as Family

Professor Uriel Simon relates that once, when he was seven years old, he was sick and had to stay home from school. There were no children's books in his home, and when he asked his father what he should do during the day, his father gave him a Bible. He recalls poring over the text and coming to the story of Joseph and his brothers. When he read of the brothers' cruelty, he says, he was shocked and began to cry. Almost seventy years on, Simon grappled with the story and discovered that, ultimately, it is optimistic: "A tale of change, relating how its heroes overcame their natures and mended their ways, is, more than anything else, a moral story, infused with optimism."[1] Let us examine, in general terms, Simon's argument.[2]

The source of all of Jacob's hardship is the preferential treatment he gives Joseph, which provokes anger and jealousy in his

---

1. *Seek Peace and Pursue It*, 58.
2. See ibid., 58–85.

other sons. As the Midrash notes (Genesis Rabba 84:8), "One must not treat any of his sons differently, for it was due to the coat of many colors that they 'hated him' (Gen. 37:4)." Jacob's special love for Joseph is due both to his status as the eldest of Rachel, Jacob's favorite wife, and to his being the son of Jacob's twilight years, the long-awaited one. The relationship is mutual: Jacob makes a coat of many colors for Joseph, who, in turn, brings evil reports of his brothers to his father, a sure indication that Joseph prioritizes his relationship with Jacob over his relationship with his brothers.

Fueled by hatred and jealousy, the brothers viciously harm not only Joseph in selling him into slavery, but also their father. They bring him the blood-soaked coat and say, "Know now whether it is your son's coat or not" (37:32). By the end of the story, Benjamin, Rachel's second son, becomes Jacob's new favorite. When Joseph's brothers descend to Egypt in search of grain with which to survive the famine in Canaan, Joseph frames Benjamin as a thief and threatens to enslave him. It is then, in the story's climactic moment, that Joseph witnesses a profound reversal in his brothers, especially Judah.

Judah, well aware that Benjamin has taken on the status once accorded Joseph, is faced with the same choice as on the day he sold Joseph into slavery so many years earlier. But this time, he sacrifices himself to save the favorite, out of consideration for his father (44:33). When Joseph witnesses that sacrifice, he can no longer hold back his emotion. Then comes what is perhaps the most dramatic moment in the Bible, when the ruler of Egypt reveals his true identity: "And he wept aloud; and the Egyptians heard, and the house of Pharaoh heard. And Joseph said to his brothers, 'I am Joseph; does my father yet live?' And his brothers could not answer him, for they were stunned at his presence" (45:2–3).

It is not just Judah who shows a nobility of spirit; Joseph, too, overcomes any vengeful feelings he may have harbored toward his brothers and treats them warmly, kissing them and weeping with them (45:15). He even attempts to assuage their guilty feelings: "And now be not grieved, nor angry with yourselves, that you sold me here; for God did send me before you to preserve life" (45:5). The *haftara* for *Parashat Vayigash* is a prophecy about the future amity between the descendants of Joseph and those of Judah: "Behold, I will take the stick of Joseph…and I will put them and it together with the stick of Judah, and make them one stick, and they shall be one in My hand" (Ezek. 37:19).

The implications of the positive ending to the story of Joseph and his brothers are clear when considered in the context of the entire Book of Genesis. A major theme of the book is sibling rivalry. The first set of brothers, Cain and Abel, come to murder. Then there are Ishmael and Isaac, Jacob and Esau, and Joseph and his brothers. Each of the stories ends in a denouement of sorts, with a thematic thread whose progress can be traced from one story to the next.

In the case of Isaac and Ishmael, for example, we learn that after the forced separation of the brothers they reunite to bury their father (25:9). With Jacob and Esau, too, there is a scene where the brothers come together to bury Isaac in the Cave of the Patriarchs (35:29), alongside descriptions of their earlier reconciliation (33:4–15). But Joseph and his brothers undergo a profound change, going beyond a mere détente. As Simon writes, the evolution of brotherly relations culminates in the Book of Exodus, which opens with another pair of brothers, Moses and Aaron, who represent an ideal model of amity and partnership. The Midrash (*Tanhuma Shemot* 27) goes so far as to say that the verse "Look, how good and how pleasant it is for brothers to dwell together in unity" (Ps. 133:1) is a description of Moses and Aaron.

A Family Man

Why does Genesis focus so intensively on sibling relations? Surprisingly, the book, which provides the underpinning for the emergence of Jewish peoplehood, does not deal with political incidents or the establishment of a nation, but rather with familial interactions: relationships between siblings, husbands and wives, and parents and children. This is due, I think, to one of the Jewish people's most special qualities: the fact that we are not only a nation but a family.

The association of family with peoplehood begins with Abraham's election as the father of "a great and mighty nation," by whom "all the nations of the earth shall be blessed" (Gen. 18:18). Abraham's election is based not only on his leadership qualities, but also on confidence in his faculty as a family man, in his ability to instill values in his children and the members of his household. As the ensuing verse says, "For I have known him, to the end that he may command his children and his household after him, that they may keep the way of the Lord, to do righteousness and justice." In Judaism, the family is seen as a focal point for the transmission of heritage. The Torah includes many reiterations of the commandment to "tell your son" (Ex. 13:8), "teach ... diligently to your children" (Deut. 6:7), and "teach them your children" (Deut. 11:19).

But beyond cultivating the importance of the family unit, the Torah also fosters the idea that the entire Jewish people is a single family. The term "brother," which permeates Jewish law, is not a semantic quirk; it signifies a quality that underpins all interpersonal relations. Among strangers, a more rudimentary social contract – live and let live – is sufficient. But a brotherhood entails solidarity and mutual support. Hence the injunction to heed the other's distress: "You shall not see your brother's ox or his sheep driven away, and hide yourself from them; you shall surely bring them back to your brother.... You shall not see your brother's ass or his ox fallen down by the way, and hide yourself from them; you shall surely help him to lift them up again" (Deut. 22:1, 4).

Since I did not grow up in Israel, I do not take for granted the solidarity that is such a fundamental aspect of life here. The public's solidarity with prisoners of war is one expression of the sense that we are all members of a single family. I do not recall Americans having a similar attitude regarding Vietnam POWs. That selfsame solidarity also seems to be the source of the sometimes-shrill tone of our debates – we even quarrel like family members. In the US, the discourse may be more sober, but I believe such politeness stems not from intimacy but from distance. Native Israelis often become aware of this aspect of the Israeli experience only when they go abroad. I remember that in India, the Israeli backpackers' tendency to stick together was very apparent.

The Jewish familial quality is twofold: first, the importance of the family unit, and second, the attempt to extend a sense of kinship to broader circles. Recent history has seen nations and countries attempt the opposite. Natan Sharansky, in his book *Fear No Evil*, tells of a Soviet boy who became a hero for daring to inform on his father, who had defied austerity measures by stashing away for his family grain he had been required to hand over to the authorities. After the father was caught and sent to Siberia, the boy was murdered by his family, and the regime lionized him as an exemplar for putting national solidarity above kinship. But the Bolshevik assumption that eroding familial solidarity would boost citizens' loyalty to the state turned out to have been false. A case in point is the famous joke about the Soviet boy who is asked about the identity of his parents and replies that his father is Stalin and his mother is Russia. He is then asked what he wants to be when he grows up and replies, "An orphan."

The Torah, in contrast, directs us to establish familial relations with all of society. Take, for example, the verse, which appears at the end of *Parashat Toledot*: "And Isaac sent away Jacob; and he went to Paddan-aram to Laban, son of Bethuel the Aramean, the brother of Rebecca, Jacob and Esau's mother" (Gen. 28:5). Rashi asks why the Torah notes that Rebecca is the mother of Jacob and Esau when the reader is already well aware of that fact. I heard a good answer to the question from my teacher the late Rabbi Aharon Lichtenstein: sometimes, power struggles within a family leave all sides resentful and in conflict. The Torah makes a point of noting that Rebecca is the mother of both Jacob and Esau in order to emphasize that while she supports Jacob and his struggle for the birthright, she still identifies as Esau's mother too. When Rebecca tells Jacob of her fear that Esau will murder him, she concludes, "Why should I be bereaved of you both in one day?" (27:45). She is afraid not only of losing Jacob, but of losing Esau, too, if he were to become a killer. The same is true among ourselves: we can argue, quarrel, and hold diametrically opposed views, but we dare not forget that we are family.

Religion as Family

The Jewish people's familial quality is a feature not only of its national identity, but of its religious identity as well. Just as we relate to one another as family, so we relate to God as kin.

Judaism's novelty lies not only in its monotheism, but also in its belief in mankind's ability to maintain a personal, familial relationship with the divine. In the story of the Exodus from Egypt, God tells Moses to "say to Pharaoh: Thus says the Lord: Israel is My son, My firstborn" (Ex. 4:22). The Mishna (Avot 3:14) states that while all of humanity was created in the image of God, "Beloved are Israel, for they are called children of God; it is a sign of even greater love that it has been made known to them that they are called children of God, as it is stated, 'You are children of the Lord your God' (Deut. 14:1)."

The Song of Songs evokes another facet of the familial relationship between the Jewish people and God – its likeness to the love between man and wife. The Zohar further compares our relationship with God to the relationship between brothers. In its commentary on the verse (Ps. 133:1) "How good and how pleasant it is for brothers to dwell [also] together in unity (*gam yaḥad*)," the Zohar writes:

Those companions, when they sit as one, not separating from each other.... What does the Holy One say? "Look, how good and how pleasant it is for brothers to dwell *gam yahad*, also together!" – *gam*, also, including the *Shekhina* with them.[3] Furthermore, the blessed Holy One listens to their utterances and is pleased and delights with them... and for your sake, peace will prevail in the world, as it is written, "For my brothers' and companions' sakes, I will now say, 'Peace be within you' (Ps. 122:8)." (Zohar, *Aharei Mot* 59b)

When we treat one another as siblings, our relationship with God, too, mirrors the affinity of "brothers and companions."

Discussing our relation to God in terms evocative of human interpersonal relationship can be construed as ascribing corporeality to God. But one can also examine the issue from the opposite point of view. There are almost no familial relationships in the animal kingdom (beyond mothers' survival instinct, which drives them to protect their young). In nature there is no special significance to relationships among sibling or between fathers and their sons, and even the relationships between males and females do not often go beyond the reproductive instinct. Thus, to conceive of our relationship with God in human terms is not necessarily a projection. Rather, it acknowledges that relationships are a divine gift to humanity, and to have meaningful relationships is to actualize a powerful aspect of our divine image.

---

3. The Zohar sees the seemingly superfluous word *"gam"* as a hint that there is Another present beyond the brothers.

Vayeḥi

Eternity in This World

And the days of Israel drew near to die.

– Genesis 47:29

The Days Stand Still

Every encounter with death amplifies our sense of death's eternity and infinity on one hand, and life's finitude and transience, on the other. Such feelings can lead to a blasé approach to this world, based on the reasoning that this life is but a springboard for the true life, after death.

The Zohar on *Parashat Vayeḥi*, in its discussion of Jacob's death, reveals the secret of eternal life. But, wonder of wonders, eternal life, according to the Zohar, is attained in *this* world, not the next. The Zohar does not posit some magical object, such as Harry Potter's Philosopher's Stone, that has the power to lengthen our lives. Increased longevity, the Zohar says, brings one no closer to defeating death, for even if one were to live a thousand years, on one's deathbed one would still feel as if life had lasted no more than a single day (Zohar, *Vayeḥi* 223b). Rather, the Zohar teaches us, eternal life can be attained on this earth, and is a function not of the number of years one lives, but of the manner in which one conducts one's life:

> R. Yose said, "… For it is not written, 'The day of Israel drew near to die,' but rather 'days' (Gen. 47:29). Now, does a person die on several days? In a single moment, he dies and departs from the world. However, we have learned as follows: When the blessed Holy One desires to retrieve the spirit, all those days in which a human has existed are convened before Him and reckoned…. Happy is the share of the human being whose days draw near the King without shame, without one of those days being thrust out." (Zohar, *Vayeḥi* 221b)

The Zohar opens with a question: why does the Torah say "days," when death takes place in a single moment of a single day? It explains that the verse is not concerned with the date of death, but rather with what transpires at the moment of death (which the Zohar tenderly describes as the time at which God recalls to Him a person's spirit). When people die and ascend to heaven, every one of their days on earth ascends with them – for good or ill. They are not, as we tend to think, passing shadows; rather, each and every day, and the content with which one imbues it, remains with one forever.

To a certain extent, it seems as though this outlook is true before death as well. We are each what our life stories have made of us, what our past experiences, choices, and deeds have shaped us into, and even when we cannot recall the past, or be aware of the present, it remains etched in our bodies and souls. Yet, in the Zohar, this fact goes beyond psychological insight. Days have existential and real meaning, based upon which the Zohar defines the relation between days and an individual's identity. But before we try to understand the Zohar, let us examine the underpinnings of these ideas. In Judaism, every person has a soul, an inner essence that is eternal, existing before one is born and persisting after death. In this context it is worth mentioning the author Mary Russell, who said that the sense of desolation that one experiences when looking at a corpse is the ultimate proof for the existence of a soul in the living.[1]

The Zohar seeks to understand the meaning of the soul's sojourn in this world, i.e. the difference between its prenatal state and its postmortem state. In other words, the Zohar is after the meaning of life. The prevailing outlooks are variations on the theme of divine recompense, whereby a person who chooses good is rewarded, while one who chooses evil is punished. But the Zohar posits a far more existential approach: each day of one's life becomes an eternal "garment" for one's soul. It emerges that one's earthly life is eternal in the sense that it is a coalescence of all of one's days in this world, which accompany the soul for eternity. The body may rot away, but one's identity is defined by one's inner essence and the manner in which one lived.

Body, Soul, and In Between

The Zohar posits a novel answer to the nagging question of what a person is, of what I am. Some would answer that a person is composed of body and soul, and that because the body's existence is transitory, a person's true identity is the soul. There are spiritual outlooks, especially in the East, that seek to slough off this world and all materiality, uncovering the inner soul. The Zohar, however, claims that man is not a hybrid of soul and body, but rather an amalgamation of soul and life. The body may disappear, but our life stories – in the sense we described above – endure forever.

This conception of life after death recalls the synthesis of "being" and "doing": in this case, the element of "being" is

---

1. Mary Russell, *Children of God* (New York: Villard, 1998), 400.

represented by the soul, the inner essence, while "doing" is one's life story. This insight can help us resolve a paradox in the Mishna:

> R. Yaakov says, "This world is like a hallway before the World to Come. Fix yourself in the hallway so you may enter the drawing room." He would say, "One hour of repentance and good deeds in this world is better than all the time in the World to Come. And one hour of pleasure in the World to Come is better than all the time in this world." (Avot 4:16–17)

At first, it seems as though R. Yaakov is seeking to denude life of its existential meaning: the world, he appears to say, is only a means for attaining real meaning in the future, in the World to Come, where even a single hour of pleasure surpasses the entirely of this world. But then he pivots, saying that, in fact, the hallway surpasses the drawing room in importance, that "one hour of repentance and good deeds in this world is better than all the time in the World to Come."

According to R. Yaakov, even though some aspects of existence in the World to Come are more exalted, this world has an important advantage – the capacity for action. It is only through acting that people can change, and that ability has repercussions for one's eternal identity.

An outlook that lends ultimate reality to each and every day is very demanding. One must take responsibility and live every moment precisely, to imbue it with positive, not mundane, content. The Zohar offers a picturesque description of the danger of falling short:

> Every single day a herald emerges and proclaims – and no one pays attention! We have learned: When a human being is created, on the day he issues into the world, all his days arise in their existence. They come flying through the world,

descending, alerting the human – day by day, individually. When a day comes to alert him, if a person commits a sin on that day before his Lord, that day ascends in shame, bears witness, and stands alone outside. (Zohar, *Vayeḥi* 224a)

According to the Zohar, it is not only that a herald emerges every day, but that every day is itself a herald. Every day is a potential, waiting to be actualized. It cautions the individual to live it wisely, but sometimes, due to carelessness, the potential is squandered.

The movie *Groundhog Day* is about a man who wakes up every morning, only to discover that it is yesterday, which he had already completed. At first he fails to progress past that day, and is condemned to live it over and over again – until he learns to live it right. In real life, sadly, there are no do-overs. Every day is a unique opportunity that one can either actualize or squander.

The Zohar goes on to explain that when the Torah says Adam and Eve "knew that they were naked" (Gen. 3:7) after eating of the fruit, it means that they were without days to wear as garments, for they had sinned on their very first day in the world. In contrast, when the Torah says that Abraham was "stricken with age"[2] (Gen. 24:1), the Zohar interprets it to mean that he was surrounded by his life's days.

The Zohar teaches us the nature of eternal life, and how to shape ours. Only in this world do we have the duty and privilege to forge ourselves. Our identity emerges out of the totality of our lives, and is solidified for eternity when we die, lending everlasting meaning to each day that went into it.

---

2. The Hebrew, "*ba bayamim*," can be interpreted to mean "coming with days."

Shemot

The Deeds of the Daughters Are a Sign for Their Fathers

The Missing Name

Parashat Shemot begins with the story of Moses, who goes on to become the preeminent Jewish leader, the greatest of the prophets, and the main figure in the Exodus from Egypt and the journey to the Promised Land. But the Torah omits an essential biographical detail: nowhere does it mention the name given to Moses by his parents at birth. We know Moses only by the name given to him by the daughter of the Jewish people's greatest enemy: "And the child grew, and she brought him to Pharaoh's daughter, and he became her son. And she called his name Moses, and said, 'Because I drew him out of the water'" (Ex. 2:10). The Midrash notes the omission: "By your life, of all the names you have been called, I shall call you by just the name which Bityah, the daughter of Pharaoh, did" (Leviticus Rabba 1:3).

The key may lie in the words "and he became her son." The Midrash (*Lekaḥ Tov*) states, "When one raises the child of another, it is as if one had birthed the child." Pharaoh's daughter not only raises Moses; in drawing him out of the Nile and bringing him into her home, she rescues him from certain death. That rescue is tantamount to a rebirth, in which case the waters of the Nile symbolize a womb of sorts. But I think there is another, more fundamental reason for the fact that Moses is known only by that name. The name is derived from the most formative event of his life, and perhaps symbolizes the essence of his story. He lives only thanks to the extraordinary action of Pharaoh's daughter. She, upon being moved to compassion by a human story, is not content with watching from the sidelines and empathizing; she intervenes to prevent injustice.

The Torah omits not only Moses' original name, but also the names of his parents, Amram and Jocheved, who are referred to merely as "a man of the house of Levi" and "a daughter of Levi" (2:1), and that of Pharaoh's daughter. All are described archetypically. Thus, the Torah throws into stark relief the meeting between a "daughter of Pharaoh" and "one of the Hebrews' children" (2:5–6), highlighting her courageous choice to intervene and save the life of a boy whom her father had condemned to die.

Unable to Stand By

It is only at the age of eighty that Moses encounters God in the burning bush. Until then, the Torah chooses to relate only his interpersonal interactions. The three stories related in the *parasha* depict him as a man who is unable to stand by when he witnesses an injustice:

> And it came to pass in those days, when Moses was grown up, that he went out to his brothers, and looked on their burdens; and he saw an Egyptian striking a Hebrew, one of his brothers. And he looked this way and that way, and when he saw that there was no man, he struck the Egyptian and hid him in the sand. And he went out the second day, and, behold, two men of the Hebrews were striving

together; and he said to him that did the wrong: "Why are you striking your fellow?"... Now when Pharaoh heard this thing, he sought to slay Moses. But Moses fled from before Pharaoh, and dwelt in the land of Midian; and he sat down by a well. (2:11–13, 15)

Moses, like Pharaoh's daughter, sees and does not stand by. The Torah twice uses the word "saw," which, the Netziv explains, in this context connotes a penetrating gaze: "He looked much upon the form of their burdens, whose purpose was not the king's labor but rather their own affliction" (*Haamek Davar*, ibid.). Moses contemplates the depths of reality, sees the moral injustice, and is driven to take action for which he pays a heavy price – ultimately relinquishing a prince's life of comfort for harsh exile in the desert, a death sentence hanging over his head.

But Moses does not step in only when an Egyptian is abusing his own kin; on the following day he is compelled to intervene at the sight of a brawl involving two Hebrews, his brothers. When an outsider harms a member of our group, it is natural for us to experience that harm as personal, but it is harder for us to take sides and intervene in internal disputes, and the price we pay is more complicated. Nevertheless, Moses again cannot stand idly by. It is noteworthy that this story, like that of Moses' rescue by Pharaoh's daughter, employs archetypal terms: an Egyptian smites a Hebrew; two Hebrews strive together.

In the third story, Moses arrives at a new place where no one knows him, and immediately clashes with the locals:

Now the priest of Midian had seven daughters; and they came and drew water, and filled the troughs to water their father's flock. And the shepherds came and drove them away; but Moses stood up and helped them, and watered their flock. (2:16–17)

As in the Darwinian world, where only the fittest survive, the stronger shepherds overpower Yitro's daughters. But Moses cannot abide that, and he helps the weaker women even though he does not know them. Here is a third level of intervention: Moses is compelled to step in even in the face of a dispute between two "others," despite having no allegiance to either side.

Yet, the courage required of Pharaoh's daughter in rescuing Moses is even greater. Not only does she intervene on behalf of another; she has to take the side of an ostensible enemy, to act against the interests of her own people. Moses, in his first speech to the Israelites on the plains of Moab, makes a similar demand of his people, opening with the moral imperative of serving justice, whether in the case of one's brother, or one's other: "And I charged your judges at that time, saying, 'Hear the causes between your brethren, and judge righteously between a man and his brother, and the stranger that is with him. You shall not respect persons in judgment'" (Deut. 1:16–17).

Boundless Compassion

Moses' life story serves to illustrate the ripening of compassion, epitomizing a natural love refined and extended to ever-widening circles. In her song "You Are a Miracle," Chava Alberstein says, "To love one's country is natural/Why should love end at the border?" Indeed, love is a natural emotion, but its scope must be expanded.

There is also love that begins at the border. Sadly, in many cases love for the distant other is a function of the relative ease with which we love those we do not strive with. It is hard to love someone we are forced to care for and get along with.

On Tisha B'Av of 2005, on the eve of the disengagement from Gaza, I participated in a meeting organized by the New Israel Fund that brought together various segments of Israeli society under the slogan "For These Things I Weep." The speakers all related the things that saddened them, and each, in turn, was asked to introduce the next speaker (rabbis introduced Palestinians, left-ists introduced settlers, etc.). Last to speak was the journalist and TV personality Jacky Levy, who pointed out two things about the speakers who preceded him: one was that the bearded rabbis had used the feminine form of "I weep," as does the Bible, and the other was that the two speakers who had bemoaned a lack of humanity in Israeli society had also neglected to introduce the speakers who came next.

We all have our challenges in life. There are those of us who must work on their approach to the distant other, and those whose challenge is to open up to those closest to them.

From the Human to the Divine and Back Again

> And the angel of the Lord appeared to him in a flame of fire out of the midst of a bush; and he looked, and behold, the bush burned with fire, and the bush was not consumed. And Moses said, "I will turn aside now, and see this great sight, why the bush is not burnt." And when the Lord saw that he turned aside to see, God called to him out of the midst of the bush, and said, "Moses, Moses." And he said, "Here am I." (Ex. 3:2–4)

Moses comes face to face with the bush and sees God. Rabbi Kushner[1] explains that the burning bush is a test of Moses' capacity to take in reality in all its fullness, in all its detail. Only someone who can observe the bush over time can notice that it is not consumed.

The capacity to observe reality and see the other is emblematic of Moses. Only he, who is capable of seeing the other, can see God as well. One who cannot see other people cannot see the

---

1. *God Was in This Place*, the first note on *Parashat Vayetzeh*.

divine Infinitude. It is a recurring theme throughout the Torah: humanity is the nexus of the unbreakable link between heaven and earth, and the path to God must pass through it.

The Torah, as we noted, does not name Pharaoh's daughter. But the Midrash gives her name as Bityah, "daughter of God," which is remarkable considering the fact that the Torah portrays her biological father, Pharaoh, as the epitome of evil: "The Holy One, blessed be He, said to Bityah, the daughter of Pharaoh, 'Moses was not your son, but you called him your son. Neither are you My daughter, but I will call you My daughter'" (Leviticus Rabba 1:3). Birth is not fate. People have choice and the capacity to change, in the eyes of both God and people.

There is a circle of compassion that begins with Pharaoh's daughter, who sees Moses' suffering, expands to Moses, who sees his own brothers' suffering, and finally extends to God, who sees the Israelites' suffering and hastens to deliver them. Just as Bityah draws Moses from the Nile into a new life, the Holy One draws the children of Israel from the Sea of Reeds to a new land. The deeds of the daughters are a sign for their fathers.

Va'era

Stories That Happen to Storytellers

The Exodus is a success story with a dramatic plot – a weakling slave nation that goes up against the most powerful nation of that ancient age and wins its freedom. Some might claim that the theme of the underdog overcoming a cruel, powerful master is a stale cliché, but that would be like complaining that Shakespeare is trite. The point is that the Bible, like Shakespeare, is the source and not the imitation. The Exodus story is very vividly drawn and sparkling with special effects. It features seemingly humorous elements, like the plague of frogs, alongside ones that inspire terror – the Nile waters turning into blood, the pitch dark, etc. And then, when it seems as though all the special effects have been exhausted, we have the ultimate set piece – the Splitting of the Sea.

The setting also informs the sense of enchantment – not some backwater, but a land of magic and mystery, the Egypt of pharaohs and mummies, wizards and pyramids. The combination of setting, plot, and special effects fires the imagination. It is no wonder, then, that the movies made about the Exodus – from Cecil B. Demille's *Ten Commandments* to Dreamworks' *Prince of Egypt* – have been blockbusters.

That would seem to be a happy chance, considering that the Exodus was a foundational event in the history of the Jewish people, imparted and studied for more than three thousand years. We are enjoined to remember it daily, and to retell it as a story at the Passover Seder, so it is a good thing that we find it so agreeable to the imagination. Yet, it turns out that it is deliberate: when God tells Moses, in the beginning of our *parasha*, how the Jewish people's most formative experience – an event of patent historical significance – will play out, we learn that He will harden the heart of Pharaoh, who will refuse to free the Israelites despite the plagues that will afflict his people. Why does God harden Pharaoh's heart?

When I was a child, I thought the purpose is to punish Egypt, but the biblical text offers an entirely different reason: "And that you may tell in the ears of your son, and of your son's son, what I have wrought upon Egypt" (Ex. 10:2). It is not enough for God to bring the Israelites out of Egypt; He wants a monumental story that will be told for posterity, and thus has to quell Pharaoh's freedom of choice so that he will not free the Israelites too soon.

A Story About a Story

The novelist Paul Auster once wrote that "stories happen only to those who are able to tell them." It is an insight that can be extended to storytelling nations as well. The events of the Exodus take place so that there will be a story to tell, and the Jewish people's retelling of the story throughout the generations – each formulating its identity by reading its own experiences in light of the foundational narrative – spins ever more secondary tales. "In every generation a person must regard himself as though he personally had gone out of Egypt," the Mishna (Pesaḥim 10:5) says. Rabbi Jonathan Sacks, the former chief rabbi of Britain, once said that the relation between the Jewish people and the Exodus was not a nation that has a story but a story that has a nation.

One example of inspiration drawn from the Exodus is the protests calling for the release of Soviet Jewry, which were always accompanied by cries of "Let my people go!" Another is the civil rights struggle in the US, led by Martin Luther King, in which the Exodus was a major theme. But the story left its mark on individuals as well as movements: the story of my family also came to pass thanks to the Exodus.

My wife's grandfather, Israel Prize laureate Professor Akiva Ernst Simon, a descendant of Rabbi Akiva Eiger, was born in Germany to an assimilated Jewish family. Until the age of seven he did not even know he was Jewish; and growing up, he was just like any other German boy, his Jewishness only a minor component of his identity. When World War I broke out, he joined the German army, where he first encountered brutal and cruel anti-Semitism. The encounter with his comrades was the first sign that his place in German society was destined to change. One evening, Simon learned that the Jewish soldiers were holding a Passover Seder, a ritual that was utterly foreign to him, and decided to join them. Toward the end, several participants got up and exclaimed enthusiastically, "Next year in Jerusalem!" When Simon asked the young man seated next to him why they were standing, he was told, "Those people are Zionists. They want to emphasize that the Jewish people should return to the Land of Israel."

"At that moment, my life changed," Simon would relate when recalling the story over the years. "I, too, rose to my feet, slowly, and thought, *I want to be a Jew. I want to be a Zionist. I want to immigrate to the Land of Israel!*" As soon as he was discharged, he began to learn Hebrew, study Torah, and take on mitzvot, and a few years later he fulfilled his dream of moving to the Land of Israel.

Between Egyptian Immortality and Jewish Eternity

I once heard Rabbi Sacks tell of two ancient nations that sought eternity and found it. The Egyptians immortalized themselves by building magnificent monuments to withstand the winds of time – the pyramids, which stand to this day throughout the desert. The Israelites, too, found their way to eternity, but through a different approach. In his first address to the children of Israel, even before the Exodus is completed, Moses entreats his flock to tell their children and their children's children what they have seen. Since then, every generation has carried out Moses' will, and the Jewish tradition is thus maintained through the living bond between parents and children. The Jewish eternity is handed down for posterity.

Once, during a family visit with my parents in the US, my wife, Michal, took our children to the department of Egyptian art at the Met in New York. As soon as they entered the gallery, my youngest ran to a large Sphinx sculpture and sat between its paws. Of course, from that moment onward, one of the museum guards, an older, heavyset man, followed them around, keeping a close watch wherever they went. Michal told the children about the sculptures and about Egyptian culture, lowering her voice so as not to disturb the guard, but he only leaned in to listen more closely. When they emerged from the Egyptian art wing, he approached them and asked with amazement, "Is that Hebrew your children are speaking?"

The guard, a devout Christian, was well versed in the Exodus story. Yet, he was astounded, thousands of years after the fact, to meet a Jewish family from Israel whose children still speak the language of the Bible – the same language spoken by their forefathers as they made their way from Egypt to the Land of Israel. The Jewish people's victory over Egyptian culture is undeniable: Egypt's immortality lies behind glass in museum displays, while the Jewish eternity is alive and vital.

Life as a Story

When we understand that God shapes reality in order to tell a story, we gain insight into life itself and into God's place in it. *Sefer Yetzira* tells us that the Holy One created the world with storytelling (1:1). A story is not only derived from reality, it is the force shaping it.

Auster, in asserting that "stories happen only to those who are able to tell them," apparently refers to the storyteller's tendency to look at life from a special perspective. The storyteller understands that life itself is a story, one that he learns to read and plumb for meaning. By approaching life as a story, and searching for our place within that story, we learn to embrace the challenges mounted by life and "play" our part in them.

I enjoy stories immensely, but beyond that, I ascribe great significance to their power to guide me and generate new stories. I often find myself in situations where I am compelled to come up with a course of action. Whenever I see similarities between a situation and a story that once excited me, I know what I have to do, even if it is difficult. A good story is a story that helps me to be better.

The encounter with God in life, the sense that I can see His hand guiding my life, is a fundamental religious experience. In the *Modim* blessing of the daily *Amida* prayer, we say, "We will thank You and declare Your praise ... for Your miracles, which are with us every day, and for Your wonders and favors at all times, evening, morning, and noon." We must see God not only in the past, but in the present, too – in our very lives – and we must tell the story.

Bo

The Ḥametz of Idleness

For hundreds of years, the children of Israel await the day when they will be liberated from the yoke of slavery. When that day finally arrives, they are forced to get up and leave immediately – otherwise the Egyptians will have a change of heart and the opportunity will be missed. The Exodus teaches us not to miss opportunities, a goal that is generally very difficult to achieve. In our day-to-day lives we tend to become entrenched in our routines, growing ever more gnarled and sluggish, so that every change, no matter how small, becomes a major complication. By the time we examine the opportunity, make a decision, and initiate action, the window of opportunity has often closed. The etymology of the word "opportunity" (from the Latin *opportūnus,* from *ob-* "toward" + *portus,* "port") recalls a ship coming into harbor. Sometimes, by the time we decide to come aboard, the ship has already sailed for sea, never to return.

Conversations with the Evil Inclination

The Passover prohibition against ḥametz, or leavened food, is a response to that very human weakness. The Israelites decamp from Egypt in such a hurry that there is not enough time for their dough to leaven and rise. They must accede to life's vagaries and suffice with matzot. They leave as they are, and embark on their journey toward freedom. Yet, among the children of Israel, it seems, there are those who cannot conceive of setting out without bread. When the time comes to hurry up and leave, they do not heed the call, instead dallying in preparing provisions for the road. But as soon as they finish packing their freshly baked rolls, they learn to their surprise that they are alone in Egypt – the exit gates are closed, the opportunity is gone.

Our sages liken ḥametz to the evil inclination. We tend to think of the inclination as a monster, a horned man-devil who goads us into sin, so it seems odd to compare it to ḥametz, which is useful, tasty, and nutritious. But the comparison brings us face to face with a far more formidable enemy. In the Talmud we find the following prayer: "Master of the universe, it is known full well to You that our will is to perform Your will, and what prevents us? The yeast in the dough" (Berakhot 17b). Rashi explains that the "yeast" is the evil inclination, which lies in our heart – "the dough" – and "ferments" it. The Hebrew word for "ferments," "maḥmitz," relates to both ḥametz and "haḥmatza," or "missed opportunity." The evil inclination, with which we strive constantly, does not necessarily convince us to do outright evil. But whenever we arrive at a significant crossroads, it tempts us to choose the easy, comfortable fork, to dally and miss the opportunity rather than make an effort and change.

On Passover we read the Song of Songs, which, behind the pretty words, is the tragic story of missed opportunity – a thwarted lovers' tryst. The final verse begins with the words "Make haste, my beloved" – the meeting is missed, the moment slips away. Earlier, we learn of the beloved's longing for her lover's presence: "I sleep, but my heart wakes." And then she hears him: "Hark! My beloved knocks. 'Open to me, my sister, my love, my dove, my undefiled.'" But instead of jumping out of bed and running to open the door for her beloved, she lounges about: "I have put off my coat; how shall I put it on? I have washed my feet; how shall I defile them?" By the time she is done dallying and finally rises to open the door, her lover is gone: "I opened to my beloved; but my beloved had turned away, and was gone. My soul failed me when he spoke. I sought him, but I could not find him; I called him, but he gave me no answer" (5:2–3, 6).

The Song of Songs teaches us to listen for the songs of our own lives. There are those whose entire lives pass them by as they wait to "find love" or "attain enlightenment"; to encounter their "big story," or someone who knows their purpose or their soulmate – things that do not always arrive. Often those who wait are disappointed to find that the world seems walled off to them, that no one is offering them an opportunity to grow. They are unable to heed the clarion call of life opening its gates for them. The word "*hametz*" relates to missed opportunity, and the prohibition against it on Passover teaches us not to pass by opportunities for personal development. As the Midrash says, "Just as one should not be slow to make the matza, lest it leaven, so one should not be slow to perform a religious duty. Rather, if a religious duty comes your way, perform it immediately" (*Mekhilta Bo, 9*).

Fear of Missed Opportunity

Our generation emphasizes spiritual work motivated more by love and joy than by fear, or *yira*. My wife taught me that the *yira* driving true spirituality is in fact the fear of missed opportunity. Life is so special, every day is so valuable, and it is so easy to miss an opportunity.

A realistic evaluation of life requires the kind of perspective that, sadly, sometimes arrives too late – at death's door. The introspection brought about by the knowledge of imminent death is a recurring trope in our culture. In Tolstoy's classic novella *The Death of Ivan Ilyich*, the eponymous hero's terminal illness causes him to reevaluate the emptiness of his life. Only too late does he grasp that his all-consuming focus on climbing the Russian bureaucratic ladder and becoming a "good bourgeois" had kept him from living his life as he truly wanted.

But sometimes people get a second chance. One of the leading candidates in the Democratic Party's presidential primary in 1992 (which was eventually won by Bill Clinton) was Paul Tsongas. During the campaign, Tsongas learned that he had cancer, and decided to back out of the race. A while later it emerged that it had been a mistaken diagnosis and he was fit to run, but he passed up the opportunity. Tsongas explained that he wanted to devote more time to his family. "Nobody on their deathbed has ever said, 'I wish I had spent more time at the office,'" he said. I recall a sign I once saw that sums it all up nicely: "What is the point of being on the fast track when there is no one to hug you at the end?"

Ultimately, we must learn to differentiate between the substantial in life and the trivial, and through that realization to grow. The belief in an afterlife must not erode the understanding that the arena for action is this world. The next world is static; it is only in this reality that life affords us the opportunity to affect our destiny through action.

Between Ḥametz and Turkish Snuff

One Passover eve, Rabbi Levi Yitzhak of Berditchev, who was known as the "defense attorney for the Jewish people," assigned a task to two of his followers. He asked the first to go door-to-door and spread news of a sick man who was in need of *ḥametz* to eat. Then he asked the second to collect Turkish snuff for the sick man (at the time, Ottoman goods were outlawed in Russia, where the rebbe lived, due to the war between the two superpowers). A short while later, the first man returned and apologized – he hadn't been able to find any *hametz*, for it had all been burned ahead of Passover. A few hours passed and the rebbe's second follower made his entrance, followed by a long convoy of people, all bearing sacks of Turkish snuff. Rabbi Levi looked at his two followers and raised his eyes heavenward. "Master of the universe!" he exclaimed. "Do You see the extent of Your children's love for You? The czar has posted police at every corner to ensure that there is no Turkish snuff, and yet everyone is well stocked. You, on the other hand, have not a single police officer to ensure that there is no *hametz*, and behold – all of the homes are devoid of it."

Beshallaḥ

Life as a Painting

There was once a painter who resolved to create his magnum opus. Although in his time it was customary to paint portraits of the gentry, this painter thought that rather than paint the king, it would be more interesting to paint his horse. He toiled long at his work, until finally the task was complete. The painter loved to receive praise – it's only human nature – so he decided to hang the painting in a hall of the royal place and wait for the compliments to pour in. But to his disappointment, many people passed by the painting, but almost no one spared it a glance. Needless to say, none were impressed by it.

When he could no longer contain himself, the artist approached one man and asked his opinion of the painting. "I am sorry," said the man, who was embarrassed by the question, "but I cannot see the painting, for it is obstructed by the king's horse." The painter, immediately realizing the problem, walked up to the painting, tore it down the middle, and hung the halves a few inches apart. It was only then that people realized it was a painting, and were duly impressed.

Rabbi Shlomo Kluger would use the above story as an allegory for the main occurrence in *Parashat Beshallaḥ* – the Splitting of the Sea of Reeds. In the reality of our lives, he taught, we are blind even to that which lies right before our eyes; we expect to see what we have become accustomed to seeing, and are therefore oblivious to the way things really are.

How much of the vast reality surrounding us do we truly see? How much of the immense wonder, sublime beauty, and wisdom of creation lying before us at any given moment do our senses apprehend? Very little. We are oblivious to it all because we are used to seeing it. The wonder that everything around us inspired in us as children wears thin as the years go by, and we are left only with what our eyes perceive. That is the main reason for the inaccessibility of true reality: it is there – in every beautiful sunset, in every child born, in the life gushing through our veins – but our senses are oblivious.

The story of the painter teaches us, first and foremost, to overcome the primary obstacle – our inability to discern creation and our attendant blindness to the beauty of life and the world. It reminds us to look at that beauty with new eyes; to understand that the entire world is a work of art and allow ourselves to be moved by it.

Life's great adventure, as formulated by Marcel Proust, is not to discover new landscapes, but rather to see old landscapes with new eyes. The next stage is to discern that the landscape has a Creator, to realize that God indwells in reality, in creation: in the beauty of the ocean and its swells, in the power of the mountains, and in the vitality of nature. As the Talmud says, "There is no artist like our God" (Berakhot 10a). What can help awaken us and open our eyes to this hidden reality? Only the changing or shattering of reality itself. Just like the painting, the Splitting of the Sea allowed us to see it as it is, and kindled our desire to sing a hymn to God, the Song of the Sea. The Splitting of the Sea flooded us with fresh wonder, with the astonishment that only nature can inspire.

I heard the allegory of the painter at a memorial for Ilana Blidstein of blessed memory, a dear woman whose life was brief but rich with meaning. The eulogizer linked it to her capacity to truly be moved by every meeting with another human being and by every moment in life. He concluded by noting that the Mourner's Kaddish prayer does not deal directly with death, but rather opens with praise for heaven: "May His great name be exalted and sanctified." It seems that this is due to the fact that when faced with death, one gains a heightened capacity to contemplate life and stop taking it for granted. The death of another is an opportunity to set aside our routines and reflect on our own lives. It is through such contemplation, and wonder at God's creation, that we glorify God's name in the world.

The moral of the allegory of the painter has played a crucial role in my life, because it drives me to perceive the beauty of the world and life's light, and to apprehend God's presence therein. While in previous *parashot* we found representations of life as a story, in our *parasha* it seems more akin to a painting.

God and Aesthetics

When the Israeli sculptor Daniel Kafri created a piece he felt was among the most significant in his oeuvre, he expected reactions and criticism, but they did not come. The indifference frustrated him – a feeling he shared with a hitchhiker he picked up one day. During the drive, Kafri expressed his disappointment with what he said was Israeli society's ingratitude toward its artists. The hitchhiker remained silent throughout. It was only when it was time for him to get out of the car that he turned to Kafri and said, "You know, you complain about people's ingratitude toward you. Are you not grateful to God for giving you life?" Years later, Kafri would describe the encounter as a formative moment in his life, one that set him on the path to becoming religious.

Kafri's story recalls the allegory of the painter in that it conveys a moral imperative to contemplate creation in depth. Moreover, this story later led Kafri to an insight that can be said to underpin the allegory. Darwin's theory of evolution, according to which only the best-adapted survive, offers no explanation for the abundance of beauty in the world. Kafri, as an artist, knew how hard it is to create beauty, and the radiance of the world became his proof for the existence of God. That may not be the most convincing proof of God's existence, but it is certainly the most beautiful.

Yitro

The Model Father-in-Law

Yitro, Moses' father-in-law, is one of the most positive characters in the Torah. In the *parasha* that bears Yitro's name, it turns out that even the great Moses has something to learn from him. Yitro brings Moses his daughter Tzippora and his grandsons, and the Torah tells us of the excitement during the meeting: there are kisses and conversation, and Moses even bows before his father-in-law.

Already on the following day, Moses goes back to judging the people from dawn to dusk. Yitro witnesses the heavy burden on Moses' shoulders, and fears that his son-in-law will collapse. Knowing Moses well, he adds a personal element to his appeal, arguing that, ultimately, keeping all of the authority concentrated in Moses' hands will be detrimental to the people: "And Moses' father-in-law said to him, 'The thing that you do is not good. You will surely wear away, both you, and this people that is with you; for the thing is too heavy for you; you are not able to perform it yourself alone'" (Ex. 18:17–18). Yitro thus counsels Moses to share the burden with worthy individuals, and Moses takes the advice, giving rise to the Jewish justice system.

As we have seen in previous *parashot*, Moses' tendency to pursue justice above all things, and refusal to abide any injustice, exacts a heavy price from him. Yitro seeks to lay down a limit for Moses' generosity, because giving without boundaries can prove destructive to both giver and receiver. For some reason, it is only Yitro, the outsider, who can see the problematic aspects of Moses' conduct. Perhaps it is this distance that affords him the perspective to perceive what Moses cannot. Or maybe it is rather his closeness to Moses that allows him to identify his human frailty and realize that there is a limit even to his capacity. And then there is the personal aspect: Yitro speaks as a father and a grandfather. When he brings his daughter and grandsons to Moses, he is thinking of their care. Thus, he ensures that the price they pay for Moses' public service is not too high. It is no coincidence that it was my father-in-law who taught me that a husband is only considered a king so long as he considers his wife to be a queen.

Instructive in this regard are the safety instructions demonstrated by flight attendants before takeoff: "If cabin pressure should change, panels above your seat will open revealing oxygen masks; reach up and pull a mask toward you…. Secure your own mask first before helping others." According to Rachel Remen, embedded in these instructions is a profound spiritual truth – that you cannot help others if you neglect yourself. It is only after you have ensured your own steady oxygen flow that you can look around and see who else needs your help.

There is a price to boundless giving that is often paid by the family. In her book, Remen tells the story of a recovered cancer patient who decided to dedicate the remainder of his life to an issue he cared deeply about – nature conservation. But his zeal for the cause ultimately tore his family apart. His wife and children left him.[1]

---

1. *My Grandfather's Blessings*, 20–21.

I once heard the son of a famous leader allude bitterly to the high personal price he paid due to his father's dedication to public service, mentioning the midrash on Moses' grandson becoming a idolatrous cleric (Rashi on Deuteronomy 17:6). The Torah says nothing about Moses' relationship with his sons. The only mention is in a negative context: Moses is en route to Egypt to rescue the Israelites, and it emerges that he has neglected his most basic fatherly duty; having forgotten to circumcise his sons, he has placed them in mortal danger. Tzippora, who is not a daughter of Israel, is the one who saves the family by circumcising her sons (Ex. 4:24–26).[2]

Also relevant to the issue is the following anecdote: Once on the eve of Shavuot, a rabbi in the yeshiva where I teach was scheduled to give a lecture in the beit midrash. But because the evening meal went on longer than planned, the lecture started very late. A few minutes after the rabbi began his discourse, his young son entered the beit midrash in order to study with him, one on one. The rabbi cut short his lecture and apologized to the large crowd: "You may be many and he only one, but to him I am a father," he said, and sat down to study with his son.

Do and Listen

The main event in *Parashat Yitro* is the Giving of the Torah, about which the children of Israel say, "All that the Lord has spoken will

---

2. The episode contains implicit criticism of Moses. We have the message God instructs him to convey to Pharaoh: "Thus says the Lord, 'Israel is My son, My firstborn. And I have said to you, Let My son go, that he may serve Me; and you have refused to let him go. Behold, I will slay your son, your firstborn'" (4:22–23). Then, immediately afterward, the Torah relates the following episode: "And it came to pass on the way at the lodging-place, that the Lord met him, and sought to kill him. Then Tzippora took a flint, and cut off the foreskin of her son, and cast it at his feet; and she said, 'Surely a bridegroom of blood are you to me'" (4:24–25). The Torah contrasts God's relation toward His sons, the children of Israel, and Moses' treatment of his own sons. See also the discussion of Moses and the circumcision of his sons in Nedarim 31b.

we do, and listen" (24:7).[3] According to our sages, the prioritizing of "doing" over "listening" underpins the entire relationship between the Jewish people and God. As the Talmud says, "When the Israelites gave precedence to 'We will do' over 'We will listen,' a Heavenly Voice went forth and exclaimed to them, 'Who revealed to My children this secret, which is employed by the Ministering Angels?'" (Shabbat 88a).

Why is the antecedence of action such an important principle? During a talk I once gave to a group of soldiers, all of them immigrants from the former Soviet Union, I discussed the way in which Judaism contains both the element of "doing" and the element of "being." One soldier was unimpressed. "It is simple," she said. "The Torah explicitly states both 'do' and 'listen.' 'Do' is the practical action – 'doing' – while 'listen' conveys the value of paying attention, meaning 'being.'" That insight, while self-evident to her, was to me a novel interpretation of a familiar concept.

In the biblical text, on the face of it, the antecedence of "doing" is an expression of unconditional devotion, a primal readiness to answer the call. Rabbi Yaakov Leiner of Izhbitza, in his commentary on the first verse of Leviticus, explains the relation between calling out to someone and speaking: "Hearing a [friend's] call compels us to draw close and devote all of our attention. Afterward, when the friend speaks to us, it is completely personal. Similarly, there is a call by which every Jew devotes himself entirely to the Lord" (*Beit Yaakov, Bo*). It is like replying "Sure," when a friend asks for a favor – even without first finding out what favor is required. There is immense value in devotion and a fundamental responsiveness.

The first stage is to commit to doing, but afterward we must also "listen." Action may be unconditional, but there is more than

---

3. The verse appears after *Parashat Yitro*, but Rashi says it describes events that take place during the Giving of the Torah.

going through the motions. Rather than aspire toward rote performance, we yearn for "listening," for a place of profound understanding that facilitates experience, and a deep identification with the actions we take.

There is an insight attributed to Rabbi Nahman that is relevant to any spiritual journey: "Doing" refers to anything I can achieve in the present, to all of the places that I can currently reach. "Listening" refers to the spiritual qualities that lie beyond my grasp but that I should be aware of, so that my yearning for them will be stimulated and I will be moved to go beyond my current place. Hopefully, that which today is still "listening" to me will one day be my "doing."

Mishpatim

Who Deserves Justice?

Everyone talks about peace, no one talks about justice," the Israeli pop star Muki sings. But the Torah does talk about justice. *Parashat Mishpatim*, which is devoted to building a just society, is proof of the crucial importance of justice.

Parashat Yitro concludes with the Giving of the Torah, God's most significant revelation in the history of the world. Immediately afterward, in *Mishpatim*, the Torah sets out some of the mitzvot given during the Revelation at Sinai, and chooses to highlight those that relate to justice and jurisprudence. Rashi sees the juxtaposition as an expression of the fact that "judgment is of supreme importance, for the Torah juxtaposed it with the Ten Commandments, as it is written, 'And these are the ordinances'" (Ex. 21:1) (Rashi on Mishna Avot 1:1). Furthermore, our *parasha* begins with the word "and," indicating its powerful connection to *Parashat Yitro*. Revelation is bounded by jurisprudence on both sides: the beginning of *Yitro*, too, before the Giving of the Torah, deals with the appointment of judges and the establishment of a justice system. The link between the two issues points not only to the importance of jurisprudence but also to a profound connection between revelation and justice.

Yet, I think the main question is not the importance of justice, but rather what justice *is*, and to whom it can be applied. The Torah addresses this question at length as well. It does not suffice with proscribing infringements of others' rights to property based on a "live and let live" outlook, but requires that we actively help others, returning their lost objects (23:4) and helping them to unload their pack animals (23:5).

The most germane question, which constantly comes up in public discourse in Israel, is who is included in these laws. In early 2011, a public uproar was sparked by a letter, published by a group of rabbis, prohibiting the rental or sale of homes to non-Jews. That ruling, to my mind, is diametrically opposed to the Torah's core values.[1] The idea that the principles of justice do not apply only to our kinspeople is reiterated many times in the Torah: for instance, in Abraham's prayer for the people of Sodom, and in Moses' rescue at the hands of Pharaoh's daughter and his intervention to save the daughters of Midian. Time and again, the Torah emphasizes our obligation to do justice by the stranger, the other. The title of one of the protests against the rabbis' letter, a petition signed by yeshiva students, was taken from our *parasha*: "And a stranger shall you not oppress; for you know the heart of a stranger, seeing you were strangers in the land of Egypt" (23:9).

---

1. In short, here are my halakhic arguments against those rabbis' ruling: they relied on the prohibition against showing mercy to the seven nations (*lo teḥonem*), which appears in Deuteronomy 7:1–2 and which the Talmud, in a play on words, interprets to forbid allowing them "to settle on the soil" (Avoda Zara 20a). The original context is the war against the seven nations when the Israelites entered Canaan. Halakhic authorities are divided on the question of whether the prohibition was only applicable in its original context, or whether it should be extended to all idolaters, or even all non-Jews. The Rashba, Meiri, and *Sefer Mitzvot Katan* all rule that the prohibition applies only to idolaters, and Rav Kook, in permitting the sale of tracts of land to non-Jews during the Sabbatical year, relied on their opinions.

The source of many Jews' negative attitude toward others is clear: after thousands of years of persecution, and in the midst of an existential struggle with another nation, it is only natural for there to be suspicion and even hostility toward non-Jews. But there is another way to deal with the trauma of the past and the challenges of the present. In Egypt, too, our forefathers suffered from indignities and prosecution. Yet, the Torah, instead of drawing negative energy from that experience, directs us to empathize with the stranger, to identify with him, based on our own memories of being others in society. Elsewhere, we are enjoined not only to refrain from harming the stranger, but to open our hearts to him:

> And if a stranger sojourn with you in your land, you shall not do him wrong. The stranger that sojourns with you shall be to you as the home-born among you, and you shall love him as yourself; for you were strangers in the land of Egypt: I am the Lord your God.

Justice for Animals

The imperative to do justice relates not only to interpersonal relationships, but also to our approach to animals. The Talmud (Bava Metzia 85a) relates the story of a calf that escaped while it was being taken to the slaughter. It hides under the shirttails of Rabbi Yehuda HaNasi, and begins to wail, but he says to it, "Go, for this were you created." Rabbi Yehuda's callousness is seen as a sin, and he is punished for it with prolonged suffering. One day he sees his maidservant sweeping rat pups out of the house and asks her to leave them alone, citing the verse that says that God's "tender mercies are over all His works" (Ps. 145:9). Only then does his suffering subside.

The value of compassion toward animals is thus a theme in our *parasha*, which extends the commandment to rest on Shabbat to animals (23:12), and prohibits cooking a kid in its mother's milk

(23:19) and sacrificing an animal younger than seven days old – so that it can spend that time with its mother (22:29). Furthermore, we are enjoined to let the land lie fallow in the Sabbatical year so that, among other reasons, wild animals can eat the fallen fruit (23:11). *Mishpatim* is also cited as a source for the talmudic prohibition on cruelty to animals (Bava Metzia 32b). But the ethical treatment of animals entails not only rights but also responsibility: when an ox gores a person to death, it is given a trial of sorts and stoned to death (21:28).

Justice for Plants

There are those who take the assertion that God's "tender mercies are over all His works" to mean that compassion should extend only to the animal kingdom. But Rabbi Aryeh Levin would recall that once, as he was walking with Rav Kook, he plucked a flower from the tree. Shocked, Rav Kook exclaimed, "Believe me: in all my days I have taken care never to pluck a blade of grass or a flower needlessly."[2]

As they often do, that story engendered another: In the summer of 1992, when I was teaching in a Moscow yeshiva, I met a young man by the name of Alexander who had traveled all the way from Ukraine in order to learn about Judaism. Even though he had come from afar, Alexander only stayed at the yeshiva a single Shabbat. At one point, I sat with him on the lawn outside the beit midrash and we talked about God and the mitzvot. Throughout our conversation, Alexander picked leaves of grass, and I felt torn: on one hand, picking grass is forbidden on Shabbat, and I was finding it difficult to talk about God, holiness, and Shabbat while the holy day was being desecrated. On the other, I felt that the finer details of Jewish practice were irrelevant to Alexander at that point in his life. But I recalled the story of Rabbi Aryeh and Rav Kook,

---

2. Simcha Raz, *A Tzaddik in Our Time* (Jerusalem: Feldheim Publishers, 1989), 108.

and told it to him. Deeply moved, he immediately stopped picking the grass. We continued our conversation, and when Shabbat was over he left.

A year later I made *aliya* to Israel. The cab from the airport took me directly to Har Etzion Yeshiva, where I wanted to study. I arrived at lunchtime and entered the dining room, and from the other end of the hall, a man saw me and immediately bounded over and embraced me. At first I did not recognize him, but then I realized it was Alexander. He told me that not long after the Shabbat we had spent together in Moscow, he decided to immigrate to Israel. Oddly enough, it turned out I had no cause for concern regarding his picking grass: Alexander may have been interested in Judaism, but he was not a Jew, and the prohibition did not apply to him. But his encounter with Judaism convinced him to move to Israel and convert. A few months after my arrival, I was privileged to be on the panel of three *dayanim* who were present when Alexander immersed himself in a *mikve* and joined the Jewish people.

An Eye for an Eye and the Image of God

Our *parasha* also features one of the most well-known laws in the Torah: "An eye for an eye" (21:24). This precept is infamous mostly in Christian circles that believe in turning the other cheek. They find the idea of measure for measure to be an expression of vindictiveness, and corporal punishment seems to them to be barbaric. But that approach stems from a misconception. First, measure for measure is a principle that applies not only to punishment; rather, it is the manner in which providence manifests divine justice, a truth that is apparent in many biblical stories, including the ones in Genesis that we discussed above. The Jewish karma of measure for measure is not about exacting revenge, but rather about teaching the individual. In the story of Judah and Tamar, for example, Judah can only change after he endures an experience similar to the one he inflicted on his father. Second, measure for measure facilitates atonement and forgiveness, and there is justice in that.

Paradoxically, corporal punishment relies on an appreciation for the sanctity of the body. The late Professor Moshe Greenberg, a recipient of the Israel Prize for Bible studies, points out that the Torah never prescribes corporal punishment for property crimes. Conversely, the punishment for injuring another person is never financial.[3] The implication is that a person's body and belongings exist on separate planes that cannot converge. Greenberg focuses this idea by examining legal codes throughout history on the question of someone who gouges out another's eye. According to the Laws of Eshnunna, someone who gouges out an eye must compensate the victim. The Code of Hammurabi, several hundred years later,[4] takes that a step further, decreeing that gouging out the eye of a commoner incurs financial compensation, while someone who gouges out the eye of a nobleman must both pay redress and lose an eye. According to Greenberg, that law is based on a stratified conception of society, where the aristocracy is above property. The next stage in the history of jurisprudence is the Torah's legal code, which mandates "an eye for an eye" and is founded on the idea that all human beings are created in God's image.

The Torah's laws reflect a novel, revolutionary outlook according to which all people are equal. Yet, in contrast with the letter of the written law, halakha does not mandate gouging out the eye of an attacker, but rather requires him to compensate his victim. In doing so, it seemingly reverts back to the Laws of Eshnunna, which predate even the Code of Hammurabi in the history of jurisprudence. But there is a world of difference between the

3. Moshe Greenberg, *Studies in the Bible and Jewish Thought* (Philadelphia: Jewish Publication Society, 1995), 25–40.
4. One of the most ancient legal codes, dating from the eighteenth century BCE in Mesopotamia.

laws of the Torah and the Laws of Eshnunna: in jurisprudence, more important than the law itself are the values that it represents.

In the Laws of Eshnunna, monetary compensation for physical injury is an expression of contempt for the body. Halakha, on the other hand, refrains from corporal punishment out of respect for the body. The written Torah calls for "an eye for an eye," and it seems that our sages' understanding – that the letter of the law should be substituted with financial compensation – stems from an aversion to corporal punishment. That distaste manifests in an extreme fashion in the Mishna (Makkot 1:10), when sages declare that were they to preside over a court of law they would never hand down a death sentence. At the root of the aversion is respect for the human body, which is created in the image of God.[5]

Although many of the laws that appear in the *parasha* are inapplicable today, an appreciation for the value system that informs them shows how important it is to examine and extract meaning from them.

Justice and Revelation

The link between revelation and justice and jurisprudence goes back as far as Abraham. Before He reveals Himself to Abraham, God says, "For I have known him, to the end that he may command his children and his household after him, that they may keep the way of the Lord, to do righteousness and justice" (Gen. 18:19). Furthermore, as we saw above, the three stories preceding Moses' election as a prophet center around his dedication to justice.

What is the nature of the connection between justice and revelation? Clearly, God abhors iniquity, and injustice distances Him from the world. But there appears to be a deeper link: our *parasha* refers to a flesh-and-blood judge as *elohim* (22:7–10), which is also one of the names of God, perhaps indicating that in

---

5. Yair Lorberbaum, *In God's Image* (Cambridge: Cambridge University Press), 197.

dedicating one's life to doing justice – a fundamental divine value – one actualizes the divine image within. The Talmud states, "A judge who delivers a judgment in perfect truth causes the *Shekhina* to dwell in Israel" (Sanhedrin 7a). God dwells within a justice-based society; He manifests in reality through the adherence to divine values, paramount among which is justice. The Zohar (*Mishpatim* 122a) sees injury to the law as an injury to God Himself.

Justice defines relationships in society based on morality rather than interests. It requires us to look beyond ourselves and heed the word of God. Every revelation is an extension and development of humanity hearing the voice of God, who speaks to those who listen.

Teruma

God's Puppet Show

At the beginning of *Parashat Teruma*, God tells Moses, "Speak to the children of Israel, that they take [for] Me an offering; of every man whose heart makes him willing you shall take My offering" (Ex. 15:2).

An ancient kabbalistic homily offers an audacious interpretation for the verse. On the face of it, the verse seems to call for gifts for the construction of the Tabernacle. So why does it say "take Me" rather than "bring Me"? *The Bahir* explains that God is not asking man to bring but rather to take. He says, "take Me," so that He is the offering, to raise Him up (the Hebrew word for "offering," "*teruma*," shares a root with the word for raising up). Man has the capacity to influence God. *The Bahir* writes:

> R. Berakhya sat and expounded: "What is the meaning of the verse, 'And they shall take [for] Me a lifted offering (*teruma*)'? It means, 'Lift Me up with your prayers.' And

whom? Those whose 'hearts make them willing...' [This refers to] the righteous and pious in Israel who raise Me over all the world through their merit."[1]

People are responsible to rectify not only the earth, but heaven as well. Professor Shalom Rosenberg likened the history of belief in God to a puppet theater. The prevailing view in the world was that man was controlled by gods, like a puppet on a string, manipulated from above by a puppeteer. According to monotheism, the next stage in the evolution of faith, man is given free will: the strings connecting the puppets to their controllers have been severed, and they can move independently. Finally, Kabbala, which represents yet another stage in the empowerment of humanity and the development of faith, places the strings in the hands of the puppets, who can now manipulate the puppeteer. Humanity influences God.

To be precise, according to Kabbala, man's influence on the divine does not extend to the divine essence, which is infinite, unchangeable, and beyond any name or definition. Rather, it manifests in God's "garments," His expressions in reality.

What do we mean when we say that man "lifts up" God? There are several possible interpretations, but I would like to focus on a more existential one, while attempting to explain *The Bahir*'s two methods for elevating God: prayer and righteous actions.

Prayer and *Tikkun Olam*

Rabbi Menahem Mendel of Kotzk was once asked where God could be found, and he replied, "God can be found wherever He is allowed to enter." Our reality is generated by our consciousness.

---

1. Kaplan, *The Bahir*, 36.

Often, the gaps between people's lives are due more to contrasts in their outlooks than to material differences.

The author Yosef Haim Brenner once asked Rav Kook, "Everywhere you look, you see only light, while I only see darkness." It would be wrong to assume that one of them is correct and the other is living in an illusion. Rather, we can say that each experienced reality in a different way. Here we encounter one of postmodernism's main insights: that the interpretation of reality is inseparable from reality itself. Whether God is part of person's existential reality, and whether His presence is detectable, is a question that largely depends on the individual's sense of the world.

Prayer is a key to shaping our outlook in this regard. Addressing God enables us to gaze upon a multifaceted reality with a perspective that is confident and cognizant of His place within it. By praying, we open ourselves and the world to God, coming face to face with the divinity that inheres throughout creation.

God can also be elevated through righteous actions. One's positive deeds make the world a better, more beautiful, more rectified place. And the elevation of the world elevates its creator, the indwelling God.

These two methods for elevating God bring us back to the two life forces – "being" and "doing." Prayer is an expression of "being," while elevating God through righteous action is an expression of "doing."

Everyone Can Be Righteous

The Bahir links those whose "hearts make them willing" and who elevate God to the famous legend of the *Lamed Vavniks*, or the Thirty-Six.

As the story goes, in every generation there are thirty-six righteous people who remain hidden and whose actions secretly sustain the world. Many generations of Jews admired these people's humility and dedication to others. The author Haim Be'er recalled meeting Rabbi Aryeh Levin when he was only nine years old. Thrilled to meet such a great man, who had become a legend in his lifetime, Be'er asked the rabbi if he was truly among the *Lamed Vav*. Rabbi Aryeh took his time responding. We can speculate that his initial impulse was to deny it, but he stopped himself so as not to let down the boy and spoil his innocent faith. Finally he said, "Sometimes, for a few minutes, and you can be one too."

In doing so, Rabbi Aryeh proved that he was a towering educator. He let the boy hold onto his admiration, which stemmed from the legend built up around the rabbi's name, while empowering him to become righteous in his own right.

A similar democratization of the figure of the *Lamed Vavnik* was put forth by the author Arthur Koestler.[2] In the 1930s, Koestler was a communist operative traversing the Soviet Union in search of material for a regime-sponsored propaganda book. But during his travels, he became aware of the corruption, malice, and blind bureaucracy that were ravaging the country. He could not understand what was keeping the USSR from falling apart. Then he recalled the legend of the *Lamed Vavniks* who sustain the world. Koestler concluded that in every spot in the Soviet empire was a righteous person who was utterly devoted to his role. That person was always in the right place at the right time, someone who made existence tolerable for others despite the corrupt system.

The continued existence of the State of Israel, too, I feel, owes much to this interpretation of the idea of the *Lamed Vavniks*. The realization that our survival depends on our commitment puts a heavy responsibility on our shoulders, but it also presents a great opportunity. In a small country with large challenges, each and every one of us has the ability to change something for the better. That, at least, was how I felt while I was making *aliya* from a large country with small challenges.

---

2. Arthur Koestler, *The Invisible Writing* (Boston: Beacon Press, 1954), 156.

Tetzaveh

The Sound of Atonement

Clothes Make the Man

Mark Twain's famous comment that "clothes make the man" reflects the understanding that the garments we wear reflect our public standing and social milieu, and even influence our self-image. *Parashat Tetzaveh* describes the special garments worn by the priests while they performed their duties in the Tabernacle. According to the Midrash, "Just as the sacrifices atone, so do the vestments" (Leviticus Rabba 10:6). But while the sacrifices atone because they are offered and entail certain rituals, the vestments are merely worn – how is atonement effected through them? Perhaps, if clothes become a part of one's identity, we can conclude that there is atonement that does not stem from our actions but rather from our essence. Put differently, there is significance to "being" as well as to "doing." Change cannot be confined to action – what we do – but must extend to existence, to who we are.

The Sound of Atonement

Further along in the midrash it emerges that every vestment is designed to atone for a different sin. The robe worn by the high priest, for example, atones for the sin of evil speech (*lashon hara*), which we all are both guilty of and the victims of.

> One who utters evil speech has no path to atonement, and yet the Torah gave him a way to atone. How does he atone? Through the trimmings of the robe, as it is written, "A golden bell and a pomegranate, a golden bell and a pomegranate.... And it shall be upon Aaron to minister; and the sound thereof shall be heard" (Ex. 28:34–35). The Lord said, "Let the sound atone for the voice." (Leviticus Rabba 10:6)

The midrash opens with the assertion that there is no atoning for evil speech. It seems there are two main reasons for that. One is that most people are unaware of the extent of the pain they inflict on others merely by speaking, and consequently do not think there is anything to atone for. While the injured party is deeply hurt, the one who inflicts the wound may think it was "nothing but talk." I have a vivid memory of a young man, the victim of unfortunate life circumstances, who was teased by another young man to the effect that no one would ever want to marry him. The words deeply affected the first man, while the other probably forgot about it – certainly he was unaware of the damage and sorrow his words had wrought.

Another unique characteristic of the sin of evil speech is the fact that we have no control over the repercussions of our statements. They say there was once a man who asked his rabbi how he could atone for evil speech. The rabbi instructed him to take a down-filled pillow, rip it open and spread the feathers in a field, and he did. Afterward he returned to the rabbi and asked if his evil speech had been atoned for. No, the rabbi said, but it would be when he will have collected every single feather.

Yet, after the midrash declares that there can be no atoning for evil speech, it states the exact opposite. If we are to resolve the contradiction, we must first understand the special relationship between the robe and evil speech. Here is how the Torah describes the robe:

> And you shalt make the robe of the ephod all of blue. And it shall have a [mouth] for the head in the midst thereof; it shall have a binding of woven work [on the lip of] the [mouth] of it, as it were the hole of a coat of mail that it be not rent…a golden bell and a pomegranate, a golden bell and a pomegranate, upon the skirts of the robe round about. And it shall be upon Aaron to minister; and the sound thereof shall be heard when he goes in to the holy place before the Lord. (Ex. 28:31–35)

In the original Hebrew, the robe is described in terminology that invokes the mouth and lips. Furthermore, like the human mouth, the robe makes sounds, by way of its golden bells.

I heard an interpretation of the midrash to the effect that knowing when to keep one's mouth shut is comparable to a tailor making a jacket that keeps the body well protected. Yet, I wish to posit the opposite interpretation: the human capacity for speech is not only a danger, but a blessing as well. Speech is an expression of what makes us human, of the divine image within us.[1] It is my understanding that the intent of the midrash is not that there is no atoning for evil speech because the past cannot be rectified; rather, that such sin is overcome not by refraining from evil speech but by making an effort to engage in positive

---

1. See Onkelos on Genesis 2:7.

speech. There is no erasing the hurt caused by evil speech, but it can be counterbalanced. The high priest, faced with the debasement of the world through evil speech, tries to offset that trend with positive speech and a gracious eye, to the accompaniment of the dulcet tones produced by his vestments as he goes about his work in the Temple.

Ḥafetz Ḥayim, the title that Rabbi Israel Meir Kagan gave to his book about evil speech, is taken from a verse in Psalms: "Who is the man that desires life, and loves days, that he may see good? Keep your tongue from evil, and your lips from speaking guile. Depart from evil, and do good; seek peace, and pursue it" (34:13–15). The first step is to "depart from evil"; after that, one must "do good" – speak well of the other and of the entire world, offer praise and thanks.

A Tale of Two Notes

One day when I picked up my daughter from daycare, her teacher approached me, beaming, and said, "Thank you so much for the note. It made my day." I did not know what she was referring to, but I had learned by then that the correct response was not to ask, "What note?" but to return her smile. When I got home I found on the floor a note that my wife had written for our second-grader son's teacher apologizing for his tardiness that morning. Inferring that there was a connection between the two notes, I called my wife to find out more. She explained that as she was writing the note for our son, his two-year-old sister began to cry out that she, too, wanted a note. In order to mollify her, my wife wrote a note expressing appreciation for the daycare teacher and thanking her for investing in our daughter. It seemed that the eight-year-old's note was not a top priority for him, so he left it lying on the floor. The littler one, on the other hand, excited to emulate her big brother, was careful to hand hers to the teacher.

Her note did not contain superfluous flattery, but rather only an honest expression of appreciative feelings for the charming and dedicated teacher. But were it not for our daughter's willfulness, we would have missed the chance to express our gratitude in writing.

In his book *Words That Hurt, Words That Heal*,[2] Rabbi Joseph Telushkin tells of a rabbi who officiated at a funeral for the wife of an elder in his community. After the ceremony, the widower insisted on saying goodbye at his wife's fresh grave. The rabbi waited patiently, and eventually said gently that he thought it was time to go. The widower replied, "You do not understand. I loved my wife." The rabbi waited a little longer and again urged the widower to leave the gravesite. "But you do not understand," the widower said, "I loved my wife, and once, I almost told her." There is so much pain and frustration inherent in the realization that one could have achieved something with mere words but will no longer have the chance – no matter how much one yearns to do so.

Air Pollution and Air Purification

They say talk is cheap. Part of the problem, when it comes to speech, is the assumption that it is trivial, which to my mind is erroneous. Speech is an expression of our personality. It carries a profound healing potential (through therapy, for example), and the power to shape reality – it can be a force for both construction and destruction.

Some speech engenders sublimity, love, and intimacy, while other speech creates an atmosphere of depravity, cynicism, and alienation. Though we cannot see the words themselves, it is speech – more than any other thing – that fills the interstices

---

2. Joseph Telushkin, *Words That Hurt, Words That Heal* (New York: William Morrow and Company, 1996), 154.

between people and shapes the space in which we live. A shift in how we speak can change our world, the very air we breathe. If the environment is important to us, let us make an effort to purify, rather than pollute, the air with our speech.

A Priestly Blessing, with Love

It is no accident that the high priest is the one to don the robe that symbolizes atonement for evil speech. It is said that Aaron, the first high priest, was beloved of the people for his ability to make peace between hostile parties. Aaron would speak to each side individually, thus laying the groundwork for reconciliation (*Avot DeRabbi Natan* 12). According to one midrash, it was thanks to Aaron that the Clouds of Glory escorted the Israelites on their journeys through the desert. Rabbi Israel of Ruzhyn offers an interesting explanation: When one person speaks, their breath forms the shape of a cloud, as we see when it is cold. When two people speak to each other, there are multiple clouds. And when two people address each other with respect, there are clouds of glory (the Hebrew for glory, "*kavod*," also connotes respect). The clouds of glory were thus created by Aaron's efforts to bring people to talk to one another.

To this day, before they bless the congregation, the priests declare their intention to "bless His people Israel with love." The loving blessing emanates from Aaron's holiness, which imbues his descendants with the capacity, and the responsibility, to walk in his footsteps on the path of peace and love.

Ki Tissa

Questioning God

The Hebrew term for the penitent, "*hozer biteshuva*," and its modern Israeli corollary, the "*hozer beshe'ela*," posit the believer as a person of answers and the non-believer as a person of questions. The original connotation of "*teshuva*," "returning," has thus taken a back seat to the more recent connotation, "answer." It follows that the penitent is no longer one who returns to God, but rather one who claims to know the answers to all of the questions of the universe.

According to the Zohar (*Bereshit* 1b), however, faith in God will always entail unanswerable questions, a fact inherent in one of His names. In Hebrew, "*Elohim*" is an anagram of the words "*mi*" ("who") and "*eleh*" ("these"). "*Mi*" is an expression of the ineffable aspects of the divine, about which one can ask questions, though they are not necessarily answerable. "*Eleh*," in contrast, refers to the facets of God that can be expressed. "*Elohim*" is thus an amalgam combing the knowable and definable with the indescribable.

Based on this idea, the Zohar suggests a novel interpretation for the sin of the Golden Calf, which appears in our *parasha*. After the Giving of the Torah, Moses tarries atop Mount Sinai, and the people of Israel, plagued by uncertainty, decide to make a statue:

> And when the people saw that Moses delayed to come down from the mount, the people gathered themselves together to Aaron, and said to him, "Up, make us a god who shall go before us; for as for this Moses, the man that brought us up out of the land of Egypt, we know not what is become of him." ... and [he] made it a molten calf; and they said, "These (*eleh*) are your gods, O Israel, which brought you up out of the land of Egypt." (Ex. 32:1, 4)

The people welcome their new deity with the words "These (*eleh*) are your gods, O Israel." The sin of the Golden Calf is in the thought that God is a mere "this," an "*eleh*" – defined and denuded of mystery, of the ineffable, of "*mi*." The Zohar says, "Based on this mystery, those who sinned with the Golden Calf said, 'These (*eleh*) are your gods, O Israel!'" The Zohar adds that "through this mystery, the universe exists," and tells of the excitement that grips R. Shimon bar Yoḥai's students after he transmits this idea: "R. Elazar and all the companions came and bowed down in front of him. Weeping, they said, 'If we have come into the world only to hear this, it is enough'" (Zohar, *Bereshit* 2a).

It appears that the Zohar touches in a profound way upon a basic element of the story: people's desire to create an accessible, tangible god, one that can be seen. The Israelites struggle to accept God's invisibility, His transcendence of material reality, and in a moment of uncertainty, when it is unclear what has happened to Moses, they lose control, give in to their desires, and create an idol.

Countering the sinners, who proclaim, "These (*eleh*) are your gods, O Israel," is Moses, who cries out, "Whoever (*mi*) is on the Lord's side, let him come to me" (32:26) – again, the "*eleh*" versus the "*mi*." But the two must ultimately be recombined; the "*eleh*" joined to the *"mi,"* restoring God's mystery, the unanswered question, the ineffable.[1] Part of the atonement for the sin of the Golden Calf is through the mitzva of the red heifer, which is considered a *ḥok,* or a law for which there is no apparent rational explanation (Rashi on Numbers 19:2).[2] The deeper rectification of the sin of the Golden Calf lies in the ability to accept the incomprehensible too.

The Ineffable God

A god that can be defined is no god at all, for definition is constriction, while divinity is infinite, encompassing everything. As Rav Kook writes:

> Any definition of the divine leads to heresy. Definition is spiritual idolatry. Even to define [the divine as] mind and will, and as divinity itself and as the name of God, is a definition. And were it not for the ultimate knowledge that all of these definitions are but scintillating sparks of that which is beyond definition, they too would lead to heresy. (*Orot* 124–125)

This insight is shared by many religions that contemplate divinity. The *Tao Te Ching* opens with the following assertion: "The Tao that can be trodden is not the enduring and unchanging Tao. The name that can be named is not the enduring and unchanging name." The ineffable underpinning reality is what lends it vitality and being. As the fox famously tells the little prince, "And now here is my secret ... what is essential is invisible to the eye."[3]

The mystery shrouding our questions about God imbues life with value and meaning. Indeed, the same mystery exists in the

---

1. My thanks to Mordechai Zeller for pointing this out.
2. My thanks to Zvi Yehuda Cohen for pointing this out.
3. Antoine de Saint-Exupery, *The Little Prince,* http://users.uoa.gr/~nektar/arts/tributes/antoine_de_saint-exupery_le_petit_prince/the_little_prince.htm.

human context as well. Many people have described to me their sense that the people around them do not truly know them. There is an external world in which they can encounter the other, but their inner worlds remain hidden, and they are unable to share them with anyone else. (The Baal Shem Tov once described the hidden as that which is not, and perhaps never will be, communicable to the other.) Yet, despite their frustration, and the feelings of alienation and loneliness that the realization engenders, these people would not relinquish their privacy and inner worlds. It seems that the key to dealing with these feelings lies in the realization that there will always be an ineffable dimension to every encounter with another human being. It is a realization that has the power to deepen and enrich the relationship, even if we cannot define it.

Questions Fuel Growth

When we receive an answer, we stop searching, but if our question goes unanswered, the world remains wide open. Questions stimulate growth. Isidor Rabi, the Nobel physics laureate, attributed his success to the education he received from his mother. Every day, upon his return from school, she would ask him not what he learned but rather what questions he had asked.

My children like to tell a story about a child who asks his father, "Why is the sky blue?" The father replies, "I am sorry but I do not know." On the following day, the boy asks, "Father, why is the grass green?" Again the father apologizes and professes his ignorance. A few days later, the child asks, "Father, do you want me to stop asking you questions?" The father replies, "But if you do not ask, how will you know?" I used to think it was a joke, but eventually I realized that there is a profound lesson to the story: because the father repeatedly holds back from answering, his son continues to search, and perhaps, thanks to his unwavering curiosity, will one day arrive at previously unknown discoveries. According to Professor Yehuda Liebes, "*mi*" is "the aspect that is always in question. It is the infinite inquiry and appeal, and it is the source of every monumental creation, including the Zohar."[4]

When it comes to the big questions of life and death and God, those people who feel they need answers are invariably frustrated, while those who do not attempt to grapple with them are doomed to lead meaningless lives. The golden mean is understanding that even when our questions remain unanswered, there is value to continuing to ask them. As the Zohar (*Bereshit* 1b) says, "'Who' (*mi*) can be questioned. Once a human being questions and searches, contemplating and knowing rung after rung to the very last rung.... All is concealed, as before." To my mind, the Zohar's intention is that although the question itself has no answer, one is elevated merely through contemplating it. In Zen traditions, one of the paths to spiritual development is *kōan*, a question that forces one to contend with oneself and venture beyond one's habitual frames of reference.

Trust

According to Rabbi Nahman, the highest level of faith is a choice to continue to believe even without answers (see, for example, *Likutei Moharan* 64). When everything is overt, there is no need for trust. It is only when there is a hidden dimension that faith can exist. Still, it is important to emphasize: the fact that we have questions does not necessitate doubt as well; despite our bewilderment and perplexity, we can choose to believe.

In the Book of Job, we read of a fundamental argument between Job and his friends: Job raises the question of theodicy in all its starkness, while his friends rebuke him for questioning the ways of God. They deny him the right to ask questions, claiming that the calamities that have befallen him were all deserved, a consequence of his sins. Ultimately, God takes Job's side in the argument and scolds his friends:

---

4. Yehuda Liebes, "Zohar and Eros," *Alpayim* 9 [Hebrew] (1994): 67.

And it was so, that after the Lord had spoken these words to Job, the Lord said to Eliphaz the Temanite, "My wrath is kindled against you, and against your two friends; for you have not spoken of Me the thing that is right, as has My servant Job." (Job 42:7)

God refers to Job as his "servant," for service of God and faith in Him do not mean ignoring and suppressing questions, but rather grappling with them honestly, while internalizing the idea that God transcends human understanding and that not all questions can necessarily be resolved.[5] The search is eternal. As the psalm (105:4) enjoins, "Seek the Lord and His strength; seek His face continually." One of the main definitions of life is a capacity for movement. The search for the face of God – expressed in the form of questions about Him that are not mere means to an end – is the essence of life, which is a journey into the beyond. Though we never arrive, we are constantly engaged in study and growth that imbue our lives with meaning and purpose.

When we examine reality, we sense within ourselves the two faces of God. On one hand, a voice emerges, asking difficult questions; on the other, there is a powerful internal conviction that nothing is left to chance – that there is a higher power guiding life. Must we silence one of those voices, or can we learn to live with both, to accept a life of complexity?

My Face Shall Not Be Seen

And [Moses] said, "Show me, please, Your glory." ... And He said, "You cannot see My face, for man shall not see Me and live." And the Lord said, "Behold, there is a place by Me, and you shall stand upon the rock. And it shall come

---

5. My thanks to my friend Rabbi Shmuel Ariel for the insight and its formulation.

to pass, while My glory passes by, that I will put you in a cleft of the rock, and will cover you with My hand until I have passed by. And I will take away My hand, and you shall see My back; but My face shall not be seen." (Ex. 33:18–23)

The protagonist in Mary Russell's science fiction novel *The Sparrow* is Emilio Sandoz, a Jesuit priest who travels with his friends to the planet Rakhat in order to encounter, for the first time in human history, extraterrestrial life. The novel relates the journey mostly from the point of view of Emilio, who is thrilled to have been chosen for the mission. But the expedition ends in disaster, and Emilio, feeling that he has been wronged, experiences a crisis of faith. He, who had devoted himself entirely to God, has been forsaken in return, his journey tragically cut short.

In the sequel, *Children of God*, Emilio returns to Rakhat after many years, and discovers what happened in the wake of that earlier disaster. He realizes that there was meaning to his suffering. He may not have received answers to the difficult questions he asked, but he understands that even the most difficult experiences he endured had purpose. Toward the end of the novel, his friend, also a Jesuit priest, quotes a verse from our *parasha*: "And you shall see My back; but My face shall not be seen." He explains that God cannot be seen head-on, meaning that His intentions are inscrutable while events are occurring, and can only be construed after the fact, from the perspective of His "back."

While reading the book, I was struck by the thematic similarities to the Jewish story, with its coupling of chosenness and terrible suffering – the hidden face of God throughout the generations. When I read interviews with the author, I found I had not been wrong: that was indeed the source of inspiration for Russell, an Italian Catholic who had converted to Judaism.

In her afterword, Russell explains that the source of the insight expressed by Emilio's friend is the Ḥatam Sofer, one of the greatest rabbis of the nineteenth century. It bears mention that the outlook expressed by the Ḥatam Sofer underpins the thought of Rabbi Moshe Hayim Luzzatto, an eighteenth-century kabbalist known by the acronym Ramhal, especially in his books *Daat Tevunot* and *Kelaḥ Pitḥei Ḥokhma*. The Ramhal theorizes that the purpose of history is to reveal God's unity, meaning to give humanity the tools to understand historical events and see how they are expressions of God's will.

Yet, we must realize that even our capacity to see God's "back" is incomplete. The Book of Genesis, for example, concludes with Joseph's words to his brothers, which contain a large degree of optimism: "And as for you, you meant evil against me; but God meant it for good, to bring to pass, as it is this day, to save a great number of people alive" (50:20).

Seemingly, here is an instance of "you shall see My back" – what first seemed bad turns out after the fact to have been good. But it is not that simple. First, the scars are still fresh – the final chapter of Genesis also describes Joseph weeping bitterly, and his sorrow over his estrangement from his brothers. Moreover, when we examine the story of Joseph's sale into slavery from the vantage of his great-grandchildren, the picture is reversed yet again, for we see that it led to the Israelites' bondage in Egypt. It is only a broader historical lens, which considers that episode of servitude essential to the construction of Jewish national identity, that casts the story in a positive light.

But who knows what yet awaits us? We have not yet come to the end of the story, and as we said, when it comes to providence, there is far more than meets the eye.

Vayak'hel

Shabbat Here and Now

Six days shall work be done, but on the seventh day there shall be to you a holy day, a Sabbath of solemn rest to the Lord.

– Exodus 35:2

Change and Awakening

If the purpose of the spiritual search is to awaken the seeker, the implication is that, spiritually, most people are sleepwalking through life. Sleep, in this sense, means a lack of awareness of life, stemming largely from the manner in which consciousness flits between past and future, between thoughts of what was and of what will be. It is only when one succeeds in concentrating and being present in the moment that one can "awaken."

There is a story in the Zen tradition about a disciple who asked his master to show him the way to nirvana. The teacher replied, "Through food and sleep." The answer puzzled the student – after all, do not all people eat and sleep? But the master explained the difference: when he eats, it is he who eats, and when he sleeps, it is he who sleeps. The capacity to bring absolute presence to every action brings one into contact with existence and forges a connection to the essence of life. That bond is the awakening that we so yearn for.

The metaphor of sleep and wakefulness is a recurring theme in the writings of Rabbi Nahman, who similarly applies it to a general lack of consciousness: "For sleep is the departure of awareness," he writes (*Likutei Moharan* 117), and adds, "There are people who while away their days in sleep... for the essence of animation is the mind... and one must be awakened from one's slumber" (ibid. 60). Elsewhere he instructs his students to focus on the present: "There is nothing in one's world but the day and moment in which one exists, for the following day is an entirely different world" (ibid. 272). Learning to wake up is thus an important lesson: to be present in life, in the moment; to treat existence with respect, and not to let it pass one by.

Rabbi Nahman's Shabbat

> "And Moses said, 'Eat that today; for today is a Sabbath to the Lord'" (Ex. 16:25). Each of the three meals is described as "today" to suggest that one is only to dine at a Shabbat meal for the sake of that day. For there are times when one eats because one has been hungry since yesterday, or so as not to be hungry tomorrow. But at each of the three Shabbat meals, one must eat only for the sake of that day, meaning that those meals are not for the present or the future. (*Likutei Moharan* 125)

Shabbat meals, Rabbi Nahman writes, have no purpose outside themselves, and one must therefore be present in the here and now when one is eating on the holy day. Sleep on Shabbat also fulfills a spiritual function of presence in the moment. One would think that on Shabbat, one ascends to the same state of nirvana described by the Zen master, where all deeds are oriented toward the present. But a more careful examination of Rabbi Nahman's words reveals further elements pointing at a connection to the present.

According to Rabbi Nahman, eating on Shabbat connects us to a more profound stratum of reality, allows us to cleave to holiness: "On Shabbat one must literally consume copious amounts of food and drink, for anything consumed on Shabbat is pure divinity, pure holiness" (ibid.).[1] Being in the present, Rabbi Nahman says, not only awakens us but enables an experience of intimacy with God.

A Day That Is All Shabbat

The understanding that Shabbat is a day of presence in the moment is also apparent in a sentence that is added to Grace after Meals on Shabbat: "May the Merciful One bestow upon us a day that is all Shabbat and rest for life everlasting." What is this "day that is all Shabbat" and for which we yearn? Is it a future reality in which Shabbat extends throughout the entire week? If so, it would seem like a simple quantitative request – that the experience be spread out beyond a single weekday. But the truth is that the essence of Shabbat is concealed from us, and unquantifiable. It is something I always yearn to find the way to, to truly experience.

First, we must understand that the "day that is all Shabbat" is Shabbat itself, and no other day. The Baal Shem Tov says that a person is wherever his consciousness is. When we think on Shabbat about things that happened to us on Friday and about our plans for Sunday, we are not in Shabbat – we do not inherit a "day that is all Shabbat." Only by isolating ourselves from the past and future,

---

1. See the description of a Friday night meal with Rabbi Nahman in *Ḥayei Moharan*: "Immediately after he ate a slice of *ḥalla*, his consciousness ascended to another plane and cleaved to the Blessed One with great intimacy and terrible awe, and he sat in silence, his eyes wide open, all night long, in a sublime and glorious state of unity."

and focusing on the present, can we be present in Shabbat. Only then can we live the day.

The Talmud states, "Long strides diminish a man's eyesight by a five-hundredth part. What is the remedy? He can restore it with [drinking] the sanctification wine of Sabbath eve" (Berakhot 43b). I heard an explanation, attributed to Rabbi Allen Schwartz, according to which "long strides" refer to the rat race, the endless routine that "diminishes our eyesight" and prevents us from truly seeing life. The antidote is Shabbat, which stops the daily race in its tracks and restores our sight.

Halakha also directs us to imbue Shabbat with that character. Making plans for the following week is forbidden on Shabbat, as is conversing about business,[2] and there is even an added stringency of refraining from thinking about weekday plans.[3]

Life Is Holiness

The experience of encountering the present as an "awakening" is pivotal to Rav Kook's conception of the essence of life:

> Holiness is a quality that transcends every process, so that there is no need to say that [a saintly person] eats in order to learn [Torah], pray, and perform mitzvot, for that is but a middling trait; rather, that eating itself, as well as speaking, and all of the processes and feelings of life are suffused with holiness and light. (*Shemona Kevatzim* 2:65)

According to Rav Kook, when food is consumed as a means to an end, no matter how virtuous, it is an expression of a "middling trait." True holiness can only be attained when one recognizes the spiritual value of eating, not only the indirect benefit that

---

2. Shabbat 113a–b, 150a–b.
3. Ibid. 150b.

it occasions. Hence, our consciousness must be wholly directed at the action we are engaged in at a given moment. The idea is rooted in the manner in which Rav Kook conceives of the relation between life and its source, as he notes several passages earlier:

> God's radiant light, which permeates all of the worlds, animating them and saturating them with the sustenance of supernal bliss from the source of life, infuses all souls and angels, all creatures, with the strength to discern the inner aspect of the sense of life. (Ibid. 2:62)

Our "sense of life" issues from the radiant light of God that suffuses all of reality. That is why "all of the processes and feelings of life are suffused with holiness and light." When we contemplate the processes and feelings of our lives, we touch life itself, and through it life's source – God.

Elsewhere, Rav Kook describes an ecstatic experience of becoming subsumed in the supernal holiness through eating.[4] As in the Zen stories, he ascribes significance to the very act of eating, and suggests, like Rabbi Nahman, that the focusing of one's consciousness facilitates an encounter with the holy.[5]

As we have seen,[6] for Rav Kook, the idea that an action's significance is a function of its being a means to an end is the "sin of the earth":

---

4. See, for example, *Shemona Kevatzim* 3:58.
5. The connection between such holiness and Shabbat appears elsewhere in Rav Kook's writings, in the context of a distinction between what he terms "sifting and refining" and "raising worlds." The spiritual work done on Shabbat partakes of "the holiness of raising worlds" (*Shemona Kevatzim* 2:47). In the following passage, he posits, "The raisers of worlds transcend process and purpose. There is purpose in every material and spiritual occurrence." The holiness that Rav Kook discusses has to do with "raising worlds," which is the spiritual work of Shabbat. He suggests that this was the dynamic at the dawn of creation and that it will resume in the end times.
6. See above on *Parashat Bereshit*.

At the dawn of creation, the taste of the tree was also worthy of being like the taste of its fruit. All means that enhance an exalted, universal spiritual process were worthy of being perceived through a spiritual sense, at the same high level of exaltedness and blissfulness with which we conceive [of the goal]. But due to the nature of the earth...only the taste of the fruit, of the final process, the ultimate ideal, is perceived with its blissfulness and splendor. (*Orot HaTeshuva* 6, 7)

But in the World to Come:

Days will come when creation will resume its original state, and the taste of the tree will be like the taste of the fruit. (Ibid.)

Bridging the dawn of creation and its completion is Shabbat, which is "like the World to Come." On Shabbat, we return to the Garden of Eden, to a world where the taste of the tree is like the taste of the fruit, where every action has inherent meaning: eat, sleep, live. To touch Shabbat is to touch life, to touch God.

To Be or to Do

Is Shabbat indeed an actualization of the grand ideal, a taste of the World to Come? Should we aspire to live each day as if it were Shabbat? Tzur Shezaf's book *Shanti Shanti Balagan* tells the story of an Israeli family's journey in India. The family meets a young man who attained nirvana after living in the presence of the Hindu guru Amma, and no longer wants to marry and have a family. His sole desire is to bask in Amma's presence. After the family takes leave of the young man, the father reflects on a recent argument he had with one of his daughters. "There is no question that if you want to keep smiling at the world, you should probably give up on family," he muses. "On the other hand, there is more to life than happiness, fulfillment, and satisfaction."[7] The individual search for happiness is dangerous in that one can become cut off from the world. The true value of life, and by extension its fulfillment, lies in connecting to reality, not isolating oneself from it.

Few loved Shabbat as much as Rabbi Shlomo Carlebach did. But he did not suffice with savoring the Shabbat experience on his own. He embarked on a mission to traverse the globe and share the holy day with the rest of the world. During Friday night prayers, when he would sing Psalm 92, he would switch to English: "The whole world is waiting, sing a song of Shabbat." The entire world yearns for Shabbat, and he believed it was his task to help the world reach it. Rabbi Shlomo would tell the story of simple Jew known as Chatzkele Lekovod Shabbos. Throughout the week, Chatzkele would dedicate his every action to Shabbat by singing "*Lekovod Shabbos*" ("For the sake of Shabbat"). Eventually it turns out that in singing about Shabbat he was not referring only to the day of rest, but also to the ultimate Shabbat, to the redemption and the rectification of the world.

The question is: Does striving during the week to prepare the world for Shabbat mean forgoing contact with the holy? And in the broader sense, must we defer happiness now so that we can experience it tomorrow?

I believe that it is this very active striving, whose purpose is to change the world and bring the future nearer, that enables a perfect experience of the present and a connection to life in the here and now. The ability to move is one of life's prime characteristics. Plants, animals, and humans are considered alive, as opposed to rocks, which do not move. It is through action and movement that people feel connected to our life- and movement-filled world – through "doing" we arrive at "being."

---

7. Tzur Shezaf, *Shanti Shanti Balagan* [Hebrew] (Tel Aviv: Xargol, 2004), 174.

"Doing" is only at odds with "being" when a person sees action as a step on the way to future meaning. Such a conception of reality prevents one from living in the present; actualization and existence are deferred to an unknown future date, and the moment loses its meaning. In contrast, the realization that the journey itself, the groundwork and preparation, is the very essence of life elevates life and reveals the holiness embedded in the six days of action.

Pekudei

The Morning Routine

What do you do when you get up in the morning?
The same things, but slow.

– Arik Einstein

It is morning, brimming with bright light, fresh air, and hope for a new beginning. According to Jewish law, we begin the day with the ritual washing, alternating between hands. The ritual can be traced back to the purification of the priests in the Temple.[1] By contemplating the priests' ritual we can glean its meaning to our own day-to-day life.

Every morning, the priests would wash their hands and legs in the laver in the Temple before beginning their holy duties (Ex. 40:30–32). The Torah refers to this activity as "washing" but our sages call it "sanctifying hands and feet" (Mishna Tamid 1:4).[2] The change is no accident. The term

---

1. Based on *Teshuvot HaRashba* 1, 191.
2. That is also Onkelos' translation of the biblical source.

"washing" could be taken to imply the removal of dirt or impurity, while the later term, "sanctifying," has positive connotations.

What is the import of the priests' morning ablutions? When Aaron and his sons are ordained into the priesthood, they immerse, don the priestly vestments, and are anointed (40:12–15). Thenceforth, every day they reenact the three main components of their initiation ceremony: immersion, donning the vestments, and sanctification with the laver water. Washing is such a crucial component of their duties that a priest who so much as enters the Temple's *heikhal* without first sanctifying himself is sentenced to death, like a common man.[3]

The Torah states explicitly that the ordination of Aaron and his sons as priests is "everlasting... throughout their generations" (40:15). If so, why do they have to sanctify themselves anew every day?

The answer, it seems, lies in a basic conception of life as a series of daily rebirths. In *Modeh Ani*, the first prayer of the day, we give thanks to God for returning our soul to us, as if that re-receiving of the soul is tantamount to a rebirth. A perspective that sees life as beginning anew every day allows us to look at our lives, and at the world around us, with fresh eyes.

The great danger lies in forgetting what it important in life, and the challenge is to live with awareness of the things that truly matter. The washing ceremony, conducted daily and encapsulating one's purpose in life, enables us to live with awareness of the questions of who we are and what our task in the world is.

The broadening of the priestly ablutions into a daily mitzva obliging every man and woman is explained by various authorities. Here is the *Kitzur Shulḥan Arukh* (2:1):

> When one arises from bed in the morning one is like a being newly created to serve the Creator, blessed be His Name.

---

3. Maimonides, *Mishneh Torah, Hilkhot Biat Mikdash* 9:1.

One must therefore sanctify oneself and wash one's hands from a vessel, like a priest, who would wash his hands every day from the laver prior to his service.

Although the Torah states that the Jewish people are "a kingdom of priests, and a holy nation" (15:6), that status is not derived from race but rather from fulfilling a purpose, from keeping God's covenant (15:5). When one is like a priest, the entire world in which one conducts one's life becomes a temple of sorts. When we sanctify our hands in the morning, we must recall the purpose and mission in life, the purpose and mission of our day.

Fingers and Sefirot

The ideas of Kabbala can further enhance the meaning of the morning handwashing and the purpose that we take upon ourselves every day. Not only is there a part of every person that is priestlike; there is a part of every person that is Godlike.

Sefer Yetzira draws a parallel between human and divine creation. Humanity was created in God's image, and therefore "in my flesh I will see God" (Job 19:26). It is an idea that is also apparent in the morning handwashing. God's creative powers are conceived of as ten Sefirot. According to *Sefer Yetzira*, our ten fingers, the basic tools with which we manipulate reality, correspond to those Sefirot, to God's creative principles (1:3).

This foundation, laid down by *Sefer Yetzira*, is key in later-day sages' understanding of the mitzva of sanctifying one's fingers in the morning (Nahmanides on Exodus 30:19). It is a commandment that emphasizes humanity's own creative power, a force that is equivalent to the divine principles with which the world was created.

We must examine our surroundings and ask what they lack and what must change. We must believe that we possess the power to change reality, to create, to actualize the divine within. The morning sanctification teaches us that we must ask these questions every day anew.

Noam's Hands and Feet

I once asked my students why, of all our organs, we are enjoined to wash our hands and feet every day. One student, Noam Apter, replied that the mitzva was originally applied to two situations: "when they go into the tent of meeting … or when they come near to the altar to minister" (Ex. 30:20). In order to approach the sacred, one must know how to use one's feet, while ministering requires the use of one's hands; therefore, one must sanctify both. This is true of life in general, Noam continued, and explained that we are required to learn how to use our legs to come to the right place, and our hands – so that upon arriving we will know what to do.

In explaining his insight, Noam was referring to himself, as someone whose Torah and life were deeply tied into the sanctification of the feet and hands, into approaching and engaging in action. He did much in his brief life, including founding the Center for Jewish Awareness, driven by the realization that rather than wait for the people to come seek out Torah in the beit midrash, the Torah must be brought to the people. It was a trait that also characterized his death. On December 27, 2002, during a Friday night meal at the Otniel Yeshiva, while students were singing and dancing in the dining room, terrorists stormed the kitchen and murdered four who were on duty there: Noam, Yehuda Bamberger, Gabriel Hoter, and Zvi Ziemen. When the shooting began, the door separating the kitchen from the dining room, meters away from the dancing students, was immediately shut and locked. That delayed the terrorists and gave the other students time to get their bearings and return fire. When the attack was over and security forces entered the kitchen, they found the bodies of Noam and his friends alongside the locked door.

Vayikra

The Beast Within

People are generally offended when they are compared to animals. But the truth is that even those who do not believe humankind is descended from apes know that there are areas in which people are no more exalted than beasts. Each of us has animalistic qualities, and that is a good thing.

Sifra DiTzniuta, one of the most ancient and important sections of the Zohar, says that the human is an amalgam of divine and beastly elements. It is an idea that many associate with the foundational text of Chabad Hasidism, the *Tanya*. But there is a significant difference between the *Tanya*'s outlook and that of the *Sifra DiTzniuta*. While the *Tanya* says that humanity is the perpetual battleground between the animal and the divine, the *Sifra DiTzniuta* posits a state of mutual containment (in the psychological sense of the word): God created us as a synthesis of these elements not so that we will neuter one of them, but rather with the intention that we will strike the proper balance between them.

In its description of the sixth day of Creation, on which God created both beasts and humans, the Torah says, "And God said, 'Let the earth bring forth the living creature after its kind, cattle, and creeping thing, and beast of the earth after its kind.' And it was so" (Gen. 1:24). The *Sifra DiTzniuta* points out that the Hebrew word for "creature," "*nefesh*," also means "spirit," and – citing the verse "man and beast You preserve, O Lord" (Ps. 36:7) – says it is a quality shared by both human and beast: "One is found in the category of the other, beast in the category of *adam*, human" (Zohar, *Teruma* 178b). In other words, humanity has something of the beast within it. Below we will attempt to unpack that statement.

Sacrificing the Beast Within

The mode of religious worship described in Leviticus is based on sacrificial offerings. The primary, profound significance of the offering lies in the idea that the sacrifice is a stand-in for the person who offers it, who, in a sense, is sacrificing himself before God. It is no accident that the Hebrew words for sacrifice, "*korban*," and intimacy, "*kirva*," have the same root: by bringing a burnt offering we draw nearer to Him.

This idea is evident in an apparent contradiction in the second verse of our *parasha*: "When any man of you brings an offering to the Lord, you shall bring your offering of the cattle" (Lev. 1:2). The verse says the offering must be "of you" as well as "of the cattle." The *Sifra DiTzniuta* resolves the contradiction by stating that the beast is included within the man, and that we sacrifice our animal nature to God. When we stand before God, we must strive to raise up to Him even our "beastly" sides, which also need intimacy with the divine. Thus, the Temple rites were not merely intellectual and emotional, but also corporeal: making the pilgrimage, sanctifying the body, and consuming sacrifices.

According to Rav Kook, it is due to this physical connection that sacrificial offerings are preferable to prayer:

Yet more full of life than prayer...which only improves one's imagination, is divine work...the holy rites...of the Temple.... Then one's will and soul will be exalted, as the luminous parts of the animal spirit raise up one's soul.[1] (*Shemona Kevatzim* 2:20)

Both Sides Now

Humankind, according to the *Sifra DiTzniuta*, was created with a dual nature: "When Adam below descended, he appeared in a supernal image: two spirits. Of two sides, right and left, is *adam* comprised – on the right, holy *neshama*; on the left, *nefesh ḥaya*." The human was created in the image of God, and it is our similarity to Him that bestowed upon us those two sides: not only is our lofty, holy soul of divine origin, but so is our animal, beastly spirit.

If humanity's animal nature is also intrinsic to us, how does sin come about?

The *Sifra DiTzniuta* explains that "Adam sinned, and the left spread." Sin is an imbalance, an expansion of the animal beyond its proper boundaries. It is an idea that recurs in the writing of Rav Kook, who does not consider material desires to be intrinsically negative. The problem is not the desire itself but rather the surrender to it:

---

1. In the same passage, Rav Kook further develops the connection between man and beast:

   Sacrificial worship is work that appeals to the common, vulgar imagination, which is paradoxically the key to its exaltedness.... The sublimation of corporeal life; the sublimation of all of the worlds; the cleaving of all life to the light of the Life of All Worlds, to the divine life that ever emanates, vivifying all, sending its light from its lofty heights to the depths of the earth, bathing man and beast alike.... The animal spirit is bound to the human spirit. When the beast's spirit is released of its mortal coil through human intention, as a burnt offering to God, it merges with a lofty spiritual intention, and exalts along with it a sublime and very rich amalgamation of life's forces. And the world stirs, ever upward.

At their emergence, the spiritual inclinations that give rise to material desires … are encompassed by holiness. When they compel one to be delivered into their rapid, propelling flow, to the extent that one's freedom and purity of self-possession are erased, they become increasingly murky. Then one plunges into the dark depths, and all of one's positive spiritual faculties are imprisoned by vulgar, worthless materialism. (*Shemona Kevatzim* 1:720)

The desire to partake of the physical world and its pleasures has its source on high. But when that drive supersedes all else, when all of one's emotional and intellectual resources are enslaved in the pursuit of one's material desires, the balance is lost: one loses self-control and "plunges into the dark depths." A state of equilibrium facilitates partnership and cross-fertilization between our various parts. As the *Sifra DiTzniuta* states, "When they cling to one another, they give birth like an animal birthing many from a single womb." In order to birth, to bring a new soul into the world, we need our body. Like childbirth, all creative arenas – from dance, sculpture, and drawing to Torah and literature – require coordination between our physical and spiritual talents, a merging of the human and the beastly. The two elements create in tandem, meaning that desire in itself is not negative, but rather an energy that must be directed and balanced.

Go to the Physical

Earlier, in *Parashat Lekh Lekha*, we learned about the various interpretations of the apparent redundancy in the verse in which God commands Abraham, "Get yourself (*Lekh lekha*) out of your country" (Gen. 12:1). Hasidic masters posited two opposing approaches. According to Rabbi Dov Ber of Mezeritch, the implication is that in order to arrive at oneself, one must become free of one's physicality ("your country"). It is no surprise, then, that the Mezeritch dynasty gave rise to Chabad-Lubavitch, which spoke of the self as a constant battleground between one's physical and divine elements.

Rabbi Naftali Zvi of Ropshitz, however, suggests another interpretation: the meaning of "get yourself (*lekh lekha*) out of your country" is that one can arrive at oneself, at the capacity for balancing one's disparate elements, by way of ("out of") one's physicality ("country"). It is not easy to be attentive to the body without falling into addictive behavior, to be cautious without self-denial, to come to a place where knowledge of one's physical strengths and drives can be a catalyst for balanced, controlled, and positive change rather than a pitfall. Self-deception is easy, leading one to justify a descent into base, vulgar physicality when it is the consequence of ostensibly lofty spiritual goals. To me it seems that in areas that carry a risk of self-deception, it is very important to adhere strictly to halakha, which determines which expressions of our physical nature are conducive to holiness and which breed impurity.

Holiness in Celibacy or Conjugality

Intimate relations between men and women can be an arena for immense holiness, for a constant exaltation of the physical. But they can also produce the opposite effect, dragging one down into ever-increasing baseness. The complexity of the conjugal relationship underpins the Zohar's daring reading of the first verse in *Parashat Vayikra*, "And the Lord called to Moses" (Lev. 1:1). In Torah scrolls, the word "called," "*vayikra*," is written with a small *alef*. Some commentators interpret it as an allusion to Moses' humility. But according to the Zohar, it is an expression of the imperfection of Moses, who felt that in order to cleave to God he had to abstain from relations with his wife. Here is how the Zohar defines completeness: "One who would ascend should link himself above and below; then he is complete" (Zohar, *Vayehi*

234b). The Zohar goes on to contrast between Moses and Adam. In the verse "Adam, Seth, Enosh" (I Chr. 1:1), "Adam" is written with an outsize *alef*, which the Zohar sees as an expression of his completeness. In contrast with Moses, "Adam [is the] consummation of male and female" (Zohar, *Vayeḥi* 239a).

Sifra DiTzniuta and the Secret of Balance

The drive to balance and contain all of the various forces within humanity and the universe is strongly present already in the first chapter of the *Sifra DiTzniuta*: "Until there was a balance, they did not gaze face to face, and the primordial kings died and their weapons vanished and the earth was nullified" (Zohar, *Teruma* 176a). Balance symbolizes the scales that keep reality on an even keel. Without such balance, reality devolves into a state of "not gazing face to face," in which kings die, the earth is nullified, and life cannot exist.

What does the Zohar mean by the death of the kings? At the end of *Parashat Vayishlaḥ*, the Torah lists all of the monarchs of Edom (Gen. 36:31–39). Unusually, seven of the verses begin with the words, "And [the name of the king] died." Yet, the Torah omits the death of the final king, Hadar. Furthermore, Hadar is the only king who is said to have had a consort. For the Zohar, the story is an allegory about the world. The relationship between the sexes symbolizes a balanced reality. A lack of connection symbolizes an imbalance in reality, a state of kings dying, in which the world cannot exist.

Based on this, let us try to understand the meaning of the state of "not gazing face to face." In Kabbala, a healthy relationship between a man and a woman is referred to as "face to face," or "*panim befanim.*" It expresses an ideal situation, when the man and woman see each other, face each other, and are aware of each other's existence. But the "face to face" balance does not relate only to couples. It also relates to the male and female principles of reality: judgment and mercy, fire and water, body and soul. Man and woman are a microcosm of all the forces in the universe and the need to balance them. When that balance is disrupted, destruction ensues.

The introduction of harmony between those poles is called peace. As Rabbi Nahman writes:

> What is peace? It is what links opposites. As our sages of blessed memory elucidated (Zohar, *Vayikra* 12b) regarding the verse "He makes peace in His high places" (Job 25:2), here is one angel of fire, and one of water – they are opposites, for water quenches fire – and the Lord, blessed be He, makes peace and binds them together. (*Likutei Moharan*, 80)

I learned this Torah from my teacher and friend Rabbi Menachem Froman of blessed memory, who, during his discourses, would clap his hands – and encourage the audience to join in – so as to bring together right and left.

In Kabbala, the story of the death of the kings is considered an allegory for the Shattering of the Vessels. In kabbalistic cosmology, as reality comes into being, the vessels of Creation shatter because they cannot contain the divine light and influx. For the Zohar, the solution is balance, mutual containment. Perhaps that is the source of the term "Kabbala," which has come to symbolize Jewish esotericism: the capacity to accept (*"lekabel"*) and contain the disparate elements of reality, to make room for them all.

Tzav

The Empty Temple

In this day and age, the Temple seems like an anachronism. We do not know of any temples or visit any temples. At most, those of us who have been to the Far East have encountered idolatrous, statue-filled temples. Once could conclude, perhaps, that temples are at odds with monotheistic thought. Yet the Temple plays a major role in Jewish worship, and especially in Leviticus. In order to understand the idea of the Temple in depth, we will visit a contemporary temple on the Indian subcontinent. It is a temple belonging to a monotheistic religion, and is thus devoid of idols and icons. A comparison between that temple and the Temple in Leviticus can help us to better understand ourselves, as well as find philosophical allies in the world of religions.

Solidarity and Equality in Sikhism

Some five hundred years ago, Guru Nanak established Sikhism in northern India. The religion (the word "sikh" means "disciple") blends elements of Hinduism and Islam. A synthesis can be a success or a failure, and Guru Nanak created a successful synthesis, taking the good from each religion and discarding their negative baggage. He eschewed, for example, Hinduism's idolatrous elements while spreading the idea of Niranjan, the worship of a single, formless God. Nanak even imported, by way of Islam, Jewish ideas, such as the conception of God watching over and steering reality, the notion of Creation as an expression of God's will (which comes from Kabbala), and the idea of equality between all human beings. Nanak opposed the caste system, which is based on the assumption that there are entire segments of society with which one must not come in contact, and whose members are doomed to spend their entire lives in hard labor.

The Sikhs also differ from the Hindus in their approach to life and family. The monastic ideal plays a minor role in Sikhism, and the adherent is instructed to marry and have a family. Furthermore, the Sikhs rejected the passivity of yogis who dedicate their lives to asceticism and meditation. The three pillars of Sikhism are *Nām Japna* (remembrance and recitation of the divine Name), *kirat karō* (honest work), and *"vand chakkō* (giving alms).

Nanak adopted from Hinduism a profound tolerance for all human beings. While Islam emphasizes the idea of jihad, or holy war, and Christianity stresses the obligation to convert heretics through missionary work (*"outside the Church there is no salvation"*), for Nanak the faithful are not only those who identify as Sikhs, but rather any who live according to the basic precepts of faith. Faith in a single God, according to Nanak, is an element that unites all of humanity. The one God is the father of all human beings. It was in a similar vein that Maimonides wrote of Islam, "The Ishmaelites are not idol worshipers in the least ... and they pay perfect tribute to God's unblemished singularity" (Maimonides' Responsa 448). It is possible that it was due to their emphasis of these elements that the Sikhs' history has been so similar to our own: they are a small, persecuted minority in India, and yet, they are also successful in a vast range of fields.

The Blessing of the Sons

In 2005, a group of Sikh leaders visited Israel. One of their goals in visiting was to learn how Judaism, one of the most ancient of world religions, succeeded in sustaining its heritage through the generations. A Shabbat meal at the home of my friend Alon Goshen, the rabbi who hosted the group, made a powerful impression on them. In his comments, Sikh leader Bhai Sahib Mohinder Singh Ji described the special meaning of the Shabbat meal, which is not only a spiritual idea, but also spiritual action: "The beauty of Shabbat showed us what we need in our family life. How inspiring to see [that] every Friday they meet with the family – that parents bless their children [with their hands]."[1] During the visit, Rabbi Eliyahu Bakshi-Doron, one of the Israeli chief rabbis at the time, noted the values shared by the two religions and called on Jews and Sikhs to learn about each other's communities.

If Islam and Christianity can be described as the daughters of Judaism, it seems that Sikhism, which was influenced by Islam, is its granddaughter. It is no wonder, then, that Jews and Sikhs get along so well – we all know that people's relationships with their grandparents are far less complicated than their relationships with their parents.

The Golden Temple

The holiest site in Sikhism is the Harmandir Sahib, also known as the Golden Temple. The gold-covered complex, which was completed in 1604, is located on an artificial island in the center of a pool in the city of Amritsar, near the India-Pakistan border. When

---

1. Lauren Gelfond Feldinger, "Lions in Zion," *The Jerusalem Post*, December 29, 2005, http://www.jpost.com/Jewish-World/Jewish-Features/Lions-in-Zion.

I visited India, I refrained from entering temples due to the Jewish law that forbids entry into places of idol worship. But the Golden Temple does not fall under that category, and when I entered it I was struck by the similarities to – but also the differences from – our own Temple.

The Jewish and Sikh temples are similar not only in what is conspicuously absent from them – idols – but also in terms of their content. The Golden Temple houses the original Sikh scripture, the Guru Granth Sahib, just as the ark in the heart of the ancient Jewish Temple contained the Stone Tablets of Moses and the first Torah scroll, written by Moses. At the center of the Sikh temple, an old man in white vestments sits and reads from the Guru Granth Sahib, surrounded by a group of elders, also clothed in white, who play music. This recalls the atmosphere in the Temple, in terms of both the white vestments of the ministers and the musical instruments, which in Jerusalem were played by the Levites.

I was impressed especially with the eating rituals in the Golden Temple. Every visitor, upon entering, receives a helping of food. The ritual has a moral implication: everyone eats together (in contrast with the prevalent attitude in Hinduism, where one does not eat with members of a lower caste). The ritual reminded me of the eating of the burnt offerings in the Jewish Temple. When it comes to the Pascal lamb for example, all Jews eat the same sacrifice in the same place, in a national meal meant to drive home the fact that we are all free.

Another similarity is the welcoming atmosphere it both temples: the Golden Temple is open from all four directions and features a hostel for non-Sikh guests. Those are expressions of an openness to all of humanity that echoes Isaiah's prophecy about the future Temple: "For My house shall be called a house of prayer for all peoples" (Is. 56:7). Indeed, already during the dedication of the First Temple, King Solomon asks God to heed the prayers of "the stranger that is not of Your people Israel" (I Kings 8:41–43).

Sanctity of Place

Yet, alongside the many similarities between the two temples, there are also differences. The Temple in Jerusalem occupies a far more central role in Jewish life – including thousands of years of mourning for the destruction of the Temple and yearning for it to be rebuilt – than the Golden Temple does in the Sikh religion, where it is of relatively minor importance.

Perhaps the difference stems from the varying meanings associated with the temple in the two religions. Sikhism does not contain a concept of sanctity of place and time. The significance of the Golden Temple is an expression of the fact that it houses the religion's original scripture. The absence of discrete holiness – such as in time or place – stems among other things from the idea that God is everywhere. Although Judaism, too, believes that no place is devoid of His presence, it retains an idea of sanctity of place. Judaism believes there are special sites that facilitate intimacy and an encounter between human and divine.

It is due to this conception of holiness that the Temple is designed in a manner that is at once welcoming and removed and exclusive. The Temple is open on one side to all – women and men, Jews and gentiles alike – and all are allowed to bring offerings, but the farther in one progresses, the more stringent the demands. Entry into the *heikhal*, the main sanctuary, is contingent on special physical and spiritual preparation, and there are places where one is forbidden from entering. In the encounter with the divine there is a constant dance between revelation and concealment, a running and returning (*ratzo vashov*).

If holiness is to dwell within a secular world, there is need for boundaries and separation. Thresholds are there to awaken our sense of the sacred.

I will illustrate this point with something that happened to my wife, Michal. One day, she received an urgent phone call from a student of hers who was studying to become a tour guide in Jerusalem. This student was standing with her tour group and waiting for the security check before ascending to the Temple Mount, and she was deliberating whether to enter or not. Michal fell silent for a moment, thinking about the best way to inform the student that according to Jewish law, it is forbidden to enter the Temple Mount without having first immersed in a *mikve*. My wife's hesitation gave her thoughts away. "I get it," the student said. "So I should not go in?" Michal replied, "It is up to you. The question is whether you consider this place a tourist attraction or a holy site, a place where one goes to see God's face." A few minutes later, Michal received a text message from the student: "They went in, I am outside."

A few days later, I attended a student's wedding. Under the bridal canopy, she told the assembled guests that after immersing herself ahead of her wedding, she ascended the Temple Mount for the first time in her life to pray. A lifetime of planning for her wedding had carved in her heart a path ascending into holiness, and then, on this most special day of intentions and preparations, she entered God's Temple Mount.

Shemini

The Spiritual Desire

I shall not float
Unreined in space
Lest a cloud swallow
The thin band in my heart
That separates good from evil.
I have no existence
Without the lightning and thunder
That I heard at Sinai.

– Zelda, translated by Marcia Falk

The Return to Spirituality

Judaism's spiritual sides have seen a renaissance of late. Kabbala, Hasidism, and mysticism are no longer the domain of the few, and their popularity cuts across society, encompassing men and women, religious and secular – even non-Jewish pop stars. This is part of a broader shift in society, which is increasingly emphasizing the experience, emotion, and imagination.

Just as the Zionist mythos sees the resurgent Jewish nationalism as a return of sorts to the days of the Bible, so too the recent emphasis on spirituality can be seen as a biblical renewal. The primary characteristic of the biblical religious experience is prophecy – the direct dialogue with God – which draws its power from the human imaginative faculty. Many have noted the deep affinity between prophecy and meditation,[1] for example, because the focus of both is the attainment of higher awareness. The Bible is suffused with poetry and hymn, and serves as an inspiration to this day. The emotional world of the biblical heroes is striking – they love, rejoice, and cry – and widely discussed.

Where Has All the Spirituality Gone?

Why do these voices of spiritual renewal hold so much power today? Why were they less dominant in previous generations? It is important to recall that these processes are not self-evident. This fact is especially apparent to me when I visit synagogues and yeshivas in the United States, and see how rational and cerebral the prevailing Torah study methods are there. The Jewish-Israeli situation is thus unique.

To Rabbi Shlomo Carlebach, this very limited willingness to engage with spirituality was linked to the trauma endured by the Jewish people throughout the generations. It was an insight he derived from the *Mei HaShiloaḥ* on *Parashat Emor*, which says that priests are forbidden from becoming ritually impure through contact with the dead because such contact and the resulting impurity repress joy, and they must be joyful when they minister in the Temple. In the wake of the Holocaust, Rabbi Shlomo explained, all Jews are considered to have been defiled by the dead. The grief was so monumental that it had far-reaching consequences – distance from God and the erosion of religious feeling and experience.

---

1. Especially Rabbi Aryeh Kaplan in his books *Meditation and the Bible* and *Meditation and Kabbala*.

When those aspects of Judaism were diminished, many Jews – seeking to quench their spiritual thirst – became drawn to non-Jewish spiritual movements.

Rabbi Shlomo devoted his life to bringing Jews back to Torah. He named his first movement TASGIG, an acronym of the verse "Taste and see that God is good" (Ps. 34:9). He loved to tell stories, sing and dance, as well as bring others close to Judaism. I believe that if we will walk in Rabbi Shlomo's footsteps, on the path of joy and sweetness in cleaving to God, we can bring Judaism back to its natural, healthy state.

Strange Fire

But things are more complicated than that: spirituality is very powerful. Our attraction to God and natural inclination to be close to Him are a full-fledged desire. The Bible tells us that the only sin the Jewish people were never weaned of was the private altars, built in high places, on which they brought burnt offerings to God. Despite the prohibition against sacrificing outside the Temple, people experienced an irresistible drive to bring burnt offerings, and did so in illegitimate ways. Spirituality is a dangerous force that is difficult to rein in and control.

In our *parasha*, this truth is manifested through the tragic death of two of Aaron's sons. At the conclusion of the dedication of the Tabernacle, in a moment of divine ecstasy, Nadav and Avihu approach God bearing "strange fire…which He had not commanded them" (Lev. 10:1). The unmediated encounter with ultimate holiness, the dangerous meeting of finite and infinite, ends in disaster. Without proper training and awareness of boundaries, the encounter can be deadly. It is a danger conveyed in a later era in the story of "the four who entered the Garden" – the sages who penetrated the depths of Jewish mysticism. The results were disheartening: one died, another lost his mind, a third became a heretic, and only Rabbi Akiva departed unhurt (Ḥagiga 14a).

Power Corrupts

But there is an even greater danger than spontaneity inherent in spirituality: corruption. We know that "power corrupts" and that "the greater the man, the greater his evil inclination" (Sukka 52a). These principles extend to spiritual power, which can also breed perversion and destruction.

The Bible epoch is known as a spiritually uplifting period, but it is also infamous for the intensity of its corruptions, especially murder, incest, and idolatry. These mortal sins, which are inspired by emotional abandon and unbridled imagination, are the dark side of spirituality. The Talmud notes that the desire for idolatry "came forth from the Holy of Holies" (Yoma 69b), meaning that idolatry itself is a perverted spirituality. In our day, too, this is a common phenomenon: the guru who starts out as a spiritual teacher and gradually begins to take advantage of his followers and create a cult of personality. Spirituality, alongside its positive, beautiful side, is not immune to pitfalls and negativity, and in some cases can lead to them.

A History of Jewish Spirituality

Rav Kook saw in the destruction of the Temple and the end of prophecy a process more profound than mere punishment. By lowering the spiritual flames and drying out the springs of prophecy, it was possible to rein in spiritual perversions and precipitate renewal. Spirituality was being undermined by a lack of boundaries and discipline, and contending with those problems entailed formulating boundaries and maintaining inner discipline while emphasizing adherence to halakha. If the prototypical First Temple religious figure was the prophet, in the ensuing centuries the Torah sage, the man of halakha and Talmud, rose to preeminence. In an ideal situation, the two models can both be integrated side by side, but it is not an easy task (*Orot* 120–121).

Many movements in Jewish history sought to restore the central role of the spiritual dimension – Christianity, Sabbateanism, Frankism – but those attempts lacked the discipline of adherence to mitzvot and all eventually broke off from Judaism. Hasidism's success in generating a spiritual awakening and a revival of religious feeling was due in large part to its refusal to renounce halakhic discipline and commitment.

In our day, alongside the return to the land, to life, and to the natural order, there is a return to spirituality. But this return, rather than undo history, must retain the qualities that Judaism cultivated assiduously over thousands of years.[2] We are lucky to live in special times. The attraction to spirituality is no passing trend, but rather a profound movement that enables Judaism to actualize its purpose. I am thankful to God for the opportunity to live in an era when I can be involved in these processes.

The Shattering and Repairing of the Vessels

A good model for the Jewish people's historical process is the myth of the shattered vessels, which we have touched on several times.[3] According to this idea, in the beginning, reality, which is likened to vessels, received an influx of divine light that it could not contain, and it shattered. The purpose of humanity is to repair the vessels so that they can receive the light without shattering.

The implication is that each individual is a vessel and the light is the spirituality that one tries to receive and contain. If one is not strong enough, that influx can be shattering. One must undergo a process of internal toughening in order to receive the light once more.

---

2. Rabbi Abraham Isaac Kook, "Derekh HaTeḥiya," in *Maamarei HaRe'iya*, http://www.daat.ac.il/daat/vl/maamaey/maamaey01.pdf.

3. See *Parashot Noaḥ* and *Vayera*.

Fear of the Lord Is the Beginning of Experience

"The fear of the Lord is the beginning of wisdom," the psalmist (111:10) says. These days, we tend to emphasize experience, so we can say fear of the Lord is also the beginning of experience. The Mishna (Avot 3:17) warns of the danger posed by wisdom: "Anyone whose wisdom exceeds his deeds, to what is he compared? To a tree whose branches are many but whose roots are few; and the wind comes and uproots it and turns it upside down." This warning holds true also in the case of those whose experiences exceed their deeds.

I apply this idea to my own Torah study. For years I have been starting every day of study with my students by noting the date and reciting the verse "This is the day which the Lord has made; we will rejoice and be glad in it" (Ps. 118:24). Having acknowledged that experience must be wedded to action, we can proclaim with joy the famous verse from Ecclesiastes (12:13): "The end of the matter, all having been heard: fear God, and keep His commandments; for this is the whole man."

Tazria

The Priestess of Life

No More Silence: On Revealing the Secrets of the Relationship Between Man and Woman

The Mishna (Ḥagiga 2:1) says, "The laws of sexual relations must not be expounded upon by three people, nor the account of Creation by two, nor the account of the Divine Chariot by one." There are thus three domains in the realm of the occult: the "Divine Chariot," Ezekiel's prophetic vision of the divine; the account of the Creation of the world; and "sexual relations," the intimate contact between men and women. The Mishna restricts the study of these issues to the very few and forbids the masses from approaching them.

Despite the Mishna's prohibition, in the twelfth century kabbalists began to divulge in writing the secrets of the Chariot and of Creation. Professor Moshe Idel explains that the kabbalists at the time felt that they could remain silent no longer. After the publication of Maimonides' *Guide of the Perplexed*, which posited competing accounts of the Divine Chariot and Creation, silence on the part of the kabbalists would have enabled those opinions to spread throughout the Jewish people unchallenged.

We see a similar process in our day in regard to the relationship between man and woman. The issue is at the heart of secular culture, and it occupies many people and movements the world over. Today, more than ever, I feel that we cannot remain silent. It is incumbent upon us to describe openly the Torah's esoteric approach to the relationship between men and women.[1]

Sensitivity to Impurity Is a Prerequisite to Holiness

One of the major issues in intimate relations, and a source of much confusion, is that of *nidda*, or the impurity of menstruating women. By Jewish law, after a woman menstruates, she must count seven days and immerse in a *mikve* before she can have relations with her partner. The implications of *nidda* impurity for the essence of the relationship between man and woman, and between a woman and her body, raise many questions and require much thought and elucidation.

Almost all the laws of ritual impurity – about one-quarter of the Mishna – relate to the Temple, for "sensitivity" to impurity, and the need to remain apart from it, can only exist in a place of holiness: "And you shall not defile the land which you inhabit, in the midst of which I dwell; for I the Lord dwell in the midst of the children of Israel" (Num. 35:34). The only arena aside from the Temple in which there is sensitivity to impurity is the relationship between the sexes. That is why to this day, even when there is no Temple, the laws of *nidda* are still practiced.[2]

---

1. Notably, this has been the subject of many books that came out recently, including *The Temple of Life* by Rabbi Dov Berkovits [Hebrew] (Jerusalem: Maggid Books, 2011); *And He Named Them Adam*, an anthology of articles put out by the Siach Yeshiva [Hebrew] (Efrat: Bina la-Itim Institute, 2005); and the books of Naomi Wolfson, *A Man Shall Cleave unto His Wife* [Hebrew] (Jerusalem: Erez Publishing, 2006) and *Touching Distance* [Hebrew] (Tel Aviv: Yediot Books, 2011).
2. As well as the prohibition against priests becoming ritually impure, a function of their connection to the Temple.

The similarity between marital relations and the Temple shows us that sensitivity to impurity does not stem from a negative view of the relationship between the sexes, but rather is an expression of commitment to the sanctity and importance of the relationship. Rabbi Akiva, one of the greatest *Tanna'im*, puts it thus: "When husband and wife are worthy, the *Shekhina* abides with them" (Sota 17a). This is also apparent in the comparison to others whom Jewish law requires to ritually immerse: the only two groups obliged to do so are priests who enter the Temple and women in relationships.

The Creation of Life and Holiness

Still, we have to ask: why does menstrual blood make a woman impure. Furthermore, if ritual immersion is indeed an expression of the sanctity of marital life, why is it an obligation of the woman but not the man? In order to an answer these questions, we must understand the essence of holiness. In Judaism, ritual impurity is linked to death. A corpse is considered "*avi avot hatuma*," meaning the primary source of defilement, and any other source of impurity is associated with death or lessening of life. Holiness, on the other hand, is associated with life, and anything that increases life and vitality is holy.

Every month, a woman's body bears the potential to create new life, and menstrual blood is an expression of that opportunity being missed, of an egg going unfertilized, of a month devoid of new life. *Nidda* impurity does not stem from a primitive taboo, from fear, but from the recognition that menstruation is an expression of a lessening of life. This is evidenced in the fact that after childbirth there is a period when the blood that comes out of the womb does not defile the woman; rather, because it is an expression of the creation of life, not its lessening, it is called "the blood of purification" (Lev. 12:4–5).[3]

---

3. As for the period after childbirth (seven days for a baby boy and fourteen days for a girl), when the man and woman are forbidden from intimate relations, there are

Purity and impurity stand in opposition to each other, which is why places that are suffused with holiness require extreme caution as to ritual impurity. The idea that menstrual blood causes impurity is linked to the assumption that, during the rest of the month, the life-creating process within the woman's body is holy.

A Cycle of Light

The halakhic system imbues biological reality with religious meaning. But those two systems are also related to a third – the cosmological cycle. There is a well-known parallel between women and the moon, both in terms of the cyclical process and in terms of its length – thirty days. The lunar phase reaches its full state in the middle of the month, two weeks before the end of the cycle, just like a woman's cycle. This affinity is also noted in halakha; for instance in the thirteenth-century book *Or Zarua*:[4] "Women who choose to refrain from work on the first day of the month are engaging in a worthy and virtuous custom…. Know that every month, the woman renews herself, immerses and returns to her husband, and is dear to him as on their wedding day. Just as the moon renews every first of the month…. That is why the first of the month is a festival for women."

A man's body, in contrast, is devoid of cyclicality. He is unable to foster new life within himself and thus cannot be a source of *nidda* impurity.[5] That is why the woman determines the period of time when the couple is forbidden from intimate contact. The prohibition against having relations begins with the process taking place inside the woman's body, while the couple's return to one another is the culmination of a process of the

---

several explanations. Rabbi Baruch Kehat suggested that after childbirth, when the infant emerges from the womb, the woman has a reduced life force.

4. *Or Zarua, Hilkhot Rosh Ḥodesh* 454.

5. Seminal emissions, which cause a man to become impure and which are also a kind of lessening of life, are happenstance rather than something the body prepares for.

woman contemplating her body during the seven clean days and immersing in the *mikve*.[6]

I once delivered a class in my home on the *Sefer Yetzira's* secret kabbalistic formula for creating a golem. My wife, Michal, overheard some of our discussion and could not help herself: "Only men could think of creating a golem!" she exclaimed. "We women do it so much better – we have actual children!" In the spirit of that statement, Michal instructs the female students at the pre-military academy she heads not to serve in combat roles but rather in other units. Women, who bring life into the world, should not, she says, be in a position to take life away. The Zohar (*Bereshit* 48b) offers a similar explanation for why it is women who light the Shabbat candles. Being the one who gives life, the woman is also the one worthy of lighting a candle that symbolizes the additional soul that one receives on Shabbat.

Immersion on Approaching the Holy

Once could say that the difference between women and men is analogous to the difference between priests and laypeople. The priest, because he is required to cleave to holiness, is more sensitive to impurity. Women, it follows, are the priestesses of life.

The transition from impurity to purity is effected by way of immersion in the *mikve*. Water purifies by virtue of its spiritual quality: in the Torah – both in the stories of Creation and in the visions of the end times – water plays a central part. When a woman immerses in water, the source of all life, she is "subsumed" in its amorphous body. There are sources that compare the *mikve*

---

6. It is worth noting that according to the letter of the Torah, it is sufficient to count seven days from the onset of menstruation. The requirement to count an additional seven days was the initiative of women: "The daughters of Israel have imposed upon themselves the restriction" (Nidda 66a). Here we have a rare instance of a law that was shaped by women.

to a woman's womb,[7] and see her emergence from the water as a symbol of the renewal of her life, as a rebirth.

The Holiness of Love

As we discussed earlier, the man-woman relationship has dual aspects, reflected in the two descriptions of Creation. In the first account, the relationship is geared toward procreation, while in the second the intimate connection between man and woman is presented as a value in itself. Just as we must understand the meaning of the laws of family purity in the context of the holiness of creating new life, so too we must examine it in the context of the holiness of a couple's intimate relations. This holiness is also manifested in the identical numerical value (13) of the Hebrew words for "love" ("*ahava*") and "one" ("*eḥad*"). Love is the yearning to be "one" with the other. As the verse says, "and [he] shall cleave to his wife, and they shall be one flesh" (Gen. 2:24). When two people become "one flesh," in body and spirit, there is holiness in them. By forming that "one," a man and a woman manifest an expression of the grand revelation of "One," within the cosmos and even within divinity Itself.[8]

The Talmud (Sota 17a) illustrates this idea using the Hebrew words for "man" ("*ish*") and "woman" ("*isha*"): those words share two letters in common – *alef* and *shin* – while "*ish*" contains another *yod* and "*isha*" another *heh*. Joining the man's unique letter, *yod*, to the woman's, *heh*, yields "*Yah*," one of the names of God.[9]

---

7. *The Beginning of Wisdom*, "Gate of Love" 11:29. Further elaboration on the meaning of water and *mikve* can be found in Aryeh Kaplan, *Waters of Eden* (New York: NCSY, 1982).

8. "For the essence of faith is…to unify all oppositions at their roots into a single oneness. And that is faith and the unification of the Tetragrammaton and the name Elohim, of male and female. It is all one, so to speak" (*Zohar Ḥai* on Zohar, *Bereshit* 49b).

9. "*Yah*" has a numerical value of fifteen. It is noteworthy that during the process of purification, the woman conducts fifteen *bedikot*, or internal examinations, to ensure

The capacity to touch the holiness within life depends to a large extent on the individual's awareness of his or her actions. Eating, for example, takes on spiritual significance through actions such as hand purification and blessings, which encourage one to pause and contemplate before consuming food. The sanctity of life also features in the realm of intimate relations. When a couple refrains from contact while the wife is menstruating, they generate an expectation and yearning that can facilitate a sense of renewal. This addresses the danger of marital life being taken for granted, of the novelty and excitement being deadened by habit. This point is formulated explicitly by the Talmud (Nidda 31b): "Why did the Torah ordain that the uncleanness of menstruation should continue for seven days? Because being in constant contact with his wife [a husband might] develop a loathing toward her. The Torah, therefore, ordained: Let her be unclean for seven days in order that she shall be beloved by her husband as at the time of her first entry into the bridal chamber."

No Crying over a Broken Glass

During the Jewish wedding, the memory of the destruction of the Temple is evoked by breaking a glass under the bridal canopy. It is astonishing that it is at that ostensibly sad moment in the ceremony that the entire assembly yells out, "Mazal tov!" One explanation is that life – and certainly marital life, which is to my mind the essence of life – is rife with crises. Sometimes these crises are painful and difficult, and sometimes they cause a couple to drift apart. But it is these very difficulties that enable the couple to renew their love, thus reconnecting from a more positive place. The Hebrew word

---

that the flow of the menstrual blood has ceased – two examinations on each of the seven days that she counts before immersing. Those fifteen checks can be said to parallel the numerical value of "*Yah*," which emerges from the connection between man and woman, as well as the fifteen Songs of Ascent in Psalms and the fifteen stairs leading up to the Temple in Jerusalem.

for "crisis," "*mashber*," is also the biblical word for a birthing chair. Crisis is what gives rise to new things.

The Kabbala tells us that man and woman were first created with their backs fused to one another. God then separated them so that they could reconnect, not back to back but face to face. The hope in a relationship is that the wedding will not be a climax but rather the beginning of a path along which the couple will ascend ever higher. A cyclicality of distance and closeness, both physical and emotional, is one path toward growth and advancement through love and mutual sharing.

How Do I Love Thee? Let Me Count the Days

The renewal of the intimate relationship after a woman counts her days of impurity can be compared to another count that culminates in renewal. In Kabbala, the days of the Omer, counted between Passover and Shavuot, are considered days of gradual spiritual buildup ahead of the special meeting between the Jewish people and God on Shavuot, the Giving of the Torah. The Zohar (*Emor* 97) compares the counting of the Omer to the seven days the woman counts from the day her menstrual blood stops until she can immerse in the *mikve*. Just as counting the days of the Omer prepares us for meeting with God, so the couple prepares to renew the intimate bond between them and contemplate the spiritual meaning of their looming reunion.

Metzora

From Biography to Biology

The Midrash (*Tanḥuma Metzora* 6), based on the story of Miriam, who was afflicted with leprosy after speaking ill of Moses (Num. 12:1–16), concludes that the disease is a punishment for the sin of evil speech (*lashon hara*). It reads the word for leper, "*metzora*," as a pun on "*motzi ra*," one who speaks ill of others (Leviticus Rabba 16:1). My friend Yehoshua Hoffman notes, based on the Torah commentator *Kli Yakar*, that the term "*motzi ra*," which literally means "extracts evil," can be seen as an expression not only of the sin but of the punishment as well. A person who speaks ill of others is someone who projects evil on others and, by extension, possesses a certain evil himself. It is this evil that leprosy extracts or uncovers. But "*motzi ra*" also alludes to the solution: the purification ceremony whereby the evil is drawn out of the leper's mind and he is freed from it.[1]

---

1. *Shnei Luḥot HaBrit* on Pesaḥim, a discourse for *Shabbat HaGadol* on *Parashat Metzora*.

The sin and its rectification are intertwined. A person's physical affliction awakens an introspective insight, and thus, through the punishment of leprosy, the leper is freed of the evil within. The punishment forces him to examine his evil and process it, like a disease that breaks out. He can deal with the problem at its source. When things do not have an outlet, problems can become exacerbated.

The Oscar Wilde novel *The Picture of Dorian Gray* teaches us about the danger inherent in a too-large gap between internal and external – when an inner evil is not manifested outwardly. Dorian is a young man blessed with good looks and virtues. His facial features radiate integrity and kindness. When his friend paints his portrait, Dorian gazes at the brilliant painting and realizes that within that frame he will forever remain young and beautiful, while in reality he will grow old and lose his good looks. So he makes a wish to change places with the portrait – that while he will remain unchanged, the painted image will grow increasingly older and uglier. His wish comes true and thus, while Dorian becomes increasingly more corrupt, other people continue to put their trust in him because of his unchanging appearance of innocence.

Our Afflictions and the Afflictions of Others

A person afflicted with leprosy is subjected to – literally, on his own flesh – the same experience he put others through. It was his speech about the other that caused people to recoil from the other in disgust – the very same disgust he is now experiencing. Leprosy causes the leper's family and friends to keep a distance from him, both due to his external appearance – his body is full of sores, his hair is wild, and his clothes are torn (Lev. 13:45) – and because of his sin, for they all know why he was afflicted with the disease.

The leper must declare publicly that he is "Unclean, unclean" (ibid.). The *Shnei Luḥot HaBrit* explains that rather than take note of the shortcomings of others, the leper is expected to see his own blemishes. The capacity to acknowledge those faults is crucial if he is to learn how to make room for the faults of others. When one lives with the consciousness that one is imperfect, one will show more empathy toward others and will be able to tolerate their limitations.

The Baal Shem Tov offers a similar explanation for the mishna that says, "A person can examine all afflictions *(nega'im)* except for [literally, outside] his own afflictions" (Nega'im 2:5). The obvious meaning is that people require an outside perspective to diagnose themselves. But the Baal Shem Tov, based on a hyperliteral reading of the Hebrew, suggests a far more profound interpretation that has to do with our capacity to apprehend reality. He says that any affliction, any imperfection, that we can see outside ourselves, is in fact our "own affliction." Anything we apprehend in the reality surrounding us is a reflection of our own conceptions of reality and the world. Thus, our criticisms of the other say a lot more about ourselves than about the other. We perceive in others the very shortcomings that we are afflicted with. "With one's own blemish one stigmatizes [others] as unfit," the Talmud (Kiddushin 70b) says.

This insight gives us a powerful tool for self-understanding. If you wish to know yourself, observe yourself observing your surroundings: if you see the good in others, you are good; if you see imperfections, you are imperfect. Furthermore, if you see someone stealing from their fellow, reflect on whether you take care with others' belongings. If you see someone lying, examine whether you are fully truthful. Such a perspective teaches us humility in the face of the other's imperfections, rather than disdain.

The process of purification from leprosy requires withdrawal from society: "All the days in which the plague is in him he shall be unclean; he is unclean; he shall dwell alone; outside the camp shall his dwelling be" (13:46). Forced loneliness causes the leper to miss the companionship of others. He will feel their absence and no longer take them for granted. Afterward he can return to society and see it with a more positive eye.[2]

The Chatter of the Birds

After the leper is cured of his affliction, the priest takes two birds, slaughtering one and setting the other free "into the open field" (Lev. 14:7). The Midrash explains the symbolic meaning that the birds fulfill in the purification ceremony: "He disseminated evil speech; therefore the Torah says 'birds,' for they conduct their voices" (*Tanḥuma Metzora* 8). Rashi (Lev. 14:4) elaborates: "Because lesions of leprosy come as a result of derogatory speech, which is done by chattering. Therefore, for his cleansing, this person is required to bring birds, which twitter constantly with chirping sounds." It seems that just as psychodrama gives concrete expression to our psychological processes, so too the birds represent the process of breaking free of evil speech, with one sacrificed and the other sent out into the distance.

Body and Spirit

With leprosy, the Torah creates a fascinating link between body and spirit. In her book *Anatomy of the Spirit,* Caroline Myss claims that our biography becomes our biology. Our emotions and thoughts, and the way we live, have a direct impact on our health. Throughout the book she sketches, based on the kabbalistic system of Sefirot and Eastern conceptions of the chakras, the basic elements of the human spirit. She contends that any harm to these elements is not solely spiritual; it will eventually leave its mark on the body as well. We all play a role in the development of the diseases we suffer from, as well as the capacity and responsibility to contribute to the process of healing them. Our physical ailments emanate from the spiritual realm, and that is where their solution lies.

---

2. My thanks to Avner Peled for this insight.

Aḥarei Mot

The Festival of Love

Many consider Tu B'Av to be the festival of love. The source for that is the mishna (Taanit 4:8) about the maidens of Jerusalem who, on that day, would go dancing in the vineyards to find husbands.

But the rest of that mishna is not as well known: it says that the maidens would dance in the vineyards not only on Tu B'Av, but also on Yom Kippur. It is a custom that many have forgotten, perhaps due to association of the Day of Atonement with immensely powerful and meaningful traditions: fasting, penance, and the priestly duties in the Temple. Yet, the mishna implies that the dancing of the maidens was no less momentous than the rest of the day's events, for it attests to the fact that "never were more joyous festivals in Israel than…Yom Kippur" (ibid.). What was the secret of the dance? And why does it express, more than all the other customs of Yom Kippur, the special joy of that day?

Yom Kippur is the only day of the year when a person was allowed to enter Holy of Holies, the most holy part of the Temple. At the heart of the Holy of Holies was the Ark of the Covenant, atop which stood the two cherubim. On Yom Kippur, the Divine Presence would reveal Itself in a cloud between them. The Talmud tells us that the cherubim were in the shape of a male and a female in a perpetual embrace, so as to equate the love between God and the Jewish people to the intimate bond between man and woman (Yoma 54a). It also relates that the ark's two staves (the wooden poles attached to its sides) jutted outward from the Holy of Holies and formed two bulges in the curtain like "the two breasts of a woman" (ibid.). The Talmud ties this idea to the verse "My beloved is to me as a bag of myrrh, that lies between my breasts" (Song 1:13).

The entrance of the high priest, who represents the entire nation, into the Holy of Holies, is likened to the intimate union of two lovers. This union is at the heart of the Song of Songs, which describes the relationship between God and His people in allegorical terms, as the relationship between the lover and his wife.[1]

These ideas can teach us about the dancing of the maidens of Jerusalem, which, it turns out, was about a lot more than solving some "shidduch crisis." Let us take a closer look at the Mishna:

> Never were more joyous festivals in Israel than Tu B'Av and Yom Kippur, for on them the maidens of Jerusalem used to go out dressed in white garments – borrowed ones, in order not to cause shame to those who had them not of their own. These clothes were also to be previously immersed. And thus they went out and danced in the vineyards, saying, "Young men, look and observe well whom you are about to choose." (Taanit 4:8)

---

1. One can find a hint of the fact that the Holy of Holies is the arena for the fulfillment of the Song of Songs in the words of Rabbi Akiva, who says that "all the Scriptures are holy, but the Song of Songs is the Holy of Holies" (Mishna Yadayim 3:5). The Song of Songs is linked to the life of the Temple. The Zohar (*Teruma* 143a) says that King Solomon recited the Song of Songs upon completing the construction of the Temple.

The white garments of the dancers are like the white vestments that the high priest wears when he enters the Holy of Holies on Yom Kippur. The halakha mentioned in this seemingly aggadic mishna – "These clothes were also to be previously immersed" – reinforces the link between the dancing of the maidens and the world of the Temple, with its stringent requirements of ritual purity.[2] The dances are directed toward God; He is the audience.[3] The priest's encounter with God is occasioned by the Temple rituals, while the women come before Him in dance.

What does their dance express? Further along, the Mishna interprets the verse from the Song of Songs that describes the wedding day as an allegory for the building of the Temple and the Giving of the Torah:

> And thus is it said, "Go out, maidens of Zion, and look on King Solomon, and on the crown wherewith his mother has encircled [his head] on the day of his espousals, and on the day of the gladness of his heart" (Song 3:11). "The day of his espousals" alludes to the day of the gift of the law, and "the day of the gladness of his heart" was that when the building of the Temple was completed.

The dance is the fulfillment of the verse in the Song of Songs about the gladness of the heart and the wedding day, which the

---

2. See also the mishna that states, "All the vessels in the Temple required immersion" (Ḥagiga 3:8).

3. We must thus find an explanation for the dancing of the maidens on Tu B'Av. One connection is that Tu B'Av was the main day when the people would bring an offering of wood that would be used throughout the ensuing year for the altar at the Temple (Mishna Taanit 4:5). Professor Pinchas Mandel concluded, based on that fact, that "on those two days especially, the powerful connection between the people – all of the people – and the Temple was readily apparent" (Mandel, "Never Were More Joyous Festivals in Israel than Tu B'Av and Yom Kippur: On the Last Mishna of Tractate Taanit and Its Metamorphoses," *Te'uda* 11 [Hebrew] (1986): 170.

Mishna links to the Temple and the Giving of the Torah. What does it mean? My friend Amnon Dokov notes that the story of the dancers contains many allusions to the Song of Songs, primarily in the description of the women as "maidens of Jerusalem," a term that appears in the Song of Songs seven times. The location of the dance – the vineyards – is also mentioned many times in the Song of Songs. In addition, in the Mishna, as in the Songs of Songs (5:15), the potential lovers are referred to as "young men," or *baḥurim*. Based on the fact that in the Song of Songs, the maidens of Jerusalem serve as bridesmaids who mediate between the bride and her beloved,[4] Dokov concludes:

> The dances are an enactment and realization of sorts of the verses in the Song of Songs – a feminine awakening on the part of the maidens of Jerusalem aimed at reinvigorating the relationship between the lover and the bride. It was no coincidence that on the same day that the high priest would enter the Holy of Holies, the maidens of Jerusalem would go out and sing the people of Israel's song of love for God.[5]

A Complicated Relationship

It seems that the dancing maidens are not merely performers and bridesmaids, but rather represent the bride herself when they perform in white before the young men. Indeed, with their clothing they correspond to the high priest who enters the Holy of Holies.[6] There is no contradiction between the characterization

---

4. See also the "maidens of Zion" who, according to the verse cited at the end of the mishna, are the bridesmaids accompanying the bride on her wedding day.
5. Published in a newsletter for Otniel Yeshiva alumni who serve in the IDF.
6. The Talmud on this mishna (Taanit 31a) discusses the future dance of the righteous around the Lord in the Garden of Eden. There the righteous are in direct contact with the blessed Holy One, which is proof that the dance of the maidens must not be seen as a mere dance of the bridesmaids, but rather as that of the bride herself.

of the maidens as bridesmaids and as brides: in many rituals one can serve in several roles at once. During *Kabbalat Shabbat*, for example, one at once approaches Shabbat like a groom proceeding toward his bride, and arouses God to unite with Shabbat: "Your God will rejoice concerning you/As a groom rejoices over a bride," says the liturgical song *Lekha Dodi*. According to Kabbala, any human action below, in the mundane plane, precipitates a parallel action above, in the divine realm.[7] Just as one can be both Shabbat's lover and the one arousing God's love for Shabbat, so too the maidens can at once represent the bride and arouse God's love for the Jewish people.

The dance shows us not only that women were active in the Temple ritual, but that the Jewish people is the feminine party in its relationship with God, just as in the Song of Songs. According to Kabbala, the image of the Jewish people as a woman[8] is behind the fact that the Jewish calendar is based on the moon, a feminine symbol, rather than the masculine sun. In the context of standing before God, a Jewish person is feminine.

A Cathartic Experience

The Mishna links the phrase "the day of his espousals" from the Song of Songs to the Giving of the Torah. According to that interpretation, the Giving of the Torah is the marital contract between God and Israel. However, this lovely analogy has a catch: if the Giving of the Torah is the marriage of God and Israel, then the sin of the Golden Calf is tantamount to a bride committing adultery under her bridal canopy (Song of Songs Rabba 8). This points us toward another level of meaning in the dance of the maidens on

---

7. See Reuven Kimelman's *The Mystical Meaning of Lekha Dodi and Kabbalat Shabbat* [Hebrew] (Jerusalem: Magnes, 2002), 58–59.
8. In the divine realm, "*Knesset Yisrael*" is identified with the *Shekhina*, meaning the feminine side of the divine.

Yom Kippur.[9] On the seventeenth of Tammuz, in the aftermath of the sin, Moses breaks the tablets he received on Mount Sinai (Mishna Taanit 5:4), but the rectification of that shattering, the receiving of the second tablets, takes place on Yom Kippur. That is why the Talmud describes Yom Kippur as a positive day for the Jewish people: "Because it is a day of forgiveness and pardon and on it the second Tablets of the Law were given" (Taanit 30b)·

The shattering of the tablets symbolized a crisis in the relationship between God and the Jewish people, and the giving of the second tablets is a healing, cathartic experience. The dance of the maidens in the vineyards represents the renewed bond between the lover and his wife, the bride and her beloved.

Yet, there is even more to the dance. When a horrified Moses witnesses the sin of the Golden Calf, he notes the "dancing" around the idol: "He saw the calf and the dancing; and Moses' anger waxed hot, and he cast the tablets out of his hands, and broke them beneath the mount" (Ex. 32:19). The dancing of the maidens before God is the remedy for the dance around the Golden Calf.

Husband and Wife, and the *Shekhina* In Between

As the Mishna tells us, the maidens also dance for a more mundane purpose – to find husbands. Yet, the intimacy and love expressed in their dance are inherent on two intertwined planes: both in the relationship between God and Israel and in the one between man and wife.[10] The Song of Songs, too, teaches us about our relation not only to the supernal world, but to this one as well. Rabbi

---

9. It is also clear why the Mishna links "the day of the gladness of his heart" to the building of the Temple. Yom Kippur is not only the culmination of the Temple rituals; it is also its rededication, in a sense. See Israel Knohl and Shlomo Naeh, "Milu'im and Kippurim," *Tarbiz* 62 [Hebrew] (1993): 17–44.

10. Regarding Tu B'Av as well, some of the commentators in the Talmud (Taanit 30b) link the dance to the relationship between man and God, while others ties it to relationships within the Jewish people, between men and women.

Akiva, who calls the Song of Songs "the Holy of Holies" (Mishna Yadayim 3:5), says, "When husband and wife are worthy, the *Shekhina* abides with them" (Sota 17a). The image of man and woman is not merely a metaphor for the relationship between God and humanity; the encounter with God is achieved via interpersonal relationships.

The Talmud (Ketubbot 62b), in discussing the commandment of *onah* (the requirement that a man have relations with his wife), tells of Rabbi Reḥumi, who would come home once a year, on the eve of Yom Kippur. The context of the story implies that he would have relations with his wife only on that day. Just as there is a special commandment to eat on the eve of Yom Kippur, so too it seems that, according to Rabbi Reḥumi (whose name means "love" in Aramaic), even though intimate relations are forbidden on Yom Kippur itself, there is a special quality to the union of man and wife in the hours leading up to it.[11]

---

11. My thanks to Kobi Weinberg for bringing my attention to this.

Kedoshim

The Art of Love

To Love or Be Loved?

The fundamental principle of the Torah, according to Rabbi Akiva (*Sifra Kedoshim* 2), is love of the other: "Love your neighbor as yourself" (Lev. 19:18). Yet it seems that most of us have the inverse wish: for the other to love us. The path laid down by Rabbi Akiva, as this short story by Hermann Hesse will show, is the way to happiness:

There was once an expectant woman who sought out a pious man to bless the fetus in her womb. The pious man promised the woman to bless her with the blessing of her choice, and she asked that all of the child's acquaintances love it. The pious man hesitated, and asked her if she was certain about her choice of blessing. But when she insisted, he blessed the fetus as she requested. The woman gave birth to a boy, and the blessing was fulfilled: everyone loved the child. Yet, that love made them pardon his bad behavior, and he grew up to become corrupt. One day, he discovered the source of his misery and went to the pious man to reverse the blessing: rather than be loved by all, he asked to love all. Thus he became a happy man.

A similar point is made by Orson Welles in his seminal film *Citizen Kane*, whose titular character grows up parentless and becomes immensely wealthy. Throughout his adult life, he uses his money to gain popularity, but ultimately dies alone in his colossal mansion, a single last word on his lips: "Rosebud." The film follows the doomed efforts of a journalist to find out who or what is "rosebud." In the end, we learn that "rosebud" is a small object from Kane's childhood, the sole thing to which he was truly connected.

It is a secret known to every parent: generally speaking, parents express love for their children far more than the other way around. Usually it is the parent who is the lover and the children who are loved, yet the exquisite pleasure of this love is experienced by the parent.

True love has value in itself, and when it is not authentic it is worthless. This is an insight that informs our behavior in many ways. Often, people will act or refrain from action, consciously or not, out of concern for their popularity. But when we are guided by commitment to loving rather than being loved, we are free to do the right thing, even if it is unpopular.

Who Is Loved? One Who Loves Others

The truth is that in order to be loved one must love. As the story goes, Rabbi Hayim of Volozhin and his students once had to traverse a dangerous forest. At one point they were accosted and surrounded by brigands who informed them that they were going to steal their money and then murder them. Rabbi Hayim asked the robbers to give him and his students a few minutes to prepare for death, during which he stared into the face of the band's leader. Soon, the leader yelled, "Run!" and Rabbi Hayim and his students escaped. When his students asked him how he had effected such a miracle, he replied, "When the brigands told us they would murder us, I was filled with anger and hate. But I did not want to leave this world feeling anger and hate, so, in order to overcome those emotions, I forced myself to empathize with the brigands. It appears that no one had ever looked at their leader with such an emotion, for he was unable to harm us."

This insight also appears in Proverbs: "As in water face answers to face, so the heart of man to man" (27:19). Rashi explains in his commentary on the Talmud (Yevamot 117a): "As with the water that one observes and sees in it a face that is like one's own – when one smiles it smiles and when he frowns it frowns – so, too, the heart of one human to another human; if one loves the other, the other loves one back."

Love for Near and Far

Christianity took Judaism to task over the verse "Love your neighbor as yourself," claiming that it limited the recipients of love to one's neighbors while, clearly, such love should be extended to all of humanity. That claim is refuted in the same chapter, when the Torah explicitly writes, "And if a stranger sojourn with you in your land...you shall love him as yourself" (Lev. 19:33–34). The stranger and the neighbor are mentioned in separate verses in order to give voice to the understanding that love begins from the natural, closer sphere and extends outward from there – from the near to the far.[1]

Indeed, some people get stuck in the first stage, their love doomed to remain confined within their immediate circle, but it seems that trying to bypass that stage only exacerbates the problem. Absent love for those who are close to us, "love for all" can become an empty, sanctimonious slogan rather than an expression of authentic emotion. The fully egalitarian approach is often

---

1. The *Sifra* on the verse opines that the "stranger in this instance is a convert to Judaism," but commentators note that the basic meaning refers to a non-Jewish resident of the Land of Israel.

permeated with alienation. As the journalist Yair Sheleg once asked: how is it that the more a society talks about humanism, the more its members are alienated from one another?

The truth is, the verse teaches us that love must begin even closer to home. The Torah tells us to love the other like "ourselves," meaning that self-love comes first. People who are not at peace with themselves, who hate and do not accept themselves, will ultimately treat the other in the same vein.

I Am the Lord

The verse that enjoins to "love your neighbor as yourself" ends with the phrase "I am the Lord." What is the connection between loving the other and God? According to the Zohar, God is present whenever there is love among friends:

> Those companions, when they sit as one, not separating from each other.... What does the Holy One say? "Look, how good and how pleasant it is for brothers to dwell *gam yahad*," "also together!" – *gam*, also, including *Shekhina* with them. Furthermore, the blessed Holy One listens to their utterances and is pleased and delights with them ... and for your sake, peace will prevail in the world, as it is written, "For my brothers' and companions' sakes, I will now say, 'Peace be within you' (Ps. 122:8)." (Zohar, *Aharei Mot* 59b)

In Mishna Avot (3:24), Rabbi Akiva – he who enshrined "love thy neighbor" as the quintessential Torah precept – teaches that "beloved is man, since he is created in the image [of God]. A deeper love – it is revealed to him that he is created in the image, as it says (Gen. 9:6): 'For in the image of God made He man.'" God's special affection for humanity is due to its divine dimension, having been created in His image. God dwells within every human being.

Emor

Cosmos and History

Two Conceptions of Time

Mircea Eliade, one of the twentieth century's foremost scholars of religion, contrasted two different approaches to time: the cosmological and the historical.

In the cosmological model, time is cyclical: what was is what will be. Time flows backward, in a constant, recurring return to a mythical age. This conception of time is derived from, among other things, the phenomena of the natural world, which repeat every year without fail. For instance, in the spring the flora bloom, during the year the plants dry out, and in the following spring they grow anew. Eliade contrasts this conception, which pervades the pagan world, with the historical view of history instilled by Judaism. According to that idea, time and the world are always marching forward.

A good example of that contrast is the story of the Flood. While many ancient cultures knew the story about the flood that drowned the world, the Bible's telling of the story not only recounts what was known, but also includes the message that the Flood will not repeat itself: the world will not be destroyed a second time, and humanity can continue to build and progress.

The importance of the historical approach lies in the fact that it makes room for morality and values. Were that not the case, nothing could change, and man's actions would be meaningless. Eliade himself, it bears noting, identified with the cosmological model: as a fascist and an anti-Semite, he was not much enamored of the historical approach.

It seems, thus, that Eliade possessed only a partial understanding of Judaism, for the truth of the matter is that the Jewish tradition did not supersede the cosmological approach, but rather added to it, maintaining a unique synthesis between the cosmic and the historical. Franz Rosenzweig nicely elaborated Judaism's complex approach to time in describing it not as a line or a circle, but as an ascending spiral.

Jewish Time

This complex conception of time and reality emerges from the descriptions of the festivals in *Parashat Emor*. The first month in the Jewish calendar is Nisan, due to its historical significance: it is the month during which we came out of Egypt, and it is when we celebrate our birth as a nation. Yet, most Jewish holidays take place in Tishrei, the seventh month after the Exodus. During that month there are four holidays and festivals, one every week: Rosh HaShana, Yom Kippur, Sukkot, and Shemini Atzeret. The link between the sanctity of Tishrei and its holidays is apparent in the Torah's use of the term "solemn rest" (*Shabbaton*) in describing them – in contrast with the holidays and festivals of other months.

The unique status of the Tishrei holidays stems from the special significance associated with the number seven in Judaism: the seventh day is sanctified as God's Sabbath; the seventh year, *Shemitta*, is consecrated as a sabbatical for the land; and the seventh month, too, is sacred.

It may seem odd, on the face of it, to compare the seventh month to Shabbat and *Shemitta*. Shabbat marks the end of the week, and *Shemitta* signifies the conclusion of an agricultural cycle, while the seventh month lies in the middle of a twelve-month year. It seems that the explanation lies in the year's cyclical structure, in that the second half of the year progresses back toward its beginning. Thus, the chronological point that is furthest from the beginning of the year is the middle day of the year, meaning the first day of the seventh month. This idea can be elucidated with the image of an analog clock: the point that is farthest from one o'clock is seven o'clock. Similarly, in the cycle of the year, the seventh month is the furthest from the first month, in which we came out of Egypt, and thus signifies the completion of the process of the Exodus.

The uniqueness of Tishrei also stems from the fact that, according to the prevailing opinion among our sages, Creation occurred during that month. In addition, in the Land of Israel, it is when the rains resume after summer. The raindrops falling on the parched ground are likened to the primordial mist that rose up from the earth and quenched its thirst: "But there went up a mist from the earth, and watered the whole face of the ground" (Gen. 2:6; Rosh HaShana 11a).

As noted above, there is a tension between history and the cosmos. In terms of human history, Tishrei represents the ending, whereas cosmically, it stands for the beginning. These two aspects of the month can also be traced in the content of the holidays and festivals.

Sukkot: History and Nature

The Sukkot festival lasts seven days and is at the heart of the seventh month. There are two sides to Sukkot: one historical and the other cosmological.

On one hand, we dwell in sukkot to celebrate a historical event, the dawn of the Jewish people: "That your generations may know that I made the children of Israel to dwell in booths, when I brought them out of the land of Egypt" (Lev. 23:43). On the other, in moving into the sukka, we celebrate nature: we leave our permanent homes behind to dwell under the sky; the sukka itself is constructed of natural materials that grow without human intervention (Mishna Sukka 1:4); during the festival, we collect four species – lulav, citron, myrtle and willow – that represent nature;[2] and in the Temple, water is brought for the altar, a symbol of the prayers for the rain to return and slake nature's thirst.

The festival's other name, the Feast of Harvest (Ex. 23:16; 33:22), further hints at its connection to nature. It is nature at its most virginal and idyllic. Talmudic literature, in describing each of the festival's commandments, employs imagery from Creation and the Garden of Eden. With respect to the return to nature on Sukkot, Rav Kook wrote:

> During the Feast of Harvest … we draw closer to nature. We sit in the sukka and take hold of a bundle of fresh branches, rejoicing in the water's gladness, in the gladness of the natural perfusion of God's blessing for the universe, which propagates through the bounded circle of nature's iron rules. (*Igrot HaRe'iya* 3, 58)[3]

An Ending Is a Beginning

There is a profound idea inherent in connecting the two timescales – the cosmological and the historical. Cosmologically, Tishrei is the month of Creation, while historically it is the seventh month after the nascence of the Jewish people and its emergence from Egypt, a point in time that signifies the completion of the

---

2. See my book *Water, Creation and Revelation – Sukkot in the Philosophy of Halakha* [Hebrew] (Otniel: Giluy, 2008), 210–214.
3. For more on this point, see ibid., 210–217.

historical process. The furthest date from the beginning of the story is the same date that marks the start of "cosmological time." One fundamental aspect of the Torah's vision of the end of days, as described, among other places, in the books of Ezekiel (47) and Zechariah (14), is the world's return to its pristine state, in which nature and physical reality are an ideal manifestation of God's revelation and kingship in the world.

The fact that the end point of the historical process marks the return of Creation to its starting point teaches us about the role of humanity and its place in the rectification of the world. The renewed Creation differs from the original one in that it is not only the fruit of God's actions. History endows humanity with the privilege and responsibility to participate in the act of Creation by rectifying and elaborating it, and that must be the purpose of human activity throughout the generations. The partnership between God and humankind sanctifies human activity, in which people actualizes their purpose as an image of God.[4]

The intersection between the cosmological and the historical is also where the two basic modes of life – "being" and "doing" – converge.

---

4. It is noteworthy that the two progressions – the cosmic and the historical – correspond to two basic modes of reality, according to Lurianic Kabbala: the circular and the linear. See *Etz Ḥayim*, gate 1.

Behar-Beḥukkotai

What Does *Shemitta* Have to Do with Chief Seattle?

In 1854, the United States government tried to convince Chief Seattle, the leader of the Duwamish Indians, to sell the tribe's land. Seattle responded in March of that year in a speech whose exact content is unknown, in part because he delivered it in Lushootseed, a language that the whites did not understand. According to one account, in turning down the US government's request, the chief explained that "the earth does not belong to man, man belongs to the earth." In the chief's eyes, all of the earth is sacred; the land is the mother and the winds of the sky imbue us with the breath of life, and when we die we return our spirit to them. Our relation to nature, Seattle said, is like the relationship between a girl and her mother.

In Leviticus, and especially in the descriptions of *Shemitta* in *Behar* and *Beḥukkotai*, the Torah treats the land not as an inanimate object but rather as a subject, a living being to which we are committed and for which we are responsible. The land lies fallow and rests one year out of every seven, just as people rest once a week on Shabbat (Lev. 25:2). The Torah warns us that if we do not let the land rest, we will be exiled until the land has completed all of the fallow years that were denied it (26:34). If we defile the land, it will vomit us out (18:25).

Like Chief Seattle, the Torah considers the land itself to be holy. Rav Kook echoes Chief Seattle's sentiment in the opening of his book *Orot*:

> The Land of Israel is not an external thing, an external national asset, a mere means toward the end.... The Land of Israel is an independent entity, bound to the nation in a bond of life, enlaced with its reality through its own innate qualities.

Rav Kook was said to have once prostrated himself on the ground and mumbled, "My Land! My Land! O holy soil of the Land of Israel!" Asked to explain his behavior, he said, "When else do I have an opportunity to chat with our motherland, who longs for her children to return to her borders?"[1]

Although there are similarities between Rav Kook's statement and the words of Chief Seattle, there are also differences. Judaism is a monotheistic religion, while the Native American conception of the land is part of a pagan worldview. Indeed, in Israeli discourse there are voices that accuse people who speak of the land's sanctity of worshiping it. What is the relationship between the belief in a single God and the belief in the sanctity of the land? At the root of that question is another: what is the relationship between God and the cosmos?

---

1. Simcha Raz, *An Angel Among Men* [Hebrew] (Jerusalem: Kol Mevaser Publications, 2003), 237.

God and the World

There are three basic conceptions of God's relationship to the cosmos. On one end of the spectrum is the transcendental outlook, according to which God is separate and removed from reality. Although there can be a relationship between them, God is beyond the cosmos and outside it. This view is associated with Maimonides, among others.

On the other end of the spectrum is the pantheistic idea, which identifies God with nature, an approach that can lead to the worship of nature. It is an outlook that pervaded the archaic, pagan world and appears, with some changes, in Baruch Spinoza's philosophy, as well as in Chief Seattle's speech.

In between those two poles is a third approach, the panentheistic, which incorporates both outlooks:

> Panentheism is an approach whereby the world is part of God, but God is not only the world but also that which is beyond it. Panentheism is similar to pantheism in that both approaches maintain an immanent conception of the divine, according to which the world is not separate from God but rather is identified with Him. Yet, in contrast with pantheism, which does not allow for the existence of anything beyond the realms of consciousness and language, and is thus materialistic at bottom, identifying God with nature alone, panentheism posits the existence of things beyond consciousness and language. It does not reduce God to nature and the world, but also includes within Him that which lies beyond. Unlike pantheism, which posits a finite God, panentheism recognizes the existence of an infinite God. (Wikipedia's Hebrew article on panentheism)

It is just such an integrative approach that lies at the heart of Jewish mysticism, from Kabbala to Hasidism to Rav Kook's ideas.

As the Midrash (Genesis Rabba 68:9) says, "[God] is the world's place, but the world is not His place." The cosmos is part of God, and not vice versa, which is why He is not reducible to it.

The Creation of the World

The differences between the various models bring us back to the story of Creation. We tend to refer to the creation of the world as *ex nihilo* – something out of nothing – or, in Hebrew, "*yesh me'ayin*." The term is generally taken to mean that before the world was created there was nothing but God, who, in the midst of total absence, created something new, a world. After Creation there were thus two separate entities: God and the world.

According to the kabbalistic approach, however, "nothingness," or "*ayin*," does not designate an absence, but rather infinite divinity, which cannot be reduced to definitions or names. Indeed, Its designation as "nothingness" is only a function of Its ineffability. Creation, in this model, is a process of emanation from nothingness into the concrete and defined. Yet, even after this "somethingness" comes into being, there remains in the world a hidden stratum of the higher reality, the "nothingness." Statements such as "No place is devoid of Him" (*Tikkunei Zohar* 122b) and the hasidic interpretation of the verse "There is none else beside Him" (Deut. 4:35) refer to this level of reality – everything is divinity.

As Professor Yehuda Liebes notes, the original connotation of the term "*yesh me'ayin*" is the kabbalistic one.[2] The source for the term is "A Crown for the King," Rabbi Solomon ibn Gabirol's poem about Creation, which likens the emanation of the world out of nothingness to a flowing of light from the eye.

---

2. Yehuda Liebes, "Rabbi Solomon ibn Gabirol's Use of *Sefer Yetzira* and a Commentary on the Poem 'I Love Thee,'" *Jerusalem Studies in Jewish Thought* 6 [Hebrew] (1987): 73–123.

The verse paraphrases *Sefer Yetzira* (2:6), which describes the process of Creation thus: "He formed substance out of chaos, and made nonexistence into existence. He carved great pillars from air that cannot be grasped."[3] Just as "chaos" and "air that cannot be grasped" are not absences but rather indefinable realities, so, too, "nonexistence" – to which they are likened and which also becomes something, "existence" – does not indicate absence.

Rav Kook discusses this debate and explains his own stance:

> It is not the idea that it is impossible to invoke something out of utter nothingness that gives rise to the theory of emanation, in the sense that everything is, and was, and is constantly emanating from, the living spirit of God; and that the true essence of the world, too, is divinity, supernal faith. Rather, it is because there is nothing preventing the possibility of conceiving of reality in this way that we have no need of other modes [of conceptualizing it]. Clearly, it is preferable to think that divinity would create everything out of what is already at hand, needing nothing beside Himself. That is why these sages are uncomfortable with the [idea of] the creation of something out of absolute nothingness in the literal sense. (*Shemona Kevatzim* 2:81)

The Big Bang

We can understand the world's spiritual reality by comparing it to our physical reality. According to science, all matter has an internal stratum, the atomic level, which, in turn, can be described in terms of energy. There are methods for detecting this nuclear energy and releasing it.

---

3. Kaplan, *Sefer Yetzirah: The Book of Creation*, 131.

This conception of the material world rests on the cosmological theory of the Big Bang, based on which the universe emerged from a single point of energy. With time, the energy coalesced into matter. Yet, that primordial energy remains the basic constituent of all matter.[4]

Thirst for the Living God

When we again compare the kabbalistic point of view to the pantheistic approach propounded by Chief Seattle, we come to the conclusion that according to the kabbalists, the land is indeed holy, but its holiness does not stand apart from the one infinite God, who unites and transcends everything. The encounter with the divinity immanent within reality gives rise to a yearning for connection with the divinity that transcends it. As Rav Kook writes in his essay "Thirst for the Living God":

> The path into the drawing room must be shown – through the gate. The gate is the divinity revealed in the world, in all its beauty and splendor, in every spirit and soul, in every animal and insect, in every plant and flower, in every nation and kingdom, in the sea and its waves … the supernal divine, which we yearn to reach, within it to become submerged, to be gathered into its light. Yet, we cannot fulfill our yearning in that way; divinity descends for our sake into the world and permeates it, and we find it and delight in its love, find tranquility and peace in its solace. On occasion it will reveal itself to us in a sublime flash of supernal light that transcends all thought and idea. The sky opens up and we see visions of God. (*Orot* 119–120)

---

4. For the connection between kabbalistic cosmology and the Big Bang, see Daniel Matt, *God and the Big Bang* (Woodstock, VT: Jewish Lights Publishing, 1996).

The immanent conception of God is important not only to the relationship between God and humanity, but also between humanity and the world. By believing that God is present in reality, we can face life with a sense of honor and awe.

Bemidbar

Each of Us Has a Name

Each of us has a name
Given by God
And given by our parents.

– Zelda

Zelda's poem reminds most Israelis of national Memorial Day ceremonies. A discourse that revolves around the number of fallen can erode the individuality of the victims. Their uniqueness is what the poem seeks to enshrine – the fact that everyone has a name. Every year, before the siren pierces the air, signaling the beginning of Memorial Day, I choose one of the too-many people about whom, sadly, I would like to think during the siren, and devote all of my attention to their life and death. I am unable to contemplate more than one person at a time.

Counting members of the nation is considered a grave sin in Jewish tradition, as we learn from the following story about King David: "And the king said to Joab the captain of the host, who was with him, 'Go now through all the tribes of Israel, from Dan even to

Beersheba, and number the people, that I may know the sum of the people'" (II Sam. 24:2). Joab, the commander of David's army, fails to dissuade him from conducting the census. Ultimately, David himself comes to rue his sin: "And David said to the Lord, 'I have sinned greatly in what I have done; but now, O Lord, put away, I beseech You, the iniquity of Your servant; for I have done very foolishly'" (ibid. 24:10). Elsewhere, the Bible writes that it is "abominable" to count the people and that it causes God to be "displeased" (I Chr. 21:6–7).

A census turns a human being into a number, a statistic; one loses one's intrinsic value. David counts the people, it seems, in order to ascertain his own might, casting every individual person as no more than an extension of their monarch. There is a story about a doctor who was preparing to operate on a boy. Before the procedure, he asked the father if the boy was his only child. The father said he was, but added that he had four other children at home.

The quantification of humanity led to the shocking atrocities of the previous century. In his book *Darkness at Noon*, Arthur Koestler argues that such an approach underpinned the twisted outlook of Bolshevism, according to which the killing of millions was just – if it meant that billions could have a better future life. Treating people as numbers entails a certain dehumanization. During the Holocaust, for example, the Nazis would tattoo numbers on the arms of Jewish camp inmates. In a far less egregious example of this phenomenon, the film *Patch Adams* portrays a doctor who rails at his colleagues for treating patients like numbers ("bed six needs blood work") and demands that they call them by name ("Mrs. O'Bannon needs blood work"). Even if numbers are more efficient than names, economy is not the measure of everything in life.

From Human Census to Divine Census

Parashat Bemidbar tells of a census conducted by Moses. The question is, why is David's census considered a sin, while here

God Himself commands Moses to count the people? One difference, according to Rashi, is in the intention. In his commentary on our *parasha*, he writes: "Because they were dear to Him, He counted them often" (Rashi on Numbers 1:1). It emerges that Moses' census is motivated by God's love for Israel, while David's census has an administrative purpose: to establish the size of the population.

There is another key difference in our *parasha*'s census: "Take the sum of all the congregation of the children of Israel, by their families, by their fathers' houses, according to the number of names, every male, by their polls" (Num. 1:2). The key word here is "names," which recurs in the descriptions of each of the twelve tribes: "According to the number of names." The Torah emphasizes that the census is not only numerical, anonymous, but rather based on the name and affiliation of every individual. It is a vehicle for expressing uniqueness and value, along with tribal and familial bonds. Here is Rabbi Yehiel Moskowitz in the *Daat Mikra*:[1]

> The counting was done with names. The census did not establish only the total number of individuals in each tribe; rather, each person was defined and associated with a family – their father's house and tribe. The number did not comprise only a figure but also a name and familial affiliation, "By their fathers' houses."[2]

There are other indications that the purpose of the census was to empower, rather than devalue, the individual. For example, in commanding Moses to conduct the census, God tells him to

---

1. Yehiel Moskowitz, *Daat Mikra: Bemidbar* [Hebrew] (Jerusalem: Mossad Harav Kook, 1988), 4.
2. The Torah makes a point of noting explicitly the names of the representatives of every tribe: "And Moses and Aaron took these men that are pointed out by name" (1:17).

"raise the heads" of the people of Israel.[3] The words "raise" and "heads" indicate that the census is designed to elevate the individual. Also noteworthy is the Torah's use of the root *pe-kuf-dalet* because, in addition to counting, it connotes memory: "And the Lord remembered (*pakad et*) Sarah" (Gen. 21:1); "neither shall it come to mind; neither shall they make mention of it; neither shall they miss it (*yifkodu*)" (Jer. 3:16).

When people conduct a census, their purpose is only the final tally; human beings cannot retain so many names in their memory. Not so when God orders the census. The number of the children of Israel is likened to the stars in the night sky (Gen. 15:5), about which it is said, "He counts the number of the stars; He gives them all their names" (Ps. 147:4). God is capable not only of counting the stars, but also of naming each and every one. In God's census, the individual is not subsumed but rather set in relief; everyone is given attention, and each has a name. It emerges that the English title for the Book of *Bemidbar*, "Numbers," misses the point.

Nonlinear Narrative

Our understanding of the meaning of the census, and of the manner in which the tribes of Israel are arranged around the Tabernacle, can resolve a conundrum posed by the *parasha*. The Torah notes that the commandment to conduct the census is given on the first day of Iyar (Num. 1:2). The Book of Leviticus ends on the first of Nisan, the eighth day of the dedication of the Tabernacle. The description of the dedication resumes in the second *parasha* of Numbers, *Naso*, which details the offerings brought by the twelve tribal princes. That ceremony, the Torah says, begins on the same day as the completion of the consecration of the Tabernacle

---

3. English-language translations of the Bible render the phrase, "*se'u at rosh*," as "take the sum" or "take a census."

and its accoutrements (Num. 7:1), meaning it lasts from the first through the twelfth of Nisan – more than two weeks before the first of Iyar, when, in the previous *parasha*, Moses is instructed to conduct the census.

Why does the Torah interrupt the chronology of the story? It seems that the break in the order is due to a desire to begin the new book, Numbers, with its main theme – the people of Israel. That is why the census and the arrangement of the tribes around the Tabernacle preface a book that will deal extensively with the people. By placing the tribal princes after the census, the Torah also conveys a democratic message – the leaders' importance is not intrinsic but rather stems from their role as public representatives.

One Prince per Day

As noted above, *Parashat Naso* describes the offerings brought by the twelve princes. Fully seventy-two verses are devoted to these offerings – six each to every tribal leader, describing his offering in detail. What is interesting is the fact that the offerings are all identical. Why does the Torah make a point of repeating twelve times what is essentially the same offering, seemingly redundantly? In light of our observations above regarding the census, we can perhaps say that there is a difference from offering to offering, based on the identity of the individual princes. When two different people give gifts, each gift is experienced differently, depending on the personalities of the givers. The Torah's message is that each offering is made special by the person who brings it. This is also the meaning of a phrase I have been seeing on a lot of t-shirts recently: "Same same but different." The idea is that by repeating the description of the offering and noting the identity of the person bringing it, the Torah teaches that we must ask not only "what," but also "who."

Naso

The Good, the Bad and the Ugly

The Good, the Bad and the Ugly is the cult Western that catapulted Clint Eastwood to superstardom. The title of the film could just as easily have been taken from our *parasha*, which features a motley variety of characters, including the leper, the thief, the adulteress, the *nazir*, and the priest. Despite the differences between the characters, there is something they share that links them through the order of their appearance. While *Parashat Bemidbar* deals with the structure of the Israelite camp – the Tabernacle surrounded by the people – *Naso* is occupied with the daily life in the camp. The approach to each of the characters hinges on the idea that God is present within the camp. The Tabernacle is not an ivory tower, removed from life, but rather a focal point whose influence is felt throughout the camp.

The actions of the thief are not only a sin against society, but also against God: "Speak to the children of Israel: When a man or woman shall commit any sin that men commit, to commit a trespass against the Lord" (Num. 5:6). In the ensuing verses (7–8 as well as a corresponding passage in Leviticus 5:21) we learn that the trespass against God is to steal from another human being. When the divine is present in life, divine values become part of reality, any perversion of which is considered an actual injury to God. The words "any sin that men commit" teach us that whatever the Torah says regarding a thief is also relevant to any other interpersonal transgression.

The Torah follows up the thief with the *sota*, or suspected adulteress. The woman is brought to the Tabernacle, where she is made to stand "before the Lord" (Num. 5:16, 18, 30). During the ensuing ordeal, she drinks a mixture of "holy water" and dust from the "floor of the Tabernacle" (5:17), into which the priest first dips a parchment inscribed with the verses from our *parasha* regarding the *sota* (5:23). The water can be either a blessing, if the woman has not sinned, or a curse, if she has. It appears that as soon as the dust from the Tabernacle floor and the words of the Torah relating to the *sota* enter her stomach, they have the power to observe the relation between her and divine reality. When there is a state of harmony, the mixture is a blessing; when there is disharmony, a direct connection with holiness damages any who desecrate it.

The *Nazir*'s Hair

The most fascinating figure in the *parasha* is without doubt the *nazir*, whose vows are an opportunity for equality. All members of the Jewish people – man or woman; priest, Levite or layperson – are eligible to distance themselves from normative practice in order to seek holiness and intimacy with God. The basic requirements from the *nazir* are abstention from wine, growing long hair, and refraining from becoming impure through contact with the dead.

In order to better understand the *nazir*, let us compare him to the priest. Both the *nazir* and the priest partake of a special kind of holiness that precludes them from exposure to death. The difference between them can be found in the thing that has come to be associated with the *nazir* more than anything else: head hair. While the priest is forbidden from growing out his hair (Lev. 21:10), the *nazir* is prevented from cutting it. The Torah makes clear that this is what defines the *nazir's* status:

> All the days of his vow of Naziriteship there shall no razor come upon his head … he shall be holy, he shall let the locks of the hair of his head grow long…. He shall not make himself unclean for his father, or for his mother, for his brother, or for his sister, when they die; because his consecration (*nezer*) to God is upon his head. All the days of his Naziriteship he is holy to the Lord. And if any man die very suddenly beside him, and he defile his consecrated head, then he shall shave his head in the day of his cleansing, on the seventh day shall he shave it. (6:5–9)

The *nazir's* holiness is expressed through his hair, which the Torah says is "his consecration to God." The Hebrew word often translated as "consecration" is "*nezer*," which in this context connoted a crown. The prohibition against contact with the dead is also derived from this holiness, which is why any such contact requires the *nazir* to cut off his hair. When a *nazir's* vow lapses, he shaves his head and burns the hair on the altar along with his offering (6:18). Like a burnt offering, the hair belongs to God. The story of Samson also drives home the idea that the main expression of Naziriteship is hair. When Delilah asks, "Wherein does your great strength lie?" (Judges 16:15), Samson replies, "There has not come a razor upon my head; for I have been a *nazir* to God from my mother's womb; if I be shaven, then my strength will go from me, and I shall become weak, and be like any other man" (16:17).

The Zohar (*Naso* 121a) sees in the holiness of the *nazir*'s hair a similarity between him and God. The hair becomes a powerful metaphor for various attributes of the divine and its connection to reality: flow, bounty, and expansion from a single point into a boundless multitude.

Wild hair is also an expression of the spiritual state of the *nazir*, whose outlook is described in the following verse: "When either a man or a woman shall clearly (*yafli*) utter a vow, the vow of a *nazir*, to consecrate themselves to the Lord" (Num. 6:2). The Hebrew word "*yafli*" comes from "*pele*," which connotes a movement above and beyond, outside the usual frames of reference. It is a movement that is expressed aptly in the *nazir*'s wild hair, which flows chaotically and unpredictably, breaking boundaries. Today, too, long hair is a symbol of rebellion among youths.

Therein is the heart of the difference between the *nazir* and the priest: the holiness of the priest is generated by a reality of normative order. Hence, the priest must be immaculate, with nary a hair out of place. The holiness of the *nazir*, on the other hand, is generated by a departure from social structures; hence its manifestation as wild hair. Another expression of a *nazir*'s departure from normative reality is the prohibition against his becoming impure through contact with the dead – including immediate family members. The *nazir* is an individualist. In the case of Samson, that individualism sometimes left him outside the consensus: fearing the repercussions of his provocations against the Philistines, the Israelites delivered him themselves into the hands of their enemy (Judges 15:11–12).

In his essay "The Souls of the World of Chaos" (*Orot* 121–122), Rav Kook describes a unique figure whose soul is hewn from chaos. Much of this essay is applicable to the *nazir*:

> Conventional conduct – integrity and righteousness, in adherence to all virtues, rules and precepts – is an expression

of the progression of the World of Rectification (*Tikkun*). Any deviation – whether in terms of frivolity and wantonness on one hand, or the ascension of consciousness and the awakening of supernal spirituality on the other – is an expression of the World of Chaos (*Tohu*).... The souls of Chaos are loftier than the souls of Rectification. They are very large, and demand much of reality – beyond the capacity of their vessels to bear. They demand a very powerful light, and cannot tolerate anything that is bounded, limited, and ordered.

Rav Kook goes on to warn of the dangers posed by these souls of Chaos:

They strive far, far beyond their capacity, strive and fall. They realize that they are imprisoned by rules, by limiting conditions that prevent them from expanding into eternity, from rising up infinitely, and they fall, doleful, despairing, and raging. Consumed by fury, they become wrapped up in malice, wickedness, baseness, ugliness, loathing, and destructiveness – all that is evil.

Samson ends his own life with an act of destruction – he smashes the foundations of a sturdy building, killing himself along with his enemies (Judges 16:30). There is a lot of power to going with the flow and overstepping boundaries, but also danger. For Samson, the danger lies in sexuality. Our sages are very critical of his behavior in this area, condemning it as a damaging rebellion (Sota 9b). According to the Mishna (Sota 1:8), he is punished for it: "Samson went after his eyes, therefore the Philistines gouged out his eyes, as it says, 'And the Philistines took hold of him and gouged out his eyes' (Judges 16:21)."

The Mishna goes on to discuss the fate of King David's son Absalom, who, according to the sages (Nazir 4b), was also a *nazir*: "Absalom was proud of his hair, therefore he was hanged by his hair. And because he had relations with the ten concubines of his father, he was pierced by ten spears." Absalom's hair is the source of his pride and the root of his rebellion against his father. Eventually, he pays with his life in a case of poetic justice: his hair becomes entangled in the branches of a tree, and David's men are able to capture him (II Sam. 18:9). The Mishna also notes Absalom's sexual transgressions – his relations with his father's concubines.

In this context we can more readily understand the ban on *nazir*s drinking wine. For someone who has a problem with boundaries, wine can be deadly. Here is the Midrash:

> God well knew that Samson would be led astray by his eyes; therefore, they warned that a *nazir* refrain from drinking wine, because it leads to lechery. Indeed we see that as a *nazir* he was led astray by his eyes, but were he to drink as well, he would have been eternally irredeemable due to the extent of his pursuit of lechery. (Numbers Rabba 10)

According to the Talmud, this is why the Torah discusses the *nazir* after the passages dealing with the *sota*: "Why does the section of the *nazir* adjoin that of the suspected woman? To tell you that whoever witnesses a suspected woman in her disgrace should withhold himself from wine" (Sota 2a). Perhaps, more than becoming a *nazir* can help one contend with the dangers of drinking wine, teetotaling is a method of dealing with the dangers of Naziriteship.

The juxtaposition of the *nazir* and the *sota* is also fascinating due to the shared motif of wild hair: "And the priest shall set the woman before the Lord, and let the hair of the woman's head go loose" (Num. 5:18). Both the *nazir* and the adulteress defy the social order, one positively and the other negatively.

Our generation has placed major emphasis on individualism. The juxtaposition of the *nazir* and the *sota*, and their vastly different fates, sends a message to those who wish to break the boundaries of normativity. Such a departure can be either a blessing or a curse, a movement upward or downward. As we have seen in regard to drinking wine, much of the outcome is determined by the boundaries that one sets for oneself.

The *Nazir* from the South

We would be remiss to discuss *nazir*s without mentioning the remarkable story of the *nazir* from the south:

> Shimon HaTzaddik said: Only once in my life have I eaten of the trespass offering brought by a defiled tear. On one occasion a *nazir* came from the South country, and I saw that he had beautiful eyes, was of handsome appearance, and with thick locks of hair symmetrically arranged. Said I to him, "My son, what [reason] did you see to destroy this beautiful hair of yours?" He replied, "I was a shepherd for my father in my town. [Once] I went to draw water from a well, gazed upon my reflection in the water, whereupon my evil desires rushed upon me and sought to drive me from the world [through sin]. But I said to it [my lust]: 'Wretch! Why do you vaunt yourself in a world that is not yours, with one who is destined to become worms and dust? I swear that I will shave you off [my beautiful hair] for the sake of Heaven.'" I immediately arose and kissed his head, saying, "My son, may there be many *nazir*s such as you in Israel! Of you the Holy Writ says, 'When either a man or a woman shall clearly utter a vow, the vow of a *nazir*, to consecrate themselves to the Lord' (Num. 6:2)." (Nedarim 9b)

The story begins with a reservation regarding the very institution of Naziriteship. The Talmud does not state explicitly why Shimon HaTzaddik has qualms regarding the *nazir*, but it does clarify further on that he is opposed to asceticism in all its forms. The *nazir* is considered a sinner "because he afflicted himself through abstention from wine. Now, does not this afford an argument from the minor to the major? If one, who afflicted himself only in respect of wine, is called a sinner, how much more so one who ascetically refrains from everything" (Nedarim 10a).

Shimon HaTzaddik, the story shows us, can set aside his opposition to asceticism and show appreciation for a form of Naziriteship. His story is antithetical to the myth of Narcissus, who, according to Greek mythology, falls in love with himself when he sees his own reflection. Eventually, he dies of hunger because he is unable to pull himself away. In contrast, the hero of our story gazes unflinchingly at the danger inherent in pride, which has the power to drive us from the world, and chooses to grapple with it by becoming a *nazir*.

Reincarnation

On the literal level, the takeaway from the story is that the purpose of Naziriteship is to overcome desire. Yet, there is a deeper level to the story, revealed in Rabbi Isaac Luria's *Gate of Reincarnations*: the *nazir* from the south is none other than a reincarnation of Absalom, David's son. Though he does not explain his reason for linking the two men, a literary reading of the story can establish the claim that the *nazir*'s character is drawn based on that of Absalom.

Like the *nazir*, Absalom is described as handsome: "Now in all Israel there was none to be so much praised as Absalom for his beauty; from the sole of his foot even to the crown of his head there was no blemish in him" (II Sam. 14:25). Absalom's beauty is manifested in his hair: "And when he shaved his head – now it was at every year's end that he shaved it; because the hair was heavy on him, therefore he shaved it – he weighed the hair of his head at two hundred shekels, after the king's weight" (14:26). The characterization of the *nazir* as having "beautiful eyes" and a "handsome appearance" is identical to the description of David, Absalom's father (I Sam. 16:12),[1] who, one can assume, is similar in appearance to his son.

As we noted, the Mishna in Sota says, "Absalom was proud of his hair, therefore he was hanged by his hair." The *nazir* from the south, too, in encountering his beautiful reflection, has vain thoughts that threaten to drive him from the world.

When he runs from his father in Jerusalem to launch a rebellion, Absalom heads south, to Hebron. That, too, is a parallel with the *nazir* in our story, who comes to Jerusalem from the south.

Yet, Absalom does not fly south only in order to plan his rebellion, as he says, but also to fulfill his vows to God. According to our sages, those vows pertain to his Naziriteship (Nazir 4b). The *nazir* from the south corrects Absalom's lie by vowing sincerely, for the sake of heaven. The *nazir* is overcome by desire when he draws water from spring, which is where kings from the dynasty of David are anointed.[2] His statement, "I was a shepherd for my father," can also hint at the relationship between Absalom and his own father, a shepherd who came to herd the flock of Israel.

The deeper purpose of the story is to contrast between a *nazir* who wanders in order to fulfill his desires under a mere pretense of holiness and a *nazir* who wanders for the sake of heaven. It is in this sense that the *nazir* from the south is Absalom's rectification. He returns to "the scene of the crime" and – precisely where Absalom sinned, succumbing to the desire and vanity kindled by

---

1. In the story's telling in the Yerushalmi Talmud, the *nazir* is also described as "ruddy," like David (Nedarim 1, 5a).
2. See I Kings 1:33.

beauty – perseveres. The Torah says that the *nazir*'s vows "consecrate him to the Lord" (Num. 6:2), which one can take to mean that the Naziriteship is for the sake of heaven rather than one's personal ends.

There once was a man who would fast all week long except for Shabbat. Rabbi Naftali Zvi of Ropshitz, suspecting the purity of the man's motives, decided to test him. One day, when he saw a child bump into the man, the rabbi scolded the child: "How dare you hurt a man who fasts every Monday and Thursday?" The man was enraged: "What do you mean, every Monday and Thursday?! I fast all week long!" Thus the rabbi revealed the man's true motives: his piety was motivated by ego rather than an authentic desire to be close to God.[3]

---

3. Rabbi Shlomo Carlebach, *Lev HaShamayim: Pesaḥ*, ed. Shmuel Zivan (Jerusalem: Kol Mevaser, 2008), 90.

Behaalotekha

Thou Shalt Not Complain

A Dream Is Dashed

Parashat Behaalotekha is one of the saddest portions of the Torah, and that is the source of its significance, which we must internalize. The dream, the ideal, the high hopes – all are dashed on the rocks of an ugly and frustrating reality. After almost a year of dwelling around Mount Sinai, the time has come to set off. Moses is bursting with expectation – soon they will all enter the Land of Israel. He entreats his father-in-law, Yitro, to stay with the Israelites and enter the land with them, reiterating to him the good that awaits them when they arrive (Num. 10:29–32). But then we learn that not only will Yitro be prevented from entering the land, so will Moses. We also learn that before things improve they will become much worse.

When the Israelite encampment sets off, Moses tenses in anticipation of the war that awaits them upon entering the land. He cries out, "Rise up, O Lord, and let Your enemies be scattered; and let them that hate You flee before You" (Num. 10:35). Little does he know that the enemies and haters are not lying in wait along the path, but rather within.

Complaints Are Worse Than Sins

Moses' call is an expression of peak expectations. Soon afterward, things begin to fall apart: we learn that the parents' generation will die off in the desert, their children fated to wander the wastes for decades. But what is the sin that ruins it all? Even the sin of the Golden Calf – an idolatrous lapse at the holiest moment in the relationship between God and the Jewish people – was not beyond atonement and rectification. What could be worse? What sin cannot be atoned for?

Our *parasha* and the ones that follow chronicle a series of negative events: the complaints of the people who lust for meat, Miriam speaking ill of Moses, the spies and the defamation of the land, and the challenge to Moses and Aaron's leadership. All of these events can be summed up with a single word: complaints. But what is so bad about complaints? There is no commandment in the Torah "Thou shalt not complain." Furthermore, what can be more human than complaining? In order to answer that question, let us examine the complaints. It will become apparent that they are not the problem, but rather what motivates them.

Past, Present, and Future

The Israelites' complaints do not begin in Numbers: as far back as *Parashat Beshallaḥ* the people moan about a lack of water and food (Ex. 15:17). However, as Elchanan Samet points out, in *Bashallaḥ* the complaints appear justified – there is indeed a dearth of food and water at the outset of the journey.[1] Even if the people could have dealt with it in a more positive fashion, the complaints are understandable. In our *parasha*, on the other hand, the complaints are of an entirely different nature.

The problems begin after Moses exclaims, "Rise up, O Lord, and let Your enemies be scattered." Shortly afterward, the Torah

---

1. Elchanan Samet, *Studies in the Weekly Torah Reading* [Hebrew] (Jerusalem: Yediot Books, 2002), 173.

says, "the people were as murmurers, speaking evil in the ears of the Lord; and when the Lord heard it, His anger was kindled" (Num. 11:1). "Murmuring" in this context signifies a complaint of sorts. But we are not told what the people complain about. That omission, it seems, conveys something that is true of the other complaints as well: the thing that the people complain about is not the source of the complaint, but at best a pretext. An inability to recognize this truth can generate the delusion that if only the complainer were to receive his "heart's desire," everything would sort itself out. It is a delusion shared by both the complainer and the party that wants to help him. But the truth is that some people's basic outlook on life is negative. This negativity underpins their entire point of view, coloring their perception of reality. They walk around with the conviction that others want to harm them, and are blind to the many opportunities for a blessed improvement to their lives. They see only what is missing and never what there is. They are always wanting, always miserable.

Here is how the Torah introduces these characters:

> And the mixed multitude that was among them fell a lusting; and the children of Israel also wept on their part, and said, "Would that we were given flesh to eat! We remember the fish that we ate in Egypt for free; the cucumbers, and the melons, and the leeks, and the onions, and the garlic; but now our soul is dried away; there is nothing at all; we have nothing save this manna to look at." (Num. 11:4–6)

The complaints are contagious – one group of the "mixed multitude" begins to bellyache, and immediately "the children of Israel also wept on their part."

Complaints can cause a person to become stuck in the sense that everything is bad, while the reality outside it always better. But how warped does one have to be to sink into such a state when the alternative is slavery in Egypt? The Egyptians, we recall, subjected the Israelites to a living hell, enslaving them with grueling labor and murdering their sons. And yet, to the complainers, Egypt appears a place of bounty, a lost paradise. The claim that the food in Egypt was given freely is ludicrous. Even if true, there was no charge for the food for the very reason that animals receive their food "for free": animals are property; they have no money, and are fed so as to better carry out their masters' wishes.

Just as the complainers cast their bad past as good, so too they manage to portray their present as negative. They scorn God's gift, the manna, and the Torah is forced, parenthetically, to devote three verses (7–9) to praising the manna and refuting their claims. God, in response to their lust for meat, gives the complainers what they want: "Until it comes out your nostrils and is loathsome to you; because you have rejected the Lord who is among you, and have troubled Him with weeping, saying, 'Why did we come out of Egypt?'" (Num. 11:20). The lust for meat causes them to reject God, but shortly thereafter they reject the meat as well. The thought that meat is what is missing from their lives turns out to be a delusion. Beyond its distortion of reality, the narrow-mindedness and pettiness of their complaint is galling: is it possible that the most important thing in life, prompting such laments and a yearning to return to Egypt, is meat?

This skewed perspective, sadly, is not a thing of the past. Hoshea Friedman Ben Shalom, who heads Beit Yisrael, a pre-military academy geared toward contributing to Israeli society, likens our present times to the generation of the Exodus. We are fortunate to live in a time where great things are happening, the most important century for the Jewish people in the last two thousand years, but people are caught up in squabbles and petty complaints. This is true not only of the national arena, but also of the interpersonal realm. I recall vividly a scene from a wedding I attended, at which the father of the groom was arguing with the staff of the venue about the table arrangement even as the *ḥuppa* ceremony was starting, instead of rejoicing in his son's big day.

In the coming *parashot*, the people's nostalgia for Egypt continues to swell. Some suggest returning to the land of their enslavement (Num. 14:4), while others heap upon it superlatives formerly reserved for the Land of Israel, "a land flowing with milk and honey" (16:13). Then the complainers move on from scorning God (11:20) to blaspheming (14:11). The skewed sense of reality is applied not only to the past and present, but also to the future – in the sin of the spies in *Parashat Shelaḥ*. The past was good, the present is bad, and the future will be even worse.

Sins of "Doing" and Sins of "Being"

The people's complaints are too much for Moses to bear:

> And Moses heard the people weeping…and Moses was displeased. And Moses said to the Lord, "Why have You dealt ill with Your servant? And why have I not found favor in Your sight, that You lay the burden of all this people on me?… And if You deal thus with me, kill me, please, out of hand, if I have found favor in Your sight; and let me not look upon my wretchedness." (Num. 11:10–15)

The relationship between Moses and the people has deteriorated sharply. After the sin of the Golden Calf, he was prepared to sacrifice himself to save them (Ex. 32:33), but now he asks to die, if only to be spared the burden of leading them. What causes this massive crisis?

The complaints are not a one-off occurrence or a temporary lapse. They are an expression and reflection of the people's life, and characteristic of a general atmosphere. A distorted perception of reality can put negativity center-stage, no matter how good things are. In hindsight, the road not taken always turns out to have been the better choice. Rashi writes that when Moses prays for the recovery of his sister, Miriam, who is afflicted for speaking ill of him, he has to keep it short: "Why did Moses not pray at length? So that the Israelites should not say, 'His sister is in distress, yet he stands and prolongs his prayer.' Another interpretation: So that Israel should not say, 'For his sister he prays at length, but for our sake he does not pray at length'" (Rashi on Numbers 12:13).

Moses cannot win: there is no one to talk to, no possibility for a relationship, nowhere to go. Moses feels he that cannot go on in such a toxic atmosphere. The sin of the Golden Calf can be overcome, but there is no overcoming a fundamentally warped worldview. Formulated in terms of "doing" and "being," if a sin is in the realm of "being" – it can be transcended. But when its root is in "being," it manifests a deep inner world, and God's forgiveness will solve nothing, because it does not catalyze inner change.

Crime and Punishment

Although the moaners and bellyachers are ultimately proven right, they do not recognize the fact that their complaints are a form of self-fulfilling prophecy. This is clearly apparent in the story of the spies, who give the following description of themselves: "And there we saw the Nephilim, the sons of Anak, who come of the Nephilim; and we were in our own sight as grasshoppers, and so we were in their sight" (Num. 13:33). It is no wonder that when the spies have low self-esteem, and see themselves as "grasshoppers," others also come to see them in the same light: "and so we were in their sight."

The punishment for the sin of the spies is the possibility that the complaints will come true. God says:

How long shall I bear with this evil congregation, that keep murmuring against Me? I have heard the murmurings of the children of Israel, which they keep murmuring against Me. Say to them, "As I live, says the Lord, surely as you have spoken in My ears, so will I do to you: your carcasses shall fall in this wilderness, and all that were numbered of you, according to your whole number, from twenty years old and upward, you that have murmured against Me." (Num. 14:27–29)

It seems that beyond the punishment, we learn that the generation of the Exodus had a model of reality that prevented them from continuing to the next stage and entering the land, necessitating a wait for the next generation. Tellingly, Caleb and Joshua, who believe that the people *can* enter the Land of Israel, eventually do reach it. Just as negative outlooks have the power to shape reality for the worse, positive outlooks can give rise to a better reality. The verse "Who is the man that desires life, and loves days, that he may see good therein" (34:13–15) can be read not just as a question but also as an assertion: Who desires life? Those who love their days and see good in them. If we are to actualize ourselves, we must see the good and have a positive view of reality.

In one of his seminal discourses, Rabbi Nahman lays out the demand that people always look for the good in themselves and in others (*Likutei Moharan Kama* 282). This extends to evil people as well: if you see the good in them and focus on it, they will change. People, like life itself, are complicated, a mixture of good and evil. Spotlighting the positive in a person can frame the way we see them and shape their identity. When people focus on the good in themselves, they can be happy with their lives and reach positive places. Focusing on the negative in the other, however, can lead to despair. Rabbi Nahman warns of this, and chooses to end the first part of *Likutei Moharan* with it.

Internal *Tikkun Olam*

Ultimately, much of the Torah's focus is on rectifying the individual's personal conduct. The Israelites' problem in our *parasha* has more to do with their inner world than with any practical aspect of life. Much of one's basic conception of reality is shaped in the very early years of one's life. The generation of the Exodus grew up in a reality of intense suffering, which can perhaps explain their pathological approach to reality, and their inability to change even when their fate changes for the better.

One of the novelties of our age is the growing understanding that our inner world and models of reality are mutable. Hasidism and Kabbala deal extensively with the inner space of the psyche, which strives to rectify not only the "doing" but also the "being." A prerequisite for changing one's model of reality is an awareness of the difference between the world and the manner in which we experience and interpret it. Only with such awareness can one see that the necessary change is not in reality itself but rather in how we conceive of it. When we realize that, we can finally ask ourselves why we choose to interpret reality negatively, and how we can open ourselves up to other perspectives.

Shelaḥ

Battling and Sweetening Desire

The Prostitute and the Tzitzit

The Talmud relates the story of a young student who, upon learning of a famous prostitute in a faraway city, is overcome with desire
and travels to meet her. Predictably, at the last moment he is spared
from sin due to his stringent adherence to the mitzva of tzitzit. But
the story does not end there, and there is a final twist that conveys
much about the approach to desire and passion:

> Once a man, who was very scrupulous about the precept of
> tzitzit, heard of a certain harlot in one of the towns by the
> sea who accepted four hundred gold [denars] for her hire.
> He sent her four hundred gold [denars] and appointed a
> day with her.
>
> When the day arrived he came and waited at her
> door... she [said], "Let him come in." When he came in
> she prepared for him seven beds, six of silver and one
> of gold; and between one bed and the other there were

ladders of silver, but the last was of gold. She then went up to the top bed and lay down upon it naked. He too went up after her in his desire to sit naked with her, when all of a sudden the four fringes [of his garment] struck him across the face; whereupon he slipped off and sat upon the ground.

She also slipped off and sat upon the ground and said, "By the Roman Capitol, I will not leave you alone until you tell me what blemish you saw in me."

"By the Temple," he replied, "never have I seen a woman as beautiful as you are; but there is one precept which the Lord our God has commanded us, it is called tzitzit, and with regard to it the expression 'I am the Lord your God' is twice written, signifying, I am He who will exact punishment in the future, and I am He who will give reward in the future. Now [the tzitzit] appeared to me as four witnesses [testifying against me]."

She said, "I will not leave you until you tell me your name, the name of your town, the name of your teacher, the name of your school in which you study the Torah."

He wrote all this down and handed it to her. Thereupon she arose and divided her estate into three parts: one third for the government, one third to be distributed among the poor, and one third she took with her in her hand; the bedclothes, however, she retained. She then came to the beit midrash of Rabbi Ḥiyya, and said to him, "Master, give instructions about me that they make me a proselyte."

"My daughter," he replied, "perhaps you have set your eyes on one of the disciples?"

She thereupon took out the script and handed it to him.

"Go," said he, "and enjoy your acquisition."

Those very bedclothes which she had spread for him for an illicit purpose she now spread out for him lawfully. (Menaḥot 44a)

At the end of the story, the prostitute comes to the man's beit midrash, to his rabbi, Rabbi Ḥiyya, and asks to convert to Judaism. The request is met with suspicion as to the purity of her motives. Rabbi Ḥiyya finds out that, indeed, the woman has "set her eyes" on one of his disciples, but is appeased by the letter she bears and accedes to her application.

It is clear that not only the man undergoes a transformation – so does the woman, and hers is the far more dramatic process. When the man leaves her alone in her bed, she worries that he has found some blemish in her and is repulsed by it. He tries to mollify her and tells her that she has nothing to worry about; on the contrary, he says, "Never have I seen a woman as beautiful as you are." But she is not satisfied by his response. Faced with the young man's impressive capacity to heed a loftier call and forgo sexual gratification, the prostitute realizes that despite her flawless exterior, she is lacking internally; her life is unfulfilled. She makes a courageous decision to leave it all behind and pursue the young man, and eventually she succeeds.

Tzitzit and Beds

To my mind, the most interesting element in the story is the prostitute's attitude toward the "tools of her trade" – the beds. We would perhaps expect that when she sells off her assets, the first things she would want to rid herself of would be those tools of her trade that symbolize her previous depraved life – that, at most, she would take one bed on which to sleep. But she chooses to take all of her bedclothes. She is not the only one who assigns great importance to the beds. The rabbi whom she approaches in order to convert encourages her to make use of the beds in her marriage to his disciple. The beds are, I think, key to the story.

First, the numbers of beds (seven) and ladders (six) are significant, in that they establish a parallel with the tzitzit. Each of the four fringes of the tzitzit is wound thirteen times: seven times with the blue thread, which symbolizes the firmaments, and six with the white threads, which denote the air between the firmaments (Menaḥot 39a). The topmost bed is made of gold, and corresponds to the final winding of the tzitzit. According to the Talmud (ibid.), that is the holiest winding.

Ostensibly, the parallel is drawn in order to highlight a contrast, an example of the idea that "God has made the one as well as the other" (Eccl. 7:14). The passage into holiness is symbolized by the topmost winding of the tzitzit, which signifies the seventh firmament; for the prostitute, on the other hand, the seventh bed stands for the passage into depravity. It is thus surprising to encounter the rabbi's positive approach to the beds further along in the story.

There is an idea put forth by the Baal Shem Tov that can help us understand the moral of the tale. He teaches that there are three stages to spiritual work when it comes to desire: overcoming (*hakhnaa*), separation (*havdala*), and sweetening (*hamtaka*). The three stages also appear in our story. First there is an overcoming of desire – a man who has come to a situation where he is in bed with a prostitute succeeds in refraining from sinning. In the second stage, separation, he returns to the benches of his beit midrash. But first, before taking leave of the prostitute, he hands her a letter: "He wrote all this down and handed it to her." The Talmud's formulation is reminiscent of a Torah verse that says that a man who wishes to divorce his wife must "write her" a bill of divorce and "hand it to her" (Deut. 24:1).

In the third stage, sweetening, the disciple and the woman marry, and "those very bedclothes which she had spread for him for an illicit purpose she now spread out for him lawfully" – meaning that desire is actualized in marriage. The story teaches us that desire is not inherently negative, but can bring people to bad places when it takes over. The point is not to neuter desire but rather to express it in a positive context, in which it can be sweetened. The etymological link between the Hebrew words for desire (*"yetzer"*) and creation (*"yetzira"*) is evidence of the positive potential of human desire.

This nuanced approach to desire is also apparent in the rabbi's first response to the woman's request to convert. Before giving his assent, he asks her suspiciously, "Perhaps you have set your eyes on one of the disciples?" An intention to marry is, to him, not a legitimate reason to convert to Judaism. Ultimately, it emerges that he is right to suspect her – for the woman has indeed been pursuing the disciple. And yet, he accepts her conversion and gives his blessing to the union. A desire to marry is not necessarily an illegitimate motive for conversion, but it must still be examined. Once the rabbi establishes that the woman's desire to marry his disciple issues from a deep place within her soul, and that she is drawn to his inner world, which led her to Judaism, he blesses their union.

Be Holy

It is no coincidence that the climax of the story is linked to tzitzit, as the spiritual growth of the protagonists mirrors the structure of the section of the Torah dealing with the mitzva:

> Speak to the children of Israel, and bid them that they make them throughout their generations fringes in the corners of their garments, and that they put with the fringe of each corner a thread of blue. And it shall be to you as a fringe, that you may look upon it, and remember all the commandments of the Lord, and do them; and that you go not

after your own heart and your own eyes, after which you go astray; that you may remember and do all My commandments, and be holy to your God. I am the Lord your God, who brought you out of the land of Egypt, to be your God: I am the Lord your God. (Num. 15:38–41).

In verse 39 we are enjoined to "remember all the commandments of the Lord, and do them," while the verse immediately following adds, "that you may remember and do all My commandments." Why the repetition? It seems that the Torah is hinting at two stages: "Depart from evil, and do good" (Ps. 34:15). First, we must overcome our desire, meaning depart from evil: "That you go not after your own heart and your own eyes, after which you go astray." It is only after the first stage, in which the mitzvot are geared toward annulling our desire, that we can do good: "And be holy to your God."

In the first stage of our story, the tzitzit keeps the disciple from being led astray by his heart and eyes. The end of the story, when the two are united and consecrated in marriage, represents the second stage: "Be holy to your God."

The structure of the section dealing with tzitzit in our *parasha* teaches us that in approaching God and holiness, we must persevere in our inward-facing work, focusing on self-control. It is only from a pure place that we can get in touch with genuine holiness. When a person is flawed, spirituality can breed perversion and crossing of the thin line between divine worship and idolatry. This idea is evident in Rav Kook's distinction between morality and holiness: "Morality is the hallway, and holiness is the drawing room" (*Shemona Kevatzim* 1:133). Morality deals mostly with departing from evil, overcoming our negative traits. To conquer evil is not itself holiness, but it puts holiness within our reach.

In his book *Mei HaShiloaḥ* (part 2, *Parashat Shelaḥ*), Rabbi Mordechai Yosef Leiner writes that the first stage casts the mitzvot in the third person, indirectly: "All the commandments of the Lord." In the second stage, they are manifested in the second person: "All My commandments." The first stage, awe, is symbolized by the tzitzit's blue thread and characterized by an oblique approach. The second stage is love, symbolized by the white thread and characterized by direct connection.

The final verse says, "I am the Lord your God, who brought you out of the land of Egypt, to be your God." We have long been free of slavery in Egypt, but the Torah propounds spiritual work that can free us from a more insidious bondage – the one within us, to desire and our base qualities. It is only when we are liberated from that servitude that we can be truly free.

Is Everyone Holy?

The verses above teach us how to be holy. In this context, many commentators note the similarity between tzitzit and the priestly vestments: both feature strands of blue and both are woven of linen and wool – a combination prohibited in all other garments. The message seems to hark back to the verse "and you shall be to Me a kingdom of priests, and a holy nation" (Ex. 19:6). Consequently, we can understand Korah's claim, with which he confronts Moses and Aaron in the beginning of the next *parasha*: "All the congregation are holy, every one of them, and the Lord is among them" (Num. 16:3).

Part of the answer is that status is not derived merely from one's lineage, and holiness can only be attained through action. It would be wrong to read the verse "and you shall be to Me a kingdom of priests, and a holy nation" without taking note of the verse that precedes it: "Now therefore, if you will hearken to My voice indeed, and keep My covenant, then you shall be My own treasure from among all peoples."

Many are drawn to spirituality and aspire to attain holiness, but few are prepared to commit themselves to the kind of action that is a prerequisite. Tzitzit teaches us that "being," or essence, is predicated on "doing," existence: "That you may remember and *do* all My commandments, and *be* holy to your God." First we must "do" and only then can we "be." Our actions have an impact not only on our surroundings but also on ourselves – they help to shape our identity. It is interesting to note that God ascribes to Himself those two stages, starting with action: "I am the Lord your God, who brought you out of the land of Egypt." Only then comes the essence: "To be your God: I am the Lord your God."

Koraḥ

Argument and Encompassment

Although the word "argument" does not appear in our *parasha*, the events that it chronicles – and especially the challenge against Moses' leadership mounted by Korah and his followers – give the term a bad name. But we would be wrong to deduce from the story that one should avoid all arguments. In one famous mishna, the story of Korah and his followers serves as an example for a negative argument. But there are also positive arguments:

> Every argument that is for [the sake of] heaven's name is destined to endure. But if it is not for [the sake of] heaven's name, it is not destined to endure. What is [an example of an argument] for [the sake of] heaven's name? The argument of Hillel and Shammai. What is [an example of an argument] not for [the sake of] heaven's name? The argument of Korah and all of his congregation. (Avot 5:17)

It is not easy to distinguish between the two kinds of arguments. My late teacher Rabbi Yehuda Amital gave voice to this complexity in his explanation for the statement "Every argument that is for [the sake of] heaven's name is destined to endure." He would say that in any argument in which all sides are certain that their motives are purely "for the sake of heaven's name," no one will concede, and the argument will thus be "destined to endure," forever unresolved. While people will in some cases give up a personal need, when they claim to represent God and fight for something that they have couched in terms of holiness, they sanctify their obstinacy and refuse to compromise or concede.

The solution cannot be to avoid arguments altogether, for debate is a core component of our identity. Is there anything more Israeli and Jewish than deliberating, debating, and arguing? True, it is a trait that has fueled many jokes about Jews, and can be a source of misery, but to relinquish it would be tantamount to relinquishing our very selves.

The Talmud tells of R. Yohanan's search for someone to take the place of his study partner, Reish Lakish, who had died. R. Yohanan is disappointed by all of the candidates, because they try to prove the veracity of his statements, as opposed to Reish Lakish, who would argue with everything R. Yohanan said, pushing him to deepen his study. Ultimately, R. Yohanan is unable to fill the void left by Reish Lakish's death. He is so frustrated that he tears his clothes, cries, and ultimately loses his mind and dies (Bava Metzia 84a). Argument is intellectual fertilizer that breeds creativity and productive thought. Let us examine the idea of argument more closely, so that we can better determine when it brings ruin and should be avoided, and when it is a source of blessing toward which we should strive.

Some Are More Equal than Others

In our *parasha*, Korah and his followers confront Moses and Aaron with the following argument: "All the congregation are holy, every one of them, and the Lord is among them; why then do you raise yourselves up above the assembly of the Lord?" (Num. 16:3). On the face of it, it is a legitimate claim, propounding a vision of a just society, founded on the idea that we are all holy – every individual is created in the image of God, and the Jewish people is a "kingdom of priests, and a holy nation."

Moses, in response to Korah's claims, falls upon his face and calls for a test that will determine who is God's chosen (Num. 16:4–5). Later, he challenges Korah and his followers, calling them "wicked" and sinners (16:26). Does Korah not deserve a more pertinent response? Clearly, Moses himself has a lot to say on the matter. In fact, judging from other sources in the Torah, it would appear that he even agrees with some of the claims Korah levels against him.

Moses chooses to ignore Korah's argument because he understands that Korah himself does not believe in its veracity, and is in fact motivated by extraneous concerns – namely, a thirst for power. His argument against Moses and Aaron's special status is designed to conceal his own ambition. Korah employs the populist demand for equality in order to marshal the people, just as in *Animal Farm*, George Orwell's satirical novel, when the pigs rally the other animals around them with the claim that "all animals are equal." With time, the animals learn the hard way the second half of the sentence: "But some animals are more equal than others."

We can find proof of Korah's insincerity in the context in which he lodges his claim. Korah and his men are already elites. As Moses notes, Korah enjoys exalted status and is set apart from the people by virtue of his Levite lineage (Num. 16:9). And the Torah describes his 250 followers as "princes of the congregation, the elect men of the assembly, men of renown" (16:2). If indeed their hearts yearn for equality, they should first have tried to turn to the masses and empower them in the vein of the titular character in the film *The Life of Brian,* who addresses his crowd of admirers and proclaims, "You are all individuals."[1]

In light of the above, we can understand the assertion in Avot that an argument that is "not for [the sake of] heaven's name ... is not destined to endure": when the argument is impure and stems from personal ambition – meaning, when it is designed to conceal the true motives of the arguer, who does not sincerely believe in the argument – nothing will come of it.

Who Am I?

Unlike in the case of Korah, whose selfish motives are patently clear, the arguments we encounter in our lives often present a more insidious danger. Many of us become agitated and angry when we argue, even when the topic is not personal and our interlocutor is someone we respect. The intensity and tension rise, and suddenly we are frightened by the ferocity of our own emotions and our fierce desire to win the argument. But why is that so?

The spiritual teacher Eckhart Tolle has a good explanation for this phenomenon. He explains that people tend to identify with their opinions, often to the extent that, even without their awareness, their opinions become their identity. Who am I? If I identify with my thoughts, then when someone argues with me and opposes my views, I will experience the argument as an existential threat. When my opinions are not accepted, by extension I, too, am rejected. Thus arguments become battles for survival; no wonder they are so freighted with emotion. At the end of the day, even ideological arguments are fueled by personal motives and are not truly "for the sake of heaven." Our innermost needs,

---

1. The irony is that the Moses, whom the Torah describes as the meekest of all men (Num. 12:3), someone who loves the people and genuinely tries to empower them, is accused of elitism, while his accusers are motivated by a desire to be above the people. How ironic that Korah's punishment is to plummet deep into the bowels of the earth.

which we are unable to see, detract from our capacity to have a genuine conversation on a matter of disagreement.

In dealing with this issue, Tolle suggests raising awareness of the fact that our inner selves lie beyond our opinions and thoughts, and are in no way dependent on them.[2] There is much truth to what Tolle says, but at the same time we must take care to not become alienated from our ideas. Some things are of existential significance, and to sever ourselves from them would be to sever ourselves from life itself.

I wish to suggest a model that posits an inner essence beyond opinions and thoughts. This fundamental awareness infuses me with a basic security in my own existence, thus establishing it in a manner that is not contingent on my opinions and thoughts. And yet, opinions and thoughts are the mediums by which I interface with reality, so that they are important to me even if I do not identify with them. In other words, it is dangerous to gaze inward when my thoughts are what defines my perceived essence. Instead, I propose a movement that is mostly outward-facing and does not disregard that which is outside of us.

The Truth Contains Everything

Maimonides propounds what I think is the most apt definition of argument, interpreting "for the sake of heaven" to denote a "search" for truth (Maimonides' commentary on Avot 5:17). This definition is founded on two elements: truth and search. The "truth" is the essential, critical thing, which is why we privilege the claim itself over any underlying ulterior motives. The "search," or "*drisha*" (also "request"), for truth is, to my mind, a quest. This means that when we are certain that we have apprehended the truth, and think that all we must do is convince the other of its merits, there will be a

---

2. This idea underpins the spiritual approach he propounds in his books (the most basic of which is *The Power of Now*).

dialogue of the deaf. There is no point to such an argument; on the contrary, it will only deepen the conflict. However, when we consider ourselves to be in a process of searching, and are open to hearing and listening to the other, arguments can become a fertile ground for growth. While we are not expected to betray our basic premises in conversation, we should be open enough to deepen and enrich our ideas through the encounter with a different viewpoint.

This complex conception of truth, which first appears in rabbinic sources and is delineated in Kabbala, is key to the process. After stating that God's "seal" is truth, the Yerushalmi Talmud (Sanhedrin 1a), expounds on the meaning of the word "truth," or "*emet*," by noting the three letters that compose it: *alef*, the first letter of the alphabet; *mem*, which is in the middle; and *tav*, which is last. The Talmud implies that any single perspective will always be incomplete, and therefore untrue. The truth contains everything. In a corollary to the Yerushalmi, Professor Uriel Simon, my father-in-law, points out that "*sheker*," the Hebrew word for "lie," is composed of three consecutive letters – *shin*, *kuf*, and *resh* – at one end of the alphabet.

The Yerushalmi's conception of truth has a lot in common with the basic kabbalistic point of view, according to which everything contains a divine spark and the truth is the correct balance between every single thing. It is interesting that oftentimes, the most boisterous conflicts in Israel are defined as disagreements between right and left. This calls to mind the ancient kabbalistic work *The Bahir*, which, after opening with the statement that Gabriel is the angel of the left side and Michael is the angel of the right, asserts, "In the middle is Truth. This is Uriel."[3]

This is not to imply that the truth must be a compromise, in which each side relinquishes half of its stance. Rather, the middle

---

3. Kaplan, *The Bahir*, 41.

is a place that encompasses the positive points of each side. Such an outlook can promote a new way of thinking regarding problems that initially lead to a seemingly intractable conflict. That thinking is the tension that has defined this book from the outset: the attempt to integrate Eastern and Western notions of spirituality; being with doing; the human and the divine; the personal God with the Infinite.

An effort to make room for the other's outlook is essential to the argument stage, at least in the sense that each side is given full expression. The argument facilitates a dialogue in which each stance, and the price it entails, is given full consideration, as part of an attempt to build something new out of a fusion of the two. The kabbalistic model of encompassment is similar to the Hegelian dialectic: at first there is a conflict between the thesis and its antithesis, but ultimately they are united through synthesis.

The prototypical positive argument, as posited by the Mishna in Avot, is the argument between the House of Hillel and the House of Shammai. The Talmud relates that a heavenly voice issued forth and stated that the rulings of both houses are "the words of the living God" (Eiruvin 13b). To my mind, that shores up our claim that a fertile argument is one in which both sides have merit. Furthermore, according to the Talmud, we must rule according to the stance of the House of Hillel, because they acknowledge the opposing opinion and recognize its value. The House of Hillel "studied their own rulings and those of the House of Shammai, and were even so [humble] as to mention the actions of the House of Shammai before theirs" (ibid.). The House of Hillel, as opposed to the House of Shammai, represents an outlook that believes in making room for the other's opinion. As a friend of mine put it, were we to rule according to the House of Shammai, the House of Hillel's opinion would have been lost.

Those who ascribe importance to the opinions of others will ultimately see their own opinions being accepted. The House of

Hillel, even after their argument with the House of Shammai, saw fit to transmit the House of Shammai's opinion to their students. The deeper truth lies with the House of Hillel.

This dynamic, which characterizes the arguments between Shammai and Hillel, is apparent in the general world of Torah study. Halakhic literature – the Mishna and Talmud – is founded on arguments. The learner delves into all of the opinions – not just those that were accepted. Often, an opinion rejected in one context shapes the halakhic ruling in a different context. It is also worth noting that the word "halakha" is spelled *heh-lamed-kaf-heh*, an anagram of *"hakhala,"* or "encompassing." Hence the fact that many Talmud tractates, all of which are laden with arguments, end with the assertion that "sages increase peace in the world." It seems as though talmudic literature – which is built on arguments and whose method of study is generally the *ḥavruta* – did not succeed despite disagreement but rather thanks to it.

Making Room, for the Sake of Heaven

The kabbalistic sense of the word "heaven" can yield a fresh interpretation of the phrase "for the sake of heaven." According to the Kabbala, "heaven" represents the sefira of *Tiferet*, which denotes peace and the mutual encompassing of left and right. As *The Bahir*[4] writes:

> Why is heaven called *"shamayim"*? This teaches that God kneaded fire and water, and combined them together. From this He made the "beginning of His word." It is thus written (Ps. 119:160), "The beginning of Your word is truth." It is therefore called *"shamayim"* – *"sham mayim"* (there is water) – *esh mayim* (fire water). He said to them: This is the meaning of the verse (Job 25:2), "He makes peace in His

---

4. Ibid., 21.

heights." He placed peace and love between them. May He also place peace and love among us.

Heaven (*shamayim*) is a portmanteau of fire (*esh*) and water (*mayim*). It encompasses both conflicting elements, and this encompassment is truth – it is peace and love. The passage in *The Bahir* ends with an appeal to God to instate peace and love below, on earth, just as He has above. Similarly, the Zohar states that the angel Michael is associated with the element of water and Gabriel with the element of fire, and that God makes peace between them, as it is written, "He makes peace in His heights" (Zohar, *Vayikra* 12b).

The Zohar, in examining the cosmological processes that take place during Creation (*Bereshit* 1, 17a), employs this insight to interpret the statement of the mishna in Avot regarding the argument of Korah and his congregation. *Parashat Bereshit* relates that on the second day of Creation, the cosmos was split by a firmament that divided between the upper and the lower waters. The Midrash states that, unlike the other days of Creation, the second day is not described as "good" because it was also the day on which arguments were created (Genesis Rabba 4:6). One of the consequences of this disagreement, of the schism within creation, is the existence of hell. During the process of Creation, the world complexified, and hell descended. As opposed to the cosmological process, Korah's argument was not for the sake of heaven; it did not aspire to encompass, to make room for the other's stance. And when there is no encompassment, an argument endures, and manifests the very same hell that swallowed Korah.

Ḥukkat

Speech and the Rod

Moses' Sin

The end is in sight. The forty years that the Israelites were decreed to spend plodding through the desert are drawing to a close. We can only imagine Moses' excitement, a moment before the culmination of a process that began decades earlier – the journey to the Promised Land, the land of milk and honey.

But Moses' dream is dashed again, this time for good: in *Parashat Ḥukkat*, in a single moment, Moses is sentenced to die in the desert.

The people once again grumble about a shortage of water, and God commands Moses, "Take the rod, and assemble the congregation, you, and Aaron your brother, and speak to the rock before their eyes, that it give forth its water; and you shall bring forth to them water out of the rock; so you shall give the congregation and their cattle drink" (Num. 20:8). But rather than speak to the rock, Moses strikes it with his rod, and God responds harshly to the deviation from His instructions: "Because you did not believe in Me, to sanctify Me in the eyes of the children of Israel, therefore you shall not bring this assembly into the land which I have given them" (20:12). How can we reconcile Moses' apparently minor transgression with the severity of his punishment?

My friend Rabbi Amnon Dokov explains that at issue is not the severity of the sin but rather a more fundamental issue – the very nature of Moses' leadership. The symbol of Moses' rule is the rod. It is an instrument of power, with which he manipulates and controls reality, bending it to his will – to the will of his creator. In Egypt the rod upends the laws of nature, and it overwhelms the enemies of the Israelites in battle after the Exodus. Indeed, at the beginning of the journey, after the Splitting of the Sea, when the people clamor for water, God commands Moses to strike the rock with his rod and cause water to gush out (Ex. 17:6).

Yet now, forty years later, a new generation has come into its own, standing on the cusp of a new era. This time God commands Moses to speak to the rock. This imperative indicates a change of direction: a leadership founded on speech rather than miracles and signs. The rock symbolizes the imperviousness of reality, and to speak to it would imply a belief that, through speech, it can be softened and induced to reveal its treasure. It is no coincidence that Moses does not speak to the rock, for he has already stated, "I am not a man of words…. I am slow of speech, and of a slow tongue" (Ex. 4:10). Moses admits that he does not possess the capacity to convey his inner world to the other; that he cannot open up the other through speech.

Rabbi Dokov's idea about the passage from the rod to speech evokes once more the duality of "being" and "doing," the gap between obtaining one's goal by manipulating the environment and actualizing it through one's own inner world. The transition from life in the desert to life in the Land of Israel requires "doing," but upon arrival, in the actualization stage, the emphasis shifts to "being."

Moses and the Buddha

It is fascinating to compare the life of Moses to the life of the Buddha. The similarity in the arcs of their lives is clear: both begin as princes in the royal palace, both leave their sheltered lifestyle behind after encountering the suffering and pain of existence, and both eventually become spiritual teachers. But there are further parallels between them that highlight a fundamental difference.

Buddhist tradition tells of the four sights, a series of encounters that Siddhartha Gautama has en route to his enlightenment, when he leaves the palace and becomes the Buddha. The first encounter is with an old man, the second is with a sick person, and the third is with a dead body. Through these encounters, he comes to the realization that human existence is steeped in pain and suffering. Finally, Siddhartha meets a man who grapples with his suffering by practicing asceticism, and from him draws hope that the problem of suffering is not insoluble. In the wake of that meeting, Siddhartha devotes his life to sharing his insights with others.

Moses, too, has a series of four encounters after emerging from Pharaoh's palace. As with the first three sights of the Buddha, Moses encounters human suffering three times: an Egyptian beating a Hebrew man, a Hebrew man beating his comrade, and a group of shepherds denying the daughters of Yitro access to a well. Yet Moses, unlike the Buddha, intervenes to right the injustices he encounters. In the fourth encounter, which is parallel to the Buddha's meeting with the monk, God reveals Himself to Moses. That encounter, too, revolves around the issue of injustice, and concludes with Moses taking upon himself the mission of returning to his people and rescuing them from bondage. He thus devotes himself to a life of action, of "doing."[1]

---

1. It is noteworthy that each of the Buddha's encounters can be linked to a commandment in the Five Books of Moses: to visit the sick, to honor the elderly, and to bury the dead – something that even a high priest, who is prohibited from becoming

The moral of Moses' sin is not that a leadership of action should give way to a leadership of speech, but rather that speech must become a component of leadership; in other words, that "being" and "doing" should complement, rather than mutually exclude, one another. A good leader must be at once a doer and a guide who can awaken the inner world of his followers. God, in commanding Moses to speak to the rock, also enjoins him to bring the rod: "Take the rod, and assemble the congregation, you, and Aaron your brother, and speak to the rock.... And Moses took the rod from before the Lord, as He commanded him" (Num. 20:8–9).

It is only in the sunset of his life that Moses attains such perfection. We learn this from the opening verse of Deuteronomy, which describes the events that take place in the week before Moses' death: "These are the words which Moses spoke to all Israel."

---

impure through contact with the dead, is enjoined to do if he encounters a dead body while en route the Temple on Yom Kippur.

Balak

A People Apart

Lo, it is a people that shall dwell alone, and shall not be reckoned among the nations.

– Numbers 23:9

A Nation of Isolation and Connection

Bilam's words above paint a picture in many of our minds of a fundamental aspect of the relationship between the Jewish people and the rest of humanity. At first glance it would seem that this relationship is characterized by antipathy and aloofness, as if Israel's isolation on the international stage – and perhaps even anti-Semitism itself – is decreed by fate. True, the Torah's commandments engender a certain isolation. The stringent observance of Shabbat and dietary laws makes it harder to fraternize with non-Jews, and generates a sense of distance from them. This schism is evident in modern Hebrew, which divides the globe into two: Israel and "outside Israel" (*"ḥutz laaretz,"* a term with clear negative connotations). Additionally, immigrants to Israel are called *"olim,"* or "ascenders," while those who migrate from the country were for a long time referred to as "*yordim*," or "descenders."

But history shows that the opposite is also true, and the Jewish people are notable for their connection to humanity at large. Jews were always interacting with other peoples in what could be described as mutually beneficial relations. For thousands of years, Jews were scattered throughout the world, a state that many consider an actualization of the Jewish people's purpose of being a "light unto the nations." As the Netziv writes: "The fact that most of our existence is in exile is due to the blessed Holy One revealing to Abraham that his children were created to be a light unto the nations, a state that is only possible when they are scattered in the Diaspora" (*Haamek Davar*, Genesis 47:28).

The term "light unto the nations" first appears in Isaiah (42:6), but the Netziv links it to the election of Abraham in Genesis, when his ultimate purpose vis-à-vis all of humanity is described: "Abraham shall surely become a great and mighty nation, and all the nations of the earth shall be blessed in him" (18:18).

What is the nature of this blessing? The following verse explains why Abraham is chosen: "For I have known him, to the end that he may command his children and his household after him, that they may keep the way of the Lord, to do righteousness and justice" (18:19). That prophecy has indeed been fulfilled: the biblical precepts of righteousness and justice – including the sanctity of life, caring for the other, the principle of equality, and the idea that humanity was created in God's image – have become essential truths for all of humanity.

Furthermore, many Jews throughout the generations were members of the scientific, technological, and philosophical elite. Figures such as Karl Marx, Sigmund Freud, Albert Einstein, and Mark Zuckerberg gave rise to global revolutions that reshaped human consciousness, even if in retrospect some had a negative contribution. One need only consider the fact that Jews have won Nobel prizes at a rate far higher than their percentage in the population to realize the scope of their contribution to humanity.

Election Generates Connection

Does the tension between particularism and universalism not indicate a schizophrenia of sorts? It seems not, for at bottom there is no contradiction between the two approaches; on the contrary, they complete each other.

The Torah does not open with the birth of the Jewish people but rather with the creation of the world and the dawn of humanity. After relating the story of the Flood, the Torah lingers on the covenant between God and humankind (Gen. 9:8–17), while the story of the Tower of Babel shows us that God seeks variety among the nations. The Bible notes that God is not only the deity of Israel, but the god of the entire world: "For from the rising of the sun until its going down My name is great among the nations; and in every place offerings are presented to My name, even pure oblations; for My name is great among the nations, says the Lord of hosts" (Mal. 1:11).

The choosing of one people does not mean the neglect of the rest of humanity. Rather, such an election lends that people a purpose that relates to humankind as a whole – as we see in the explanations for the Jewish people's chosenness that appear in the Book of Isaiah.

Paradoxically, the connection to the rest of humanity depends on a certain degree of separation from it. The Jewish people's unique status derives from its purpose and mission for the sake of humankind. This can be likened to the role of the priesthood, who are kept apart so as better to fulfill their task: to bless the Jewish people and represent them before God through the Temple rites. On a larger scale, the Jewish people serve as a priestly class for the rest of humanity: "Now therefore, if you will hearken to My voice indeed, and keep My covenant, then you shall be My own treasure from among all peoples … and you shall be to Me a kingdom of priests and a holy nation" (Ex. 19:5–6). As the verses tell us, the election of the Jewish people is not a matter of race, but rather depends on the fulfillment of the tasks that emanate from its covenant with God.

As for Bilam's assertion, "Lo, it is a people that shall dwell alone, and shall not be reckoned among the nations" – it seems that his words should be read as encouraging a separateness born of special purpose. He is an outside observer, praising the Jewish people's capacity for remaining apart by virtue of its task, not extolling the merits of aloofness.

The Heart of Humanity

It seems that Rabbi Judah Halevi put it best when he said that when we to liken humanity to a single body, "Israel amidst the nations is like the heart amidst the organs of the body" (*Kuzari* II:36). The heart fulfills a unique role in the body, in that it is connected to all of the organs and limbs. It cannot function alone because it depends on the rest of the body; yet this is a mutual dependence, for the heart provides the body with lifeblood.

The image of the Jewish people as a heart is also manifested in the territory that God chose for us. The Land of Israel is at the crossroads of three large continents, and is thus naturally an arena of interactions. It is thus clear why God sends Abraham from his homeland in Mesopotamia to a land that has always been a corridor between civilizations.

The rest of the quote in Halevi's *Kuzari* regarding the relationship between the Jewish people and the nations is fascinating: the heart, and by extension the Jewish people, he says, "can be the most sick and most healthy of all organs simultaneously." According to the *Kuzari*, this is an expression of a profound sensitivity that enables the Jewish people to resonate with the good in the world, as well as with the evil. We can find echoes of this in recent history. In the past century, three ideologies threatened humanity and tried to take over the world: fascism, communism, and radical Islam. The first to suffer from these three movements were the Jews. Anti-Semitism is not fueled by Jews' apartness from the world, but rather by their connection to it. One does not become popular through taking on a mission and asking ethical questions. One statement attributed to Hitler is emblematic of this truth: "Conscience is a Jewish invention."

Beyond History

The historian Arnold Toynbee (1889–1975) asserted that there is a pattern to the rise and fall of nations. According to the criteria he describes, the Jewish people should have disappeared long ago. But the fact of the Jewish people's continued existence in the world did not prompt Toynbee to second-guess or amend his theory; rather, he explained that the Jewish people is a "fossil" civilization. Toynbee was an anti-Zionist who opposed granting national rights to the Jews. But it seems that he was correct on one count: the annals of the Jewish people transcend the laws of nature governing history. This insight can also be found in the Talmud (Shabbat 156a), which states, "Israel is immune from planetary influence." The implication is that the principles guiding history – in the past these were believed to be the planets and the signs of the zodiac – do not apply to the Jewish people.

The Jewish People and Humanity

The Italian kabbalist Rabbi Eliyahu Benamazegh (1823–1900), in his book *Israel and Humanity*, presents his approach to the relationship between the Jews and the other nations. To him, Judaism is the source and foundation for a world religion that should be based upon the Seven Noahide Laws, including the demand to maintain a justice system and prohibitions against idolatry, sexual immorality, murder, and theft. Some of those values were transmitted from Judaism to humanity by way of Christianity and Islam. Rabbi Benamazegh interprets the final verse in the books of Prophets – "And he shall turn the heart of the fathers to the children, and the heart of the children to their fathers" (Mal. 3:24) – as a statement on the future relations between the three religions.[1]

If the Jewish people is to fulfill its purpose in the world, it must maintain its identity; for otherwise, "the Jewish people's tiny drop of blood would be subsumed in the broad arteries of humanity. The breath of Israel would be smothered, and its mission would remain unrealized. Rather, safeguarding this nation requires precautions, and, indeed, many commandments, even if that is not their exact purpose, have that effect."[2]

Vision of the Last Days

When Israel was established, the menora was chosen as the symbol of the state. Among the reasons for that choice were the prophecies of the end times, when the Jewish people will be a light unto the nations.[3] But in the ensuing years, the vision clashed with reality, and the term "a light unto the nations" has since become a joke in many circles. Still, even if we acknowledge our shortcomings, we must not despair of ever fulfilling our responsibilities. The Jewish people succeeded in sparking humanity's imagination with the visions of the prophets, with the aspiration for a rectified world in which the nations live side by side in harmony. Just as we have overcome immense adversity to realize the vision of our return

---

1. Eliyahu Benamazegh, *Israel and Humanity* [Hebrew] (Jerusalem: Mossad Harav Kook, 1967), 37.
2. Ibid., 54.
3. Rabbi S. Z. Kahane, "Menorah: The Symbol of the State" [Hebrew], http://cms.education.gov.il/NR/rdonlyres/666C370C-33C2-4BA2-8442-296B88A3E17B/202678/220.pdf.

to Zion, there is cause to believe that if we only devote ourselves to the cause, we can realize those visions as well. Yet, the success of the Jewish people in the world depends solely on the power of the spirit – politics will always fall short of realizing this ultimate vision. As the prophet Isaiah says:

> And it shall come to pass in the end of days.... And many peoples shall go and say, "Come and let us go up to the mountain of the Lord, to the house of the God of Jacob; and He will teach us of His ways, and we will walk in His paths." For out of Zion shall go forth the law, and the word of the Lord from Jerusalem ... and they shall beat their swords into plowshares, and their spears into pruninghooks; nation shall not lift up sword against nation, neither shall they learn war any more. (Is. 2:2–4)

The vision will be fulfilled, according to Isaiah, through spreading the Torah and the word of God. The Torah does not aspire to "win souls" to Judaism, but that is not due to indifference to the fate of the other nations. Rather, it stems from the conviction that every human being, Jewish or not, can reach the pinnacle of holiness. An echo of this idea can be found in the Talmud's likening of a non-Jew who studies the Torah to a high priest (Sanhedrin 59a). It is an approach that makes room for the other, for it does not threaten their fundamental identity, but rather seeks to amplify and empower it.

For thousands of years, the Jewish people was inward-facing, striving to return to the Land of Israel from the Diaspora. We have succeeded in implementing that stage and returning to our place. The next phase is to become outward-facing, from Israel out into the world. Though it will require a mental reorientation, it is in fact a direct continuation of the return to Zion, which is not a goal in itself but rather a condition for fulfilling our purpose. Many in

Israeli society yearn for a part in the fate of humanity, and often feel that Judaism comes between them and the rest of the human race. Developing the connection between Judaism and what takes place outside it could bring these people back into the fold, "and your children shall return to their own border" (Jer. 31:16).

Pinḥas

Labor of Love

You shall love your neighbor as yourself' (Lev. 19:18) – Rabbi Akiva says, 'This is a great principle of the Torah'" (*Sifra Kedoshim* 2:4). Less well known is the opinion of Rabbi Shimon ben Pazi, who states, in a midrash quoted in the introduction to *Ein Yaakov*, that the foundational principle of the Torah is a verse from *Parashat Pinḥas* that deals with the daily *tamid* sacrifice in the Temple: "The one lamb shall you offer in the morning, and the other lamb shall you offer at dusk" (Num. 28:4).

Rabbi Akiva's choice to frame love as a foundational principle appears obvious, for all of us, it seems, ascribe importance to love and see it as one of life's main values. In contrast, Rabbi Shimon ben Pazi's choice seems odd.

It seems that Rabbi Shimon does not select that verse to highlight the importance of the burnt offerings, but rather due to a value that it teaches us: persistence and consistency. There is no shortage of talk about love: everyone seeks it out and suffers in its absence. We are not generally as conscious of persistence as a value. Many people's lives are paved with difficulties due to a lack of perseverance, and could stand to benefit greatly from Rabbi Shimon ben Pazi's words.

Fun and Change

Today, more and more people are realizing – thanks to New Age practices, among other causes – that they will not attain happiness and meaning merely by improving their material conditions, but rather that they must develop their inner worlds. Yet, it seems that only few attain the spiritual experiences for which they yearn. The flaw is not necessarily in their methods, but rather in their inability to commit to, and persist in, the work. Deep, significant change is not an easy thing to sustain. No single workshop has the power to effect a transformation in life, and those who think it can are deluding themselves. A workshop is good for learning a technique, but only a regular, long-term practice can actualize a technique's potential benefits.

I have a friend who was deeply influenced by Vipassana meditation. Impressed by the change I witnessed in him, I looked into signing up for a basic Vipassana retreat, during which, over ten days and nights, participants devote themselves to breathing-based meditations. When I asked my friend what he thought of the retreat, he said that it would be an interesting experience, but that in order to effect real change I would have to establish a regular meditation practice. He once told me his secret for successful spiritual seeking: "If you want to reach water, you need to dig deep. Those who are constantly digging new holes will never make it!"

There once was a man who traveled to the famous Shaolin Monastery to study kung fu. Upon entering, he was placed before a barrel of water and instructed to slap the surface day and night. For months he complied, waiting for the day when the secrets of kung fu would be divulged to him. Finally he gave up and left. When the man arrived at his home, his family asked him what he had learned. He replied that he had not learned a thing and, venting his frustration, slapped the dinner table, which, to his utter astonishment, broke in two.

Rabbi Nahman often quotes the maxim "All beginnings are difficult." Yet, as one of my students once pointed out, the opposite is often true – beginnings tend to be easy. It does not take much effort to be excited by something new, but to practice something over an extended period of time, even when it brings tedium – that is far less enticing.

Setting Times

The daily burnt offerings, sacrificed every morning and evening, are an expression not only of persistence, but also of consistency. Without constancy and habit, it is hard to persist, and a lot of energy is wasted on finding time. When we have to fit something into our schedule, we tend to put it off. Take, for example, someone who wishes to participate in a workshop and do spiritual work. In order to generate the right atmosphere, the workshop requires a twenty-four-hour period during which one must adhere to a set of stringent guidelines. How often should someone be expected to take time off from the rat race and participate in such a workshop? Once a year? Perhaps twice? How about once a week? Such a workshop already exists, and many – including working people and parents – participate in it. It is called Shabbat.

I am afraid that if we had to decide for ourselves, every time anew, when we would like to refrain from work, Shabbat would have been a thing of the distant past. This is true of many other mitzvot as well. The mitzva is a container that, with the passage of time, hardens into a self-evident cornerstone for life. Accepting the framework frees us to pursue things in depth, rather than occupy ourselves with external questions of what, when, and how. With Shabbat, too, the laws of the day provide a general foundation and framework for the spontaneity and natural flow that come later. That is how the spiritual experiences of Shabbat are facilitated.

Some are troubled by the thought of a routine driven by rote, mindless action, but that is precisely the source of its power. A friend of mine used to run ten kilometers every Friday. Once, he told me, it was very hot outside, and he was forced to cut short his run. On the following week, he had a hard time finishing his route, because he knew that he had the option of stopping midway. The barrier had been broken. Free will is a uniquely human capacity, but we must distinguish between times when the capacity to decide serves us and when it holds us back.

They say that when a person dies and the soul rises, it is asked, "Did you set times for Torah study?" (Shabbat 31a). Why, rather than ask whether one studied Torah, is the emphasis placed on setting times? It seems that in heaven, too, it is known that without habits there can be no study.

Renewal

But what about renewal? The Greek philosopher Heraclitus famously said that one cannot step into the same river twice. It seems that there are two reasons for this. First, the river is truly not the same river, for as soon as someone persists at something, it changes. Indeed, the rate of change is slow and often not immediately apparent, but as time passes it deepens. Most of us lack the depth dimension. Second, the person is no longer the same: we change with time, so that the import of our encounter with the various elements of life is always in flux.

A good example is the weekly *parasha*. For thousands of years, Jews the world over have been reading the same Torah portions week in and week out, completing the cycle every year. Learning the *parasha* lends an element of immutability to Jewish identity and creates intergenerational continuity. Yet, the meaning of the *parashot* evolves and is renewed from one generation to the next and from one individual to another. Furthermore, those who delve deeply into the *parasha* discover that, even for the individual, it acquires fresh meaning from year to year.

Stability

In the Temple, the daily sacrifices created a sort of framework for the day. They were the first and the last offerings of every day; in between, priests would bring the rest of the mandatory and voluntary sacrifices. They were also brought on Shabbat, Rosh Ḥodesh, and the festivals, which is why the special sacrifices of those days were termed "*musafim*," literally "added on."

This is true, too, of life, whose constant elements lend it stability. Life has ups and downs, and stable and constant elements can be a firm foundation that keeps us from getting lost, enabling us to connect with our roots rather than, God forbid, become severed from them.

Love and Loyalty

So far we have been discussing the importance of perseverance as a means for growth, but it is also important as an end in itself. Earlier, we noted the significance of love. Dedication is not only a crucial element of a deepening relationship. Beyond that, the capacity to persevere even when things are not going smoothly and when we do not feel like it – even in the midst of crises – is a manifestation of true love and loyalty. This is also true of the relationship between the individual and God.

I had a student who volunteered for an elite military unit where the training is known to be especially grueling. He told me about his frustration when, at the end of each day, sapped by the training regimen, he would pray Maariv without intention. I reminded him that, according to the Talmud (Berakhot 26b), the prayers are substituted for the daily sacrificial offerings. His very capacity to battle through exhaustion and stick with his routine was an expression of the spiritual essence of the daily sacrifices.

Matot

Spiritual Initiation in the Desert

In *Parashat Matot*, the Israelites emerge from the desert. With their arrival at the cantons of the tribes of Reuben and Gad, on the borders of the Land of Israel, their initiation phase is concluded. Much has been said about the sins of the people during their years of wandering, but it is fair to say that their time in the desert also brings about spiritual maturity. We can easily understand this by examining the spiritual journeys of our own contemporaries, which pass through places that are conducive to spiritual growth. The story of Rabbi David Zeller is a good example.

In his autobiographical book *The Soul of the Story*, Zeller recounts at length his life as a *sadhu*, a Hindu ascetic who lives without possessions. The insights that Zeller reaches as an ascetic are significant to his life and to his relationship with God, and the processes he undergoes in India ultimately bring him closer to Judaism, so that he eventually becomes a rabbi. Zeller notes that he embarked on a journey only to discover that the treasure is buried in his own home. Let us examine a few of his stories.

The Meaning of Food

Zeller describes a test he passed as a *sadhu*:

> I was learning to trust that God would always provide.... One day while getting accustomed to this attitude, I ate at a temple where they fed us *sadhus* a meal, and I put a few extra chapattis in my bag, "just in case." Later that day, we were invited to a special religious feast where there was more delicious food than I could possibly consume. There had been no need to stash the extra food. There was only a need to trust in God's Providence.[1]

Zeller's is the same insight that the Israelites learn every day anew in the desert: "Then the Lord said to Moses: 'Behold, I will cause bread from heaven to rain down for you; and the people shall go out and gather a day's portion every day, that I may test them, whether they will walk in My law or not'" (Ex. 16:4). God commands the people to gather only what they need for that day. The Torah tells us that those who fail the test and try to hoard manna are not only chided by Moses, but the food they gather becomes infested with worms and is no longer edible (16:20).

So what is the point of the test? The Torah initially says that it is a test of whether the people will listen to God. However, at the end of the journey, after forty years of manna, it emerges that there is another reason for the test: "And He afflicted you, and suffered you to hunger, and fed you with manna, which you knew not, neither did your fathers know; that He might make you know that

---

1. Zeller, *The Soul of the Story*, 81.

man does not live by bread only, but by everything that proceeds out of the mouth of the Lord does man live" (Deut. 8:3).

Zeller relates another experience having to do with food:

> Another time, Sri Pad [Zeller's teacher] sent me on an unusual lesson about being detached from food. He had seen me look longingly toward a passing wagon that was loaded with delicious-looking bowling-ball-sized clumps of brown sugar, called *gur*. "Oh," he said, "would you like some *gur*? I will send you to where they make it, and you can have as much as you want!"... [Eventually] I felt sick to my stomach, overdosed on sugar in every form it came in. I had lost a lot of things over the weeks in Vrindavan. That day I lost my appetite for brown sugar – *gur*.[2]

That, too, echoes an experience that the Israelites had in the desert. Further along on their journey, the people crave meat. Zeller's words can shed light on the meaning of the response to their request: God agrees to satisfy their desire, "until it come out your nostrils" (Num. 11:20).

Who Is in Control?

Zeller relates the following nocturnal events as a turning point in his approach to life:

> Late one night... Sri Pad announced to a few of us that we had to leave right away.... Sri Pad started walking. It was so dark that I could hardly see a step ahead of me. Walking barefoot during the day is hard enough. But at night? Forget it! It was impossible. I tried my best to pierce through the dark, straining my eyes to see sharp rocks or thorns. I

---

2. Ibid.

would spot one – or at least what I though was one – and step over it, only to land directly on a real one, and it really hurt. Or I would make out the dark round shape of a cow "patty." I stepped over what turned out to be a shadow, and stepped into the real thing!

If that was not bad enough, all my tension and fear gathered into my ankles, which started swelling from the stress. And my footsteps were getting heavier and coming down harder. I was not going to last much longer. This was the night I learned to pray. "Please God, help me! I can't see where I am going. Please make him [Sri Pad] stop for the night." As if God were answering me, I realized that this was no different from walking through life in what I think is clear broad daylight. I think that I see something coming up ahead, and make various moves to avoid it, and invariably, I walk smack into the very thing I am trying so hard to avoid. I can no more control and determine the things happening in my life than I control and determine where to place my next step in the dark .... I understood that I need to let go of my desire to control, predict, and direct my life, and even to control my next step in the dark. I needed to turn over the reins to God .... Instead of looking down, I looked ahead or up. My ankles relaxed and my step lightened. I let my feet do the walking, this time at a slow, more natural, more graceful pace.[3]

This story is amazing in its honesty and directness, and foreshadows the ending of Zeller's journey, which takes him to many places he never dreamed he would be.

---

3. Ibid., 84.

The Torah, in describing the Israelites' journeys in the desert, says, "At the commandment of the Lord the children of Israel journeyed, and at the commandment of the Lord they encamped: as long as the cloud abode upon the tabernacle they remained encamped" (Num. 9:18). Based on Zeller's insight, we can see that this verse captures a fundamental spiritual truth. Just as the manna teaches us that "by everything that proceeds out of the mouth of the Lord does man live" (Deut. 8:3), the voyages in the desert teach us that our lives – whether we are stopping or proceeding – are governed by "the commandment of the Lord."

The stories of the desert bring home to us the special quality of the Jewish people's existence as it searches for its identity on the eve of entering into the land. Today we no longer live in the shade of the *Shekhina's* wings in the desert, and we will likely not visit the ashrams of India. Yet, by perusing and debating these stories, and reading them year in and year out, we internalize their messages and insights. We hear their clarion call never to rest on our laurels, and to remain ever vigilant in the effort to bring a more refined spirituality into our lives.

Masei

The Blood of the High Priest

Murder is undoubtedly a manifestation of ultimate evil. Homicides, whether premeditated in cold blood or the result of negligence, awaken in us deep feelings of rage, and we expect justice to be served and killers to be punished. But when one person kills another by accident, sometimes, instead of anger, we feel empathy toward the killer, whose life will never be the same again. Much of the empathy arises from our recognition that the same thing could happen to us: we too could inadvertently hurt another person. *Parashat Masei* discusses the Torah's approach to someone who kills accidentally, giving us tools to think about personal responsibility for our unintended actions.

The Torah's treatment of the accidental killer is complex. If we judge him purely based on his motives – there is clearly no intention to do harm – we cannot condemn him as an evil person. On the other hand, the results of his actions are horrific: he spills innocent blood, and the Torah thus brands him a "killer." There is truth to both points of view, and neither can override the other.

The cities of refuge were put in place in order to contend with these two aspects of the accidental killer. Their primary goal is to protect the killer from the vengeance of the deceased's relatives (Num. 35:11–12). But it turns out that there is another purpose to the cities of refuge. An accidental killer must remain in one of these cities until the death of the high priest (35:25) – if he escapes earlier, an avenger is permitted to kill him (35:26–27). Furthermore, the escaped killer cannot pay to commute his term: "And you shall take no ransom for one who has fled to his city of refuge, that he should come again to dwell in the land, until the death of the priest" (35:32).

Is there another purpose to the cities of refuge? On the face of it, the answer is simple: they are a punishment for the killer, based on the principle "Exile atones for everything" (Sanhedrin 37a). But the truth is more complex. The ensuing verse says, "So you shall not pollute the land where you are; for blood, it pollutes the land; and no expiation can be made for the land for the blood that is shed therein, but by the blood of him that shed it" (35:33). Exile in a city of refuge cannot atone for the killing, as only blood can atone for blood. In order to remove the stain of such a horrific act, there is need for something equally powerful and symbolically equivalent to balance it out, a type of measure for measure. On the emotional level, as well, the accidental killer has to know that, if he is to return to society, something drastic must occur. As we will see, exile is no substitute for internal processes of atonement and positive actions, but rather one of the prerequisites for them.

In the case of a murderer – someone who kills with intent – it is the blood of the killer that atones for the spilled blood, as the Torah sentences him to death. But if only blood can atone for blood, how is the accidental killer to atone for his actions? Clearly, we do not want him to die. In fact, we go out of our way to grant him refuge and save his life. It seems the answer can be found in the fact that he must remain in exile until the death of the high priest, whose blood atones for the blood spilled by the accidental killer.

The idea that one's blood – in this case the blood of the high priest – can atone for another's sin is not entirely clear. In the song "One Human Tissue," written by Moti Hamer, Chava Alberstein sings, "When I die, a part of me will die in you... because all of us are one living human tissue. And if one of us departs from us, something dies in us." When my life is connected to the life of another, I rejoice in the other's joy and feel the other's pain. This identification with the other means that when the other dies, something in me dies too. The essence of the high priesthood is intimacy and identification with the other. The priest represents the entire community before God, first and foremost during the atonement process on Yom Kippur. In order for that process to be effective, it seems that there is need for two-way identification: just as the high priest must identify with and represent the people, so too the people should feel a deep affinity for him. Thus was the relationship between the people and the first high priest, Aaron. The Torah tells us that "all the house of Israel" mourned for thirty days upon hearing of Aaron's death (Num. 20:29).

If the accidental killer can only receive atonement through the death of the high priest, why must he spend the intervening time in a city of refuge? It is instructive, in this context, to compare the case of the accidental killer to the process of collective atonement on the Day of Atonement. Indeed, during Yom Kippur, the high priest represents the people and atones for their sins, but they too must be active participants in the process. This participation takes place on two interrelated levels – body and soul. While the people afflict themselves on Yom Kippur, the fast must be complemented by an internal process of repentance (Mishna Yoma 1:8–9).

The high priest's atonement, in death, for the sin of the accidental killer corresponds to his atonement for the sins of the people on Yom Kippur. However, as on the Day of Atonement, the accidental killer must participate in the process. He goes into exile, where he must undergo a profound internal reckoning.

Devarim

The Art of Rebuke

Rebuke and criticism have always been a part of the Jewish way of life – from the admonishments of the prophets to contemporary public discourse. It is thus surprising to discover that the Torah frames rebuke as a means to overcome interpersonal alienation and hatred: "You shall not hate your brother in your heart; you shall surely rebuke your neighbor" (Lev. 19:17). Torah commentators explain that there is a contrast between the prohibition against hating the other, and the commandment to rebuke him – that rebuke is in fact conducive to peace (Rashbam). Rebuke is also an expression of love: "For whom the Lord loves He [rebukes]" (Prov. 3:12). The ensuing verse in Leviticus, "Love your neighbor as yourself," also alludes to this, while the preceding verse, "Neither shall you stand idly by the blood of your neighbor," teaches us that one who refrains from chastening others is likened to a person who sees the blood of another being spilled and stands idly by.

Sadly, in our day, rebuke has taken on negative associations. Now, reproof and criticism attain the opposite result, increasing alienation and widening the chasm between the giver and receiver of rebuke. It is easy to mishandle the giving of rebuke, whose goal is to bring the receiver to a more positive place, to stimulate growth rather than wound and offend. This requires precision and nuance on the part of both giver and receiver. Positive intentions on the part of the rebuker – only one of the conditions for a successful rebuke – are often lacking. The healing of society will not come about through the cessation of criticism and reproof, but rather by restoring their original purpose – the advancement of peace and love.

The Book of Deuteronomy opens with Moses' rebuke of the people. His words are very harsh: not only does he list their sins and justify the punishments they received (1:19–45, as well as in the subsequent *parashot Va'ethanan* and *Ekev*); he also blames them for the punishment that he has been saddled with (1:37). It is said that one of the most prominent figures in Hasidism, Rabbi Yaakov Yitzhak Rabinowicz, known as the Holy Jew of Peshischa, would learn several verses of Moses' rebuke every day, believing in the unique capacity of those words to enter his heart (*Pri Tzaddik, Devarim*). Let us examine, as well, the words of Moses, with an emphasis on their form rather than their content, and see what we can glean about the lost art of rebuke.

Timing Is Everything

When it comes to rebuke, the timing is no less important than the content. For example, rebuke directed at someone who is depressed can potentially push them over the edge. Moses is fastidious in his timing. The Torah makes a point of noting that his rebuke comes "after he had smitten Sihon the king of the Amorites ... and Og the king of Bashan" (Deut. 1:4) – in the wake of glorious victories, when the people are still elated.

It is imperative that the rebuke be delivered at a time when the receiver is open to the possibility of changing. It is difficult for people to alter their behavior when they are immersed in their routines. In that regard, too, Moses' rebuke is on the mark, for he delivers it as the people are preparing to enter the Land of Israel, on the brink of a new chapter, the next phase in their national life.

The relationship between the rebuker and the receiver of the rebuke is also key. In this context, the people's awareness of the imminence of Moses' death causes them to be receptive to his words.

Less Is More

The question of quantity is also crucial when it comes to giving rebuke. There are areas where "the more the merrier," but with rebuke the opposite is true. In the books of Exodus, Leviticus, and Numbers we see almost no rebukes of the people by Moses. When rebuke is a unique occurrence, people are open to receive it, but when it becomes commonplace, they quickly learn to close their ears. A friend of mine, a teacher, once likened rebuke to a gun loaded with two bullets. During the school year, he can only shoot twice, so he must think hard before pulling the trigger.

Begin with Criticism and Conclude with Praise

If the purpose of rebuke is to help people improve, it should also contain a positive element. Deuteronomy opens with Moses' rebuke and concludes with his blessing in *Parashat Vezot Haberakha* ("this is the blessing"). Likewise, the *haftara* of *Devarim* is a harsh rebuke (Is. 1), followed by seven consecutive weeks of consolatory and redemptive *haftarot*.

Whom Do We Rebuke?

The surprising element in Moses' rebuke is that he does not chastise the sinners, but rather their children. The parents who sinned were members of the generation that left Egypt, and by now they are all dead. The absurdity of the situation is thrown into sharp relief when Moses says, "Moreover your little ones, whom you said would be prey, and your children, who this day have no knowledge of good or evil, they shall go there, and to them will I give it, and they shall possess it" (Deut. 1:39). It is a bizarre scene: the people Moses is addressing are not the sinners, the parents who said their children will "be prey," but rather the children themselves. What does it mean?

The *Sefat Emet* on the *parasha* concludes that there is a lesson to be learned here about personal responsibility: "Every generation must rectify the sin of the previous generation, just as they inherit the virtue left them by the preceding generation." The sins of the parents are visited upon their children. But even if we accept that the children are worthy of some reproof, it is hard to understand why only they, and not their parents, are subjected to the Torah's most substantial dressing down.

Rebuke is a corrective measure. Not only is a given generation required to rectify their parents' iniquities; it is understood that they – not their parents – are the sole people capable of effecting the correction. The Talmud states a principle whereby "as one is commanded to say that which will be [heard], so is one commanded not to say that which will not be [heard]" (Yevamot 65b). Rebuke, delivered to those who cannot receive it, can be harmful, as a verse quoted by the Talmud (ibid.) states: "Reprove not a scorner, lest he hate you; reprove a wise man, and he will love you" (Prov. 9:8). Had it been delivered to the parents' generation, Moses' reproof would have fallen on deaf ears. It is only their children, who possess the perspective afforded by time, who can hear and rectify.

We all know people who have a tendency to ruin their own lives. The natural reaction of those who care about such people is to try to open their eyes to the root of their problem and to their part in generating it. Yet, when it is clear that such an intervention will be spurned, perhaps to the point of endangering the relationship, it is better to hold one's peace and give such people the only thing that they are capable of receiving: nonjudgmental warmth. If we were to adhere to that principle, rebuke would be perceived more and more as a genuine manifestation of appreciation for the other.

As the story goes, one evening Rabbi Yisrael Hager of the Vizhnitz hasidic dynasty and his attendant visited the home of a wealthy banker in their city. The banker welcomed them in, sat them in his parlor, and waited for the rabbi to speak. But the rabbi sat silently for several minutes, and then rose from his chair, thanked the banker and headed for the door.

"Why did you come?" the banker asked the rabbi's attendant in a whisper.

"I have no idea," he replied, and the two left the house.

Shortly after they emerged into the winter night, the banker, unable to contain his curiosity, burst out the door and pursued them. When he caught up with the rabbi, he said, "Dear rabbi, forgive me, but why did you visit my home tonight?"

"In order to fulfill the mitzva of rebuke," Rabbi Yisroel replied.

"But rabbi," the banker protested, "you did not say a word!"

The rabbi explained, "Part of the commandment is to refrain from rebuke when you know that the person is unable to receive it. That was the purpose of my visit – to hold my tongue so as not to rebuke you."

"But how could you know that I would not be able to receive it?" the banker pressed.

"I know you," the rabbi said laconically and turned to continue on his way.

But the curious banker kept pressing the rabbi, who finally relented. "There is a widow who is unable to pay her mortgage," he said, "and you are about to sell her house and put her out in the street in the dead of winter."

"But rabbi, you do not understand!" the banker said. "I may be a bank manager, but the debt is not mine to forgive."

"As I predicted," the rabbi said, and he and his attendant left.

A few days later, the rabbi's words pierced the heart of the banker and he paid off the widow's debt.[1]

Loving Rebuke

Before rebuking someone, we must ask ourselves if we truly *want* to do so. If the answer is affirmative, and we feel driven to rebuke another, paradoxically it is better to hold back and refrain from rebuke. If the answer is negative, we should muster the courage to proceed.

At bottom is a basic question: am I issuing my rebuke for the other's sake or my own? I could be doing it to relieve tension or release anger, or to bolster my self-esteem by patronizing the other. To do it for another's sake means helping that person move into a better place. If I feel the urge to rebuke, it is likely that the rebuke will serve my own purposes in some way. When I do not feel like rebuking, it is likely due to a reluctance to hurt the other's feelings, or a fear that if I criticize them, they will stop loving me. But if, despite everything, it occurs to me to rebuke them, I probably know that they need me. In such a case, the rebuke will come from a place of humility, sensitivity, and precision, and there is cause to hope that authentic, heartfelt words will not go unheeded.

Contemporary public discourse is far from conducive to such constructive rebuke. Unlike Moses, most people prefer to take the easy route and reserve their criticism for those outside their social group. In doing so they may gain self-esteem, and popularity in certain circles, but ultimately, not only the attacked group is harmed; the critic's group, too, suffers from the widening divides between the various factions in society.

---

1. Based on Telushkin, *Words That Hurt*, 99–101.

Preacher at the Gate

We will conclude the chapter with another story about the art of rebuke and the importance of honesty:

There was once a small town that hired the services of a man to walk the streets ahead of the High Holy Days and rebuke the community. Every year, this professional moralizer would choose a different topic: one year it was business practices, the next year it was Shabbat, and so on. Throughout the month of Elul and the Ten Days of Repentance, he would roam the markets and streets, chiding the people on the error of their ways.

But on the eve of Yom Kippur, having concluded his commission, he would convene all of the residents and tell them a story, the same one every year:

There once was a man whose son contracted a skin disease. The doctors said he would only recover if he bathed in water every day, but the bathhouse was too far from the man's village to be reached daily. The man was desperate, until one night he had an idea. On the following morning, he began to make the rounds in the village and disseminate his vision for its future. We may be a small village, he said, but if we succeed in building a bathhouse, we will be special. We will attract tourists from all over, business will boom, and hotels will spring up like mushrooms.

Finally, the man convinced his neighbors. Funds were raised, the bathhouse was built, and he was called to deliver a speech during the dedication ceremony. But as soon as he took the podium and saw the glowing faces in the audience, he realized that he could no longer keep secret his real motives.

"My dear friends," he said, "I truly hope that this bathhouse will be a boon for us all. But I must tell you the truth: I shared my vision with you mostly for my own personal ends, which I was unable to realize on my own."

The preacher concluded his story and looked out at the residents of the village, and they realized that it was about them.

Va'ethanan

To Love Is to Listen

The Organs of Love

Sefer Yetzira (The Book of Creation) deals extensively with the importance of speech. In evoking the three "organs of love," it lists the heart and ears before the mouth (6:3). The implication is that love should be expressed in words, but that in order to arrive at the pinnacle of love, there is need for listening as well. This important idea is often overlooked in relationships: while speech is for some reason considered an act of giving, listening is perceived as a passive receiving. Thus, if a man loves his wife and wants to give to her, he talks to her. Inevitably, we often find one partner waiting anxiously for the other to finish so that they, too, can have their turn at talking and giving.

But the opposite is true: listening is the ultimate expression of love, and a lack of listening is a sign (and cause) of love's absence. When we love someone, we care about what they have to say, and thus can – and want to – listen to them.

Listening is not passive; it requires much effort, and there are countless levels and nuances to it. I recall a young groom telling me with embarrassment that he could not understand what his wife wanted from him. She was complaining that he did not listen, while he insisted that listening was all he ever did: every evening she would talk for hours and he would sit beside her and listen. It turned out that the young man thought it was enough to hear the words coming out of his bride's mouth, while she was looking for true listening.

What is true listening? In one word: presence. The quality of the listening is a function of the degree and quality of the listener's presence. While listening to another person, we must set aside our thoughts and ignore the distractions, so that we can be completely open to the other. Addressing a listener who is present enables the speaker to dispel their existential loneliness, giving them the feeling that they are not alone with their feelings and personal narrative. When we truly listen, and allow the other's words to suffuse our own beings, we encompass the other and accept them. And that is the meaning of love.

During the traditional Jewish wedding ceremony, the groom is the one who speaks and gives the bride a ring. Based on the insight above about the meaning of listening, we can deduce that it is the bride who takes on the more senior role in the ceremony: listening to the words of the groom and receiving the ring from him are expressions of acceptance and encompassment. The Hebrew word for bride, "*kalla*," comes from the same root as "*hakhala*," or "encompassment."

Listening is originally a divine attribute. During the High Holy Days prayer service, we say, "Exalted God, who understands and hears...and listens." Our prayers often go unanswered in reality, but even when the answer is negative, the faith that God is present and listening allows us to always experience His love for us.

Hear, O Israel

The basic demand of every Jew is to listen: "Hear (*Shema*), O Israel: the Lord our God, the Lord is one" (Deut. 6:4). By listening we arrive at love: "And you shall love the Lord your God with all your heart, and with all your soul, and with all your might" (6:5). In these verses we find two of the organs of love cited by *Sefer Yetzira*: the ears and the heart.

While reciting the *Shema*, it is customary to cover one's eyes. We can find an explanation for this in the book *The Little Prince*: "It is only with one's heart that one can see clearly. What is essential is invisible to the eye."[1] Closing our eyes enables us to concentrate deeply, and when we truly listen, we can see with our hearts.

Love and Commitment

The listening invoked by the *Shema* must take place "when you sit in your house, and when you walk by the way, and when you lie down, and when you rise up" (6:7). This means that no matter where we go, the experience is identical: God is one. The deeper implication of this experience is not only the understanding that there is not a plurality of gods in the world, but that "there is none else beside Him" (Deut. 4:35) and "no place is devoid of Him" (*Tikkunei Zohar* 122b). God is present in everything, and His unity is the source of all unity, which in turn gives rise to love. To experience unity wherever one goes is not only to maintain awareness of God's proximity, but also to understand that one is a part of *the One*, of the ultimate unity. The numerical value of *"ehad,"* the Hebrew word for "one," is thirteen, just like the value of *"ahava,"* or "love." To love another is to unite with them, as in the story of the Garden of Eden, which portrays the ideal intimate relationship: "And [he] shall cleave to his wife, and they shall be one flesh" (Gen. 2:24).

---

1. Saint-Exupery, http://users.uoa.gr/~nektar/arts/tributes/antoine_de_saint-exupery_le_petit_prince/the_little_prince.htm.

In "My Freedom," Chava Alberstein sings of a man mourning the loss of his freedom, a bound man. Toward the end of the song, we learn that the power that binds him is love. True love tethers us; it demands commitment; it requires that we fulfill our promises even when we do not want to. I once attended a wedding at which the rabbi read the *ketuba* – a legal document delineating the husband's responsibilities toward his wife – to the tune of the Song of Songs. Commitment and responsibility are the foundation of love.

The connection between love and commitment is also evident in the *Shema*, where, along with affirming that "the Lord is one," we state that the Lord is "our God" and accept the yoke of His sovereignty.

A woman once told me that she did not understand the significance of commitment to halakha. She maintained that, no matter what she did, God would love her. I replied that I too believed that God's love to us is unconditional. The real question, I said, was not the extent of His love for us, but of our love for Him.

It is true that commitment can be interpreted as a loss of personal freedom, but at the same time, a lack of commitment can be seen as an expression of alienation and solipsism.

The power of love lies in the feeling that the other is not alien to us, but is rather "bone of my bones, and flesh of my flesh" (Gen. 2:23), and that together we are "one flesh." The intensity of our connection to God comes from the understanding that we were all created in His image, that He is not external or alien to us. Our connection to God does not erase our inner identity, but rather reveals it, highlighting the profound link between commitment and love, between "our God" and "the Lord is one."

Ekev

From Knowledge to Consciousness

The internet provides us with access to practically infinite information. However, in order to see change in our lives, increasing our knowledge is not enough; there has to be a shift in consciousness, in the means by which we observe reality and experience it. A shift in consciousness can come about by reshaping the elements underpinning our perception of reality. Knowledge is indeed one of the means through which we can shape those elements, but it must be internalized deeply.

Appropriately, the Hebrew word for knowledge, "*yeda*," connotes not only a receiving of information, but also a connection to it. The *Tanya* (chapter 3) sees significance in the Torah's use of the word "*yeda*" to describe intimate relations: "*Daat* (knowledge) derives from 'And [Adam] knew (*yada*) Eve his wife' (Gen. 4:1) and connotes connecting and bonding, the establishment of a very firm and powerful connection of the mind." This idea is also manifested in the link between "*yeda*" and "*muda'ut*" (awareness or consciousness), a far-from-obvious relation that is unique to Hebrew. In English, for instance, there is no etymological affinity between knowledge, or information, and consciousness.

In fact, it is the very unceasing flow of information that inhibits our ability to concentrate on the truly important things. Often, rather than generate a deeper consciousness, knowledge saddles us with a surfeit of information. This corresponds to interpersonal relations in our global village, where, despite all the tools and media designed to help us stay in touch with so many people, most of us remain alienated from one another.

The Knowledge of the Heart

Ekev is the fourth and final *parasha* to mention tefillin, a mitzva that epitomizes the link between knowledge and consciousness. The four passages inscribed in the tefillin's parchments include the four foundational elements of Judaism: (1) belief in a single God and (2) His love, (3) commitment to keep the mitzvot, and (4) the memory of the Exodus from Egypt. Yet, it is not enough to know these four elements; one must internalize them, in keeping with the verse "Know this day, and lay it in your heart, that the Lord, He is God in heaven above and upon the earth beneath; there is none else" (Deut. 4:39).

This recalls the story of the young man who left his home for many years to study with a famous hasidic rebbe. When he finally returned, his father asked him what he had learned. "That the Lord is God," the son said. The father was disappointed. "But everyone knows that the Lord is God," he railed. "It took you all these years to figure that out?" The son replied, "Everyone says it, but I know it."

The purpose of tefillin is to transmute information into consciousness, by conducting knowledge into the heart and the soul. "Therefore shall you lay up these My words in your heart and in your soul; and you shall bind them for a sign upon your hand, and they shall be for frontlets between your eyes" (Deut. 11:18). This is also the context for understanding the verses that one recites while wrapping the tefillin straps around the finger (Hos. 2:21–22): "And I will betroth you to Me forever; yea, I will betroth you to Me in righteousness…. And I will betroth you to Me in faithfulness; and you shall know the Lord." There is knowledge that springs from a connection so deep it is likened to betrothal, and that connection is expressed through tefillin.

The Tefillin of the Arm and Head: To Do and to Be

There are two tefillin (the singular form is tefilla), one worn on the arm and the other on the head. The two parallel the basic modes of existence that we have dealt with extensively: "doing" and "being."

The arm symbolizes being. Based on the juxtaposition of two statements – "Therefore shall you lay up these My words in your heart" and "And you shall bind them for a sign upon your hand" (Deut. 11:18) – the Talmud (Menaḥot 37b) concludes that the tefilla of the arm should be parallel to the heart; hence its position on the bicep. The implication is that a person's actions should be motivated by the heart.

The head is emblematic of awareness, of "being." Just as the tefilla of the arm corresponds to the heart, the tefilla of the head corresponds to the soul: "Therefore shall you lay up these My words … in your soul … and they shall be for frontlets between your eyes" (ibid.). When it discusses the tefilla of the arm, the Torah uses a verb – "you shall bind" – to denote activity, while the tefilla of the head is described in more passive terms –"and they shall be."

The tefilla of the arm directs us toward dealing with the practical question, "What am I doing?" while the tefilla of head evokes the existential question, "Who am I?" I wish to address further the second question: what can tefillin teach us about the essence of humanity?

The Lord's Tefillin

"There are three rungs, interlinked," the Zohar (*Aḥarei Mot* 73a) writes, "the blessed Holy One, Torah, and Israel." The Ramhal, in his commentary on the "*Idra Rabba*" section of the Zohar, illuminates the nature of this profound bond: "The Torah, the Jewish people, and the blessed Holy One are one." The tefillin are emblematic of the ontological link between humankind, God, and the Torah.

According to the Talmud, God also wears tefillin (Berakhot 6a). Where the Jewish people's tefillin contain the verse "Hear (*Shema*), O Israel: the Lord our God, the Lord is one" (Deut. 6:4), God's tefillin are inscribed with the verse "And who is like Your people, like Israel, one nation in the earth?" (II Sam. 7:23). This midrash is evocative of the Zohar's statement above: when Jews wear tefillin they are bonded to God, and when God wears tefillin He is bonded to the Jewish people.

But it seems that tefillin are more than an expression of a connection to God; they are also an expression of God's revelation through us. In interpreting the verse "And all the peoples of the earth shall see that the name of the Lord is called upon you; and they shall be afraid of you" (Deut. 28:10), the Talmud (Menahot 35b) writes: "R. Eliezer HaGadol says, 'This refers to the tefilla of the head.'" The implication is that when one wears tefillin one assumes the appearance of the Lord, who also dons tefillin, thus manifesting the fact that the name of the Lord is called upon him.

The Talmud then goes on to comment on the verse "And I will take away My hand, and you shall see My back; but My face shall not be seen" (Ex. 33:23): "Said R. Ḥana b. Bizna in the name of R. Shimon Ḥasida, 'This teaches that the Holy One, blessed be He, showed Moses the knot of the tefillin.'" Rashi ties the Talmud's two statements together, saying that "and they shall be afraid of you" describes the reaction of idolaters upon seeing the tefilla of the head, which is a reflection of the tefillin worn by God.

Tefillin are perceived as being part of God, and seeing them is like witnessing His presence. Hence the fear of Israel among the peoples of the earth: a person who puts on tefillin is likened to the tefillin-wearing God. The name of the Lord is called upon one who wears tefillin not only because the housing of the tefilla of the head is inscribed with one of His names – *shin-dalet-yod* – but also because tefillin are part of the Lord's garments.

Tefillin and Torah

Elsewhere, the Talmud deduces the laws of the Torah scroll from the laws of the tefillin (Makkot 11a). The comparison is based on the idea that tefillin are essentially tiny Torah scrolls: like a Torah scroll, they are written with ink on parchment, and they too contain portions from the Torah. The tefillin bind one's body to the Torah.

The *Mekhilta* (13:9) takes this idea a step further: "When one is wearing tefillin, it is as if one is reading from the Torah, and one who reads from the Torah is exempt from tefillin." At first glance, it seems odd that wearing tefillin would exempt one from reading from the Torah, and vice versa. Reading from the Torah has to do with studying and understanding – it is a mitzva of the mind. Wearing tefillin, on the other hand, does not contain any element of study. It seems that the answer lies in the fact that Torah study, like tefillin, is meant to *forge a connection* to the Torah. With tefillin, that connection is not effected by way of the mind, but rather through the body. When one places the tefillin – which stand for a Torah scroll – on one's body, one connects to the Torah in an immediate and physical way.

There is no contradiction between tefillin being a symbol for the Torah and the Torah being a symbol for tefillin. "We possess an authentic tradition showing that the entire Torah consists of names of God," Nahmanides writes in the introduction to his commentary on the Torah. The source for this mystical idea is in the Talmud (Berakhot 21a): "Where do we find that a blessing before studying the Torah is ordained in the Torah? Because it says, 'For I will proclaim the name of the Lord; ascribe greatness unto our God' (Deut. 32:3)." To study Torah is to proclaim the name of the Lord.

Tefillin and Humankind

The tefillin straps are wrapped over a person's upper body – the head and the arm. According to Jewish law, the straps, housings (*battim*), and parchments must be made of leather. Thus, the tefillin can be seen as an extension of a person's body, a part of his skin. In ancient times, tefillin would be worn throughout the day, and thus become part of the wearer. The Zohar (*Kedoshim* 1:1) writes that only a person who wears tefillin is complete and can be called "one."

The connection between tefillin and the body shows us that the elements represented by tefillin are not external to the person, but are rather intrinsic to him. Tefillin, as a name of God, are a revelation of the inner essence of every human being who was born in the image of God. Tefillin are likened to a Torah scroll, an object that is held up as an expression of the sanctity of humankind – every individual is a Torah scroll. This idea is manifested in the law according to which: "He who stands by the dead at the parting of the soul is bound to rend [his garments]: [for] what does this resemble? A scroll of the Law that is burned" (Shabbat 105b). The purpose of tefillin is not to change who we are, but rather to awaken us to our true essence.

The Tefilla of the Head

A story is told about a rabbi who was targeted with an arrest warrant by the czarist police. When officers entered his home to apprehend him, they came upon him when he was bedecked with tefillin. Frightened, they backed away and left. The rabbi explained the secret to his success, citing the Talmud: "'And all the peoples of the earth shall see that the name of the Lord is called upon you; and they shall be afraid of you'.... R. Eliezer HaGadol says, 'This refers to the tefilla of [in] the head (*shebarosh*)'" (Menaḥot 35b).

The captain of the bandits in the rabbi's town heard the story and decided that he, too, would wear tefillin, thinking that police would leave him alone if he did. But it was to no avail, and he was soon arrested. Later, the rabbi explained his mistake to him: the Talmud does not refer to "the tefilla on the head," but rather to "the tefilla *in* the head." The key is the tefillin within the individual, the place in one's soul in which reside the elements represented by the external tefillin.

Re'eh

What Does God Have to Do with Social Justice?

The Torah addresses both interpersonal relations and the individual's relationship with God. There are those who think the human, social realm is more important, and others who insist that the religious life is preeminent. To my mind, Judaism's unique message is not these two aspects on their own, but rather the profound connection between them – the insight that one's relationship with God influences one's relationship with others, and vice versa.

Shemitta is a good example of this cross-fertilization. For six years we till the land, but on the seventh it is given a sabbatical and lies fallow. The Torah mentions the mitzva of *Shemitta* three times: *Parashat Mishpatim* expounds its social aspects, *Behar* gives the religious angle, while *Re'eh*, our *parasha*, blends the two approaches. Let us examine these three instances so that we can better understand the two aspects and the connection between them.

Mishpatim: Social *Shemitta*

> And six years you shall sow your land, and gather in the
> increase thereof; but the seventh year you shall let it rest
> and lie fallow, that the poor of your people may eat; and
> what they leave the beast of the field shall eat. (Ex. 23:10–11)

On the seventh year, we are enjoined to relax our grasp of
the land for the sake of the poor. Furthermore, we are called upon
to think of the animals as well, for they claim the food that goes
uneaten by the poor. Thus a parallel is drawn between *Shemitta*
and the social vision of Shabbat, as it appears in Exodus 23:12:
"Six days you shall do your work, but on the seventh day you shall
rest; that your ox and your ass may have rest, and the son of your
handmaid, and the stranger, may be refreshed." Shabbat addresses
the needs of the weaker strata of society – strangers and slaves – as
well as those of the animals: the oxen and asses. It is noteworthy
that the name of God is absent from the passage above – a glaring
absence in comparison to the passage in *Parashat Behar*.

Behar: A Sabbath of the Land

> And the Lord spoke to Moses at Mount Sinai, saying, "Speak
> to the children of Israel, and say to them, 'When you come
> into the land which I give you, then shall the land keep a
> Sabbath to the Lord. Six years you shall sow your field…
> But in the seventh year it shall be a Sabbath of solemn rest
> for the land, a Sabbath to the Lord.'" (Lev. 25:1–4)

At the outset, the Torah emphasizes that God addresses
Moses at Mount Sinai. Rashi famously asks, "What does *Shemitta*
have to do with Mount Sinai? Were not all the commandments
given at Sinai?" The question "What does *Shemitta* have to do with

Mount Sinai?" has become an idiom used to express skepticism when someone tries to link two apparently unconnected things.

It seems, however, that the very premise of the question is in doubt. The word "*Shemitta*" does not appear once in *Parashat Behar*, and indeed, there is no special significance to Mount Sinai vis-à-vis *Shemitta*. Rather, the *parasha* says that "the land [shall] keep a Sabbath." When we rephrase the question as "What does a Sabbath of the land have to do with Mount Sinai?" it loses its bite. Indeed, the covenant over the land is sealed at Sinai.[1] We already know that Shabbat is an expression of the covenant between the Jewish people and God: "Therefore the children of Israel shall keep the Sabbath, to observe the Sabbath throughout their generations, for a perpetual covenant" (Ex. 31:16). It emerges that a Sabbath is an appropriate expression of the covenant over the land, as sealed at Sinai.

In this vein, Ibn Ezra explain that *Behar* and *Behukkotai* are the "book of the covenant" mentioned in *Parashat Mishpatim* (Ex. 24:7): "It concludes the covenant that was mentioned in *Parashat Mishpatim*. It appears here, out of order, to connect…the conditions under which the land was given" (Ibn Ezra on Leviticus 25:1). By relinquishing the land into God's hands on every seventh year, we internalize the idea that the land was given by God and that its use is contingent on fulfilling the covenant. It is noteworthy that at the end of the seventh year, when the land again reverts to humanity, the people assemble for the *Hak'hel* ceremony, during which parts of the Torah are read. The description of the assembly (Deut. 31:10–13) is rife with parallels to the revelation at Sinai. This is an expression of its purpose: to renew the covenant between the people and the land at the conclusion of the *Shemitta* year.

---

1. Throughout Deuteronomy, the Torah emphasizes that the covenant at Sinai is largely a covenant between the Jewish people and the land. See for instance 5:2–3, 30; 6:2; 8:1.

To break the covenant, and especially the Sabbath of the land, is to forfeit the land, as we learn in *Parashat Beḥukkotai*. In the Book of Chronicles, the number of years the Jewish people spend in exile in Babylon is tied to the number of times they failed to observe the *Shemitta* year (II Chr. 36:21).

The varying meanings ascribed to the *Shemitta* year also give rise to practical differences. Thus, according to *Parashat Mishpatim*, the purpose of *Shemitta* is to better the lot of the poor, which is why the fruits of the field are reserved for them. In *Parashat Behar*, in contrast, letting the land lie fallow expresses acknowledgment of God's ownership of it. It follows that the fruits are a gift from God to all of humanity: "And the Sabbath-produce of the land shall be for food for you: for you and for your servant" (Lev. 25:6).

The Midrash offers a creative explanation of the above contradiction by blending the two values, the spiritual and the social: "'That the poor of your people may eat' – by implication, only the poor. How do we learn that the rich [also may eat]? The Torah teaches us: 'And the Sabbath-produce of the land shall be for food for you.' Why, then, does it say 'the poor of your people'? [To teach us that] most of it is for the poor" (*Mekhilta DeRabbi Shimon* 23:11).

Re'eh: The Lord's *Shemitta*

> At the end of every seven years you shall make a release (*She-mitta*). And this is the manner of the release: every creditor shall release that which he has lent to his neighbor; he shall not exact it of his neighbor and his brother; because the release [to the Lord] hath been proclaimed. (Deut. 15:1–2)

The unique formulation "the Lord's *Shemitta*" combines the terminology found in *Parashat Mishpatim* with that found in *Behar*. As in *Mishpatim*, we have a "*Shemitta*," meaning the emphasis is placed on the person releasing (there it is land, here it is debt), and as in *Behar*, the Torah notes that the *Shemitta* is "to the Lord."

Parashat Re'eh links between social statutes and the religious life. There are two consequences to the demand for debt forgiveness: financially speaking, it allows borrowers to start afresh every seven years, and socially, it undoes the problematic situation whereby creditors control (emotionally as well) their debtors. In effect, it prevents the long-term enslavement of borrowers. We learn of this sensitivity from the formulation "he shall not exact it of his neighbor and his brother," which means that one must not compel or pressure the other.

The purpose of *Shemitta* is thus social, but the explanations for it are theological:

> But there shall be no needy among you – for the Lord will surely bless you in the land which the Lord your God gives you for an inheritance to possess it.... Beware that there is not a base thought in your heart, saying, "The seventh year, the year of release, is at hand"; and your eye is evil against your needy brother, and you give him nothing; and he cries to the Lord against you, and it is sin in you. You shall surely give him, and your heart shall not be grieved when you give to him; because for this thing the Lord your God will bless you in all your work, and in all that you put your hand to. (Deut. 15:4, 9–10)

It is not only the force of divine decree that compels us to help the other, but also the Torah's conception of reality. The belief that God granted the land, and continues to direct the course of life within it, prompts us to take a different view of our property. The very notion of property rights is cast in a new light when we realize that God is the source of all that we have ("the land which the Lord your God gives you") and, ultimately, retains ownership of it. This can be seen in the idea that people's continued presence on the land is contingent upon their behavior ("Beware...") and that on the seventh year the land reverts to God (*Parashat Behar*). The awareness that the land belongs to God can make it easier for us to share its bounty with others, for when we know that our future situation is determined by our ethical conduct in the present ("because for this thing the Lord your God will bless you"), we are more able to open our hearts to others. Helping the other is not merely a matter of divine decree; it is human nature.

Shofetim

The Second Innocence

You shall be innocent with the Lord your God.

– Deuteronomy 18:13

The Hebrew word for "innocent" in the verse above, "*tamim*," can also be translated as "naïve" or "guileless," and derives from the same root as "*tam*," the simpleton son in the Haggada (who is imbued with the quality of "*temimut*").

According to the dictionary definitions, innocence is often synonymous with naiveté, artlessness, and gullibility; with ignorance as to the ways of the world. It is inconsistent with sophistication and a critical outlook. Indeed, there are sources that put the two qualities in opposition, including, famously, the Rabbi Nahman story "The Sophisticate and the Simpleton (*tam*)."

But *temimut* also evokes integrity, in the sense of both moral purity and completeness, a connotation that Onkelos favors in his translation of the above verse. On the face of it, the two connotations are contradictory; indeed, the *temimut* associated with the Torah is described as having the capacity to grant wisdom to the simpleton: "The [Torah] of the Lord is perfect (*temima*), restoring the soul; the testimony of the Lord is sure, making wise the simple" (Ps. 19:8). The Midrash even considers *temimut* a divine attribute that people should strive to emulate:

> Do you wish for the blessed Holy One to be with you? Embrace *temimut* ... for God prizes *temimut*, as it is written, "You shall be innocent (*tamim*) with the Lord your God" – just as He is *tamim*, as it is written, "The Rock, His work is perfect (*tamim*)"; and His Torah is perfect, as it is written, "The [Torah] of the Lord is perfect (*temima*)." (Midrash on Psalms 119)

What, then, is the innocence connoted by *temimut*? Is it wisdom or the lack thereof? Is it the sublime and profound or perhaps the trivial and superficial?

From First to Second Innocence

The kabbalistic reading of the word "*tam*" sheds light on the link between the two connotations of innocence:

> Through the merit of Abraham, who was worthy of the attribute of Kindness, Isaac was worthy of the attribute of Fear. And because Isaac was worthy of the attribute of Fear, Jacob was worthy of the attribute of Truth, which is the attribute of Peace. God bestowed to him according to his measure. It is thus written (Gen. 25:27), "Jacob was a complete man (*tam*), dwelling in tents." The word "complete" means nothing other than peace. It is thus written (Deut. 18:13), "You shall be innocent (*tamim*) with the Lord your God," and [Onkelos] renders this, "You shall be *shlim*

[at peace or complete]." The word *"tam"* refers to nothing other than the Torah.[1]

The Bahir identifies the *tam* with peace and truth. The kabbalistic idea of truth and peace, as we have already established,[2] is harmony between contrasting aspects of reality. *The Bahir* identifies this quality with Jacob, the innocent man, who represents completion and balance between the right, the loving-kindness associated with Abraham, and the left, the fear and judgment associated with Isaac. Jacob is the synthesis of the two.

The sixteenth-century kabbalist Meir ibn Gabbai, author of the *Tolaat Yaakov*,[3] identifies *temimut* with the oral Torah, because it encompasses everything. The oral tradition is multifaceted, containing myriad interpretations, and that is the source of its completeness.

If we were to offer a definition that is consonant with both connotations of the word, we would say that the *tam* is a person devoid of cynicism and sophistication, one who is capable of believing and accepting anyone and anything. Every day such a person looks upon life with fresh eyes, humbled and awed by the world.

Such a personality can arise from two separate sets of life circumstances. The first option is an innate lack of complexity, as in the case of the eponymous simpleton in Rabbi Nahman's story. But it can also stem from another source, what the philosopher Akiva Ernst Simon calls "second innocence." Sometimes, the very realization of the complexity of reality can bring one to a state of true acceptance. Awareness of the awesomeness and power of life breeds humility.

---

1. Kaplan, *The Bahir*, 51.
2. See especially *Parashat Ḥayei Sara* and *Parashat Koraḥ*.
3. In the section titled "The Secret of Shabbat."

Those who are in the first state of innocence do not see any of the flaws in the other and in the world because they do not possess a penetrating view of life. They accept reality at face value. One who is in a state of second innocence, on the other hand, sees the problems, the difficulties, and the ugliness, but is able to encompass them. The capacity to encompass stems from the understanding that flaws and limitations are inherent to the world and to human life. The *tam* thus does not treat others with condescension when he perceives their flaws, because he knows that he too is afflicted with those very same imperfections. He can accept and appreciate the other, for his holistic view of reality enables him to avoid attachment to negative things, and instead to see the good in them.

For the first *tam*, life and the world are an unfathomable mystery; for the second *tam*, the sense of mystery is generated by a profound internalization of the complexity of reality. He understands that there are many things whose nature and purpose he can never grasp.

The Four Sons

One of the four sons who appear in the Passover Haggada is wise; another is a simpleton. The four archetypes can be seen as representing four stages in the life of an individual. At first one is incapable of asking. Then one becomes a simpleton who is willing, due to one's naiveté, to accept simplistic answers to life's big questions. These answers fail to plumb the depths of the perplexities and difficulties, but the simpleton is unbothered: he lives a life of harmony in which everything is fundamentally coherent and in order. There is charm and tranquility in such a state of innocence, but ultimately it is an illusion. The world and reality are complex, and the child will one day grow up and realize that there is more to life.

The wicked son is emblematic of the next stage in life, the realization that the questions are more compelling than the answers, which can lead to a crisis. He is angry at those who, he thinks, fed him lies, and contemptuous of those who still hold by the explanations that to him seem superficial and incomplete (if not outright falsehoods). He loses faith in the society that raised him and the culture that surrounds him. When he was a simpleton he believed everything; now he believes in nothing.

But ultimately, he wises up. Like the wicked son, the wise son is aware of the complexity of reality, but that insight leads him to very different conclusions. Indeed, the world may be complex and full of contradictions, and the expectation of absolute explanations is an illusion. But the limited capacity to explain is very much a function of the nature of reality. The easy option is to throw it all away. It is harder to search for the hidden light and truths that can be found everywhere and in every person, and make meaning out of them. The wise son faces the world with humility, and mines beauty from the unknown, from those very hidden depths that defy explanation. That is the innocence to which we aspire, which has the power to "restore the soul." As the hasidic proverb says, "Innocence is greater than wisdom, but one must be very wise to be innocent."

Ki Tetzeh

Behold, You Are Special to Me

We often hear that these days, it is harder than ever to get married. It seems that the reason it is so difficult to find a suitable husband or wife is the weight of the expectations people have from the spousal relationship. This relationship is one of the novelties pioneered by our generation. True, couples of previous generations shared love and empathy, but in more recent years, people's expanded self-awareness and psychological insight, along with changes in gender dynamics, are allowing couples to maintain a qualitatively different kind of connection. Men are opening up to areas that in the past were reserved to women, while women are participating in activities that were long off-limits to them, especially when it comes to education and the workplace. Men take a more active role in the home, and women are more present in arenas outside the domestic.

The growing number of shared experiences enables more dialogue and listening than in times when men and women lived in what were practically different worlds. Furthermore, people's growing awareness of their inner lives generates deeper mutual sharing of their worlds. We mentioned above the famous story about Rabbi Aryeh Levin, who once told the doctor, "My wife's leg hurts us." These days, it seems, men can say, "My wife's soul hurts us." A growing number of conditions and mechanisms are leading toward a state where the couple is "one," thus fulfilling the Torah's vision for the spousal relationship.

The world's religions offer a broad range of outlooks regarding conjugal life: some see the relationship as a compromise to be lived with, while others see in it an ideal. Judaism's point of view on the subject is unique, and infuses couplehood with sublime ontological and existential meaning.

"When a Man Takes a Wife"

We learn of the marriage ceremony from the verse in our *parasha* that begins "When a man takes a wife" (Deut. 24:1). The verb "takes" is laden with associations from the world of property rights, and indeed the first mishna in Tractate Kiddushin begins, "A woman is acquired." My friend Rabbi Dov Berkovits devoted his book *Who Made Me a Man* to elucidating the idea of "acquisition" in the context of marriage. He shows that its meaning has to do with generating a special connection – not a commercial or legal act. Among other things, he notes that the root of the Hebrew word for "is acquired" ("*nikneit*") – *kuf-nun-heh* – first appears in the Bible in the context of the creation of new life: "And the man knew Eve his wife; and she conceived and bore Cain, and said, 'I have gotten (*kaniti*) a man with the help of the Lord'" (Gen. 4:1). Indeed, the very name of the ceremony, "*Kiddushin*," or "consecration," denotes a spiritual, rather than a material, link.[1]

---

1. Rabbi Dov Berkovits, *Who Made Me a Man* [Hebrew] (Tel Aviv: Yediot Books, 2008), 43.

I wish to posit another explanation for the Torah's choice of the word "takes," or "*yikah*" in Hebrew, whose root – *lamed-kuf-het* – appears three times in the description of the creation of Eve: "And He took (*vayikah*) one of his ribs.... And the rib, which the Lord God had taken (*lakah*) from the man, made He a woman... 'because she was taken (*lukaha*) out of Man'" (Gen. 2:21–23). The description of the creation of Adam and Eve teaches us that at first they were one, then they were separated, and ultimately they become one again: "And the man said, 'This is now bone of my bones, and flesh of my flesh; she shall be called Woman, because she was taken (*lukaha*) out of Man.' Therefore shall a man leave his father and his mother, and shall cleave to his wife, and they shall be one flesh" (2:23–24).

When the Torah says, "Therefore shall a man leave his father and his mother," we learn that the story is not only about the relationship between Adam and Eve – for they had no parents – but is also a foundational myth of the conjugal bond. Because the woman is taken out of the man (*lukaha*), her return to him is described using the same root: *lamed-kuf-het*. When the man "takes" the woman, the intention is to bring them back to a state of unified togetherness.

That oneness is also apparent in the divorce ceremony. As the Torah says further along in our *parasha*, a marriage can only be annulled with a "bill of divorcement" (Deut. 24:3). The Hebrew for "divorcement," "*keritut*," connotes a severing: after two people become one, they are not easily disassociated from each another.

The biblical conception of the couple as a whole is greatly elaborated by rabbinical and kabbalistic sources. The Talmud (Yevamot 63a) writes, "Any man who has no wife is no proper man; for it is said, 'Male and female created He them and called their name Adam (Man)' (Gen. 5:2)." And the Midrash explains that "the two together are called Adam" (Genesis Rabba 17:2).

From the juxtaposition of the preceding verse – "This is the book of the generations of Adam. In the day that God created man, in the likeness of God made He him" (5:1) – we can learn that it is only when a man and a woman are together that they attain the likeness of God.

This idea also underpins Rabbi Akiva's aphorism "When husband and wife are worthy, the *Shekhina* abides with them" (Sota 17a). The Hebrew words for "man" ("*ish*") and "woman" ("*isha*") share two letters in common – *alef* and *shin* – while "*ish*" contains another *yod* and "*isha*" another *heh*. Joining the man's unique letter, *yod*, to the woman's, *heh*, yields "*Yah*," one of the names of God.

From the Song of Songs to *The Little Prince*

We mentioned above the verse "And the man said, 'This is now bone of my bones, and flesh of my flesh; she shall be called Woman, because she was taken out of Man'" (Gen. 2:23). The first words attributed to the first man have to do with the conjugal relationship. The verse has a lyrical progression, and according to the Zohar, is a paean to the essence of love:

> The man said, "This is now…" Behold the fragrance of words, to draw love with her, draw her toward his desire, arouse passion together. See how sweet, how full of love: "Bone of my bones, flesh of my flesh," showing that they are one, inseparable. Now he begins praising her: "She shall be called Woman." This one is unparalleled, glory of the house! All women compared with her are like an ape compared with humans. Certainly, "she shall be called Woman," perfection of all, this one and no other. (Zohar, *Bereshit* 49b).

One of the most destructive things we can do in a relationship is to compare our partner to others. When we understand that our partner's uniqueness emerges from our relationship when we are together, one in body and soul, we realize that there is no room for comparison – only for acceptance and love. When the Zohar states, "'She shall be called Woman.' This one is unparalleled," we learn that the basic assumption is that she is peerless. The Zohar continues, "'She shall be called Woman'…this one and no other." It is as if the man tells his wife, "For me there is only one woman in the entire world: you."

The Torah links the word "woman" to the unique connection between her and the man: "She shall be called Woman, because she was taken out of Man." From the perspective of the man, the woman is the one with whom he actualizes a relationship of "bone of my bones, flesh of my flesh." This insight regarding the marital bond is the secret divulged by the fox in the book *The Little Prince*, in a process that begins when the prince discovers that his rose is not the only rose in the world:

He was standing before a garden, all a-bloom with roses. "Good morning," said the roses.

> The little prince gazed at them. They all looked like his flower…. And he was overcome with sadness. His flower had told him that she was the only one of her kind in all the universe. And here were five thousand of them, all alike, in one single garden![2]

At first we may think that the rose loved by the little prince is not very special; indeed, there are thousands like her. But further along, he meets the fox and realizes his oversight – that the very connection between him and the rose is what makes her one of a kind:

---

2. Saint-Exupery, http://users.uoa.gr/~nektar/arts/tributes/antoine_de_saint-exu-pery_le_petit_prince/the_little_prince.htm.

"What does that mean – 'tame'?"

"It is an act too often neglected," said the fox. "It means to establish ties."

"To establish ties?"

"Just that," said the fox. "To me, you are still nothing more than a little boy who is just like a hundred thousand other little boys. And I have no need of you. And you, on your part, have no need of me. To you, I am nothing more than a fox like a hundred thousand other foxes. But if you tame me, then we shall need each other. To me, you will be unique in all the world. To you, I shall be unique in all the world..."

"I am beginning to understand," said the little prince. "There is a flower.... I think that she has tamed me..."...

"Go and look again at the roses. You will understand now that yours is unique in all the world. Then come back to say goodbye to me, and I will make you a present of a secret."...

"Goodbye," said the fox. "And now here is my secret, a very simple secret: it is only with the heart that one can see rightly; what is essential is invisible to the eye.... It is the time you have wasted for your rose that makes your rose so important."

"Men have forgotten this truth," said the fox. "But you must not forget it. You become responsible, forever, for what you have tamed. You are responsible for your rose."

Like the woman in the Garden of Eden, the little prince's rose is also special thanks to its relationship with its lover.

Adam and Eve are alone in the world, and so are the little prince and the rose. The challenge in the relationship is for the man to always see his wife as the only woman in the world – even in a world that is unbridled and vulgar.

Yet, we must not confuse the vision and its actualization. The vision depicts a potential that we can only realize through hard work. The most nuanced, and gratifying, truth that a newlywed couple can learn is that the wedding is not the pinnacle of the relationship, but rather the beginning of a joint journey.

Ki Tavo

Happiness Here and Now

"And They Lived Happily Ever After"

The Torah is full of stories about deferred promises, obstacles that prevent expectations from being fulfilled. Our forefathers are always on the path, their rest and contentment not even on the horizon. But then, near the end of Deuteronomy, we learn about *bikkurim*, and the ending of the story is given away:

> And it shall be, when you have come into the land which the Lord your God gives you for an inheritance, and possess it and dwell therein; that you shall take of the first of all the fruit of the ground…. "And the Lord brought us out of Egypt with a mighty hand…. And He brought us to this place, and gave us this land, a land flowing with milk and honey. And now, behold, I have brought the first of the fruit of the land, which You, O Lord, have given me." And you shall set it down…. And you shall rejoice in all the good which the Lord your God has given to you. (Deut. 26:1–2, 8–11)

The above verses are laden with future-tense verbs: possess, dwell, take, set down. The mitzva of bringing *bikkurim* to the Temple is portrayed as a continuation of the conquering and settlement of the land. Thus, the tone is not imperative or legalistic, but rather fits into the description of future life in the Promised Land. Bringing *bikkurim* is an inseparable part of the happy ending to the people's desert wanderings, an expression of rejoicing and thanks over the fulfillment of the divine promise, a state of fairytale bliss: "And they lived happily ever after."

While on the face of it, the person is the giver and God is on the receiving end – and indeed giving is mentioned multiple times in the verses – it is God who is giving to the person:

> And it shall be, when you have come into the land which *the Lord your God gives you* for an inheritance… *"and gave us* this land, a land flowing with milk and honey. And now, behold, *I have brought* the first of the fruit of the land, *which You, O Lord, have given me."* And you shall set it down.… And you shall rejoice in all the good which the Lord your God *has given to you.*

The Lord is the giver, and the person receives and brings *bikkurim* to the Temple, in an expression of joy over those gifts.

Joy Is in the Present

Judaism is often occupied with memory of the past and anticipation of the future. One can learn from the past, and it is good to know what future to strive for, but one cannot overlook the present. The ability to focus on the present and the capacity for joy are closely related. The statement "Everything will be okay" is not a blessing – not only because it denies the good that already exists in the present, but because it also negates the future good. Those who ignore the present in favor of future hopes may not notice when all the good they yearned for comes to pass.

Yet, the link between the present and joy is even more profound. A person's capacity to be present in the present, to be aware of the moment and work with it, is the capacity to experience life itself, for only the moment is where life happens. A direct connection to life is the basis for joy. It is apparent that when we are happy we feel full of life, and when we are sad we are bereft of life. Joy over our reality in the here and now is what we learn from *bikkurim*:

> And gave us this land, a land flowing with milk and honey. *And now*, behold, I have brought the first of the fruit of the land, which You, O Lord, have given me.... And you shall rejoice *in all the good* which the Lord your God has given to you, and to your house.

Life Is Joy

Once during Rosh Ḥodesh prayers, I found myself saying the verse from Hallel, "This is the day which the Lord has made; we will rejoice and be glad in it" (Ps. 118:24). I wondered what day the verse was referring to, even though it is generally taken to be about the anniversaries of historical events, such as Passover, Independence Day, and Jerusalem Day. I was filled with delight at the thought that "this is the day" could be taken to apply to every single day. Such an interpretation of the verse reflects the understanding that life itself – not necessarily what occurs in life – is the source of happiness. On the other hand, when we chase after "reasons" for joy, we lose the capacity to find happiness in life itself and enjoy what is already there. Just as true love is unconditional (as affirmed by the Mishna in Avot 5:16), so too true joy is unconditional. When my children return from childcare, they always seem happy, but when I ask them what they did all day, I almost invariably get the same answer: "Nothing!"

The film *In America* tells the story of a family that loses a son. In one scene, the father runs into a neighbor, who says he wishes he could change places with him. "Are you in love with [my wife]?!" the father rails.

"I am in love with you," the neighbor replies, "I am in love with you. And I am in love with your beautiful woman. And I am in love with your kids…. I am even in love with your anger!"

"Oh," the father says, "you're dying."

Our appreciation for the inimitability of life, for the beauty of the entire spectrum of its emotions and experiences, is greatly compounded in the face of death. It is then that the true value of each and every detail stands out in fresh relief. But there is reciprocity in the relationship between joy and life: just as life forms the basis for joy, our joyful moments are the ones in which we feel most "alive."

When people are frustrated, they expend a lot of energy dealing with themselves. Their actions are designed to provide a solution to their frustrations and needs. In contrast, when people find joy in life itself, their existence does not depend on anything else, and they are freed to engage in actions they deem meaningful. Because they no longer see such action as a means for achieving personal happiness, they act out of a very authentic place.

When I am sad or frustrated, I remind myself, "This is the day which the Lord has made; we will rejoice and be glad in it." It is a teaching I relate to my students constantly – every day we begin our faith lesson with "This is the day…"

Nitzavim-Vayelekh

The Good Urge and the Comfortable Urge

T he month of Elul, the last of the year, is a time of reflection and repentance. The word Elul – spelled *alef-lamed-vav-lamed* – is said to be an acronym for the verse "*Ani ledodi vedodi li*" ("I am my beloved's, and my beloved is mine" [Song 6:3]), which teaches us that the first step in any process of repentance has to come from us. Only afterward does God reciprocate. This is also apparent on a literal level in the verses in *Parashat Nitzavim*, which is usually read on the first Shabbat in Elul: "And [you] shall return to the Lord your God, and hearken to His voice according to all that I command you this day, you and your children...that then the Lord your God will turn your captivity, and have compassion upon you" (Deut. 30:2–3).

Underlying this call for a person to return to God is the assumption that humans possess free will. The capacity to choose is part of the basic definition of what it means to be a person, which sets us apart from the animals on one hand and the angels on the other. After calling for repentance, the Torah presents the individual with a choice between two options: "See, I have set before you this day life and good, and death and evil" (30:15).

Before I present one of the foundational insights of my life regarding repentance and choice, I want to tell the story that led me to it.

Better for a Person Not to Have Been Created

On December 27, 2002, during a Friday night meal at the Otniel Yeshiva, while students were dancing in the mess room and singing "O give thanks to the Lord, for He is good, for His mercy endures forever" (Ps. 136:1), terrorists stormed the kitchen and murdered four students who were on duty there: Noam Apter, Yehuda Bamberger, Gabriel Hoter, and Zvi Ziemen. The contrast between the words of the song and the horrific attack was excruciating. Yet, at the memorial services, despite their unfathomable pain, the bereaved fathers danced together and sang, "O give thanks to the Lord." Where did they draw the strength to continue to thank God?

> Our Rabbis taught: For two and a half years were the House of Shammai and the House of Hillel in dispute, the former asserting that it were better (*noah*) for man not to have been created than to have been created, and the latter maintaining that it is better (*noah*) for man to have been created than not to have been created. They finally took a vote and decided that it were better (*noah*) for man not to have been created than to have been created. (Eiruvin 13b)

The Talmud's conclusion seems to cast life in a pessimistic light. But Rabbi Mordechai Yosef Leiner, in his book *Mei HaShiloah* (*Likutim* on Eiruvin 13b), offers a more nuanced reading. He notes that in stating it were "better" for a person not to have been created, the Talmud uses the word "*noah*," which connotes comfort or ease, rather than the more standard "*tov.*" Indeed, the place whence we come and to which we return may be more comfortable, but it is good that we came into the world. This observation gives rise to a fundamental insight about existence: we are given life not so that we can be comfortable, but so that we can do good.

Life presents us with challenges every day, and we are constantly forced to choose. Sometimes we are aware of our choices, but more often than not we are unaware of having reached a crossroads and selected a path. These choices manifest in questions such as whether to assist someone who needs our help, whether to take responsibility for something, and whether to invest and immerse ourselves in the important things in life. Should we change? Generally speaking, we are not forced to choose between good and bad, but rather between what is good and what is comfortable. When we acknowledge that the meaning of our lives lies in doing good, rather than being comfortable, we are more able to raise our awareness of life's challenges and make the right choices.

We tend to think of people as having a "good inclination" and an "evil inclination." This dichotomy is dangerous, because it can lead us to conclude that refraining from evil actions is enough. In fact, the inclination that holds us back and prevents us from doing good is not the affinity for evil, but rather for comfort. As a society, too, I think the main weakness we must contend with is the pull exerted by this "comfort inclination."

There are people who contend in their lifetimes with challenging and extremely painful experiences. They endure such suffering that they feel, in their very bones, that it was better if they had "never been created," and lose the will to live. But this devastating conclusion does not have to be the end-all. People can pick themselves up and carry on with their lives, impelled by the realization that they must search for the good, for life's flavor and meaning, thus overcoming the greatest adversity. We must resist the urge to cease being, which is an expression of the "comfort inclination." In difficult times, we must focus on being active and finding the good, the meaning of life.

A woman whose husband was murdered once told me that in the days after the murder, she was unable to say *Modeh Ani*, the prayer uttered first thing in the morning, in which we give thanks to God for restoring our souls. She felt that she no longer wanted to live, and was thus incapable of giving thanks for her continued existence. Only later did she understand that the very fact of her survival was a sign that God had chosen her life. That basic insight drove her to search anew for her purpose in the world and to weave meaning into her life.

Some time after the terror attack in the yeshiva, at one of the memorial services, I understood for the first time that the *Mei HaShiloah*'s idea about what is good and what is comfortable is in fact the story of the attack. When the terrorists opened fire, the door separating the kitchen from the dining room, mere meters from the dancing students, was immediately shut and locked. That delayed the terrorists and gave the other students time to get their bearings and return fire. All four students who were on kitchen duty were slain, but in the last seconds of their lives they locked the door. In saving the lives of their friends, they chose the good over the easy.

Haazinu

Every Person Has a Letter

A few years ago, I spent a Shabbat at Bahad 1, the Israel Defense Force's officers' school. During the Friday evening meal, two non-religious soldiers delivered discourses on the weekly *parasha*, *Haazinu*. One cadet explained something that Rashi says. He asks why the eagle carries her young on her wings, and replies, "It is better that the arrow pierce me than that it should pierce my young" (Rashi on Deuteronomy 32:11). The cadet equated the eagle's treatment of her young to the proper conduct of an officer toward the soldiers under his command. Then one of the commanders of the courses linked the nearing end of the cycle of Torah readings to the impending graduation of yet another class of officer cadets.

I am amazed by the capacity of the weekly *parasha* to speak to the heart of every person – wherever they may be – and provide them with the existential meanings they need. There is a kabbalistic idea that says that the soul of every Jewish person is linked to a different letter of the Torah (*Zohar Ḥadash* on Song of Songs 91b), and that Hebrew word for Israel, Yisrael, is an acronym for "There are 600,000 letters in the Torah" (*"Yesh shishim ribo otiyot laTorah"*).

The number 600,000 stands for the overall number of Jews, implying that each Jew has a unique connection to the Torah. The truth is that even one's personal letter is not fixed but rather dynamic – as one's life changes so does one's reading of the Torah portions. One is constantly reading them with fresh eyes and gleaning new inspiration from them.

The Face of the Torah and the Face of Humankind

The Lord's greatness, the Mishna says, lies in His creation – out of a single person – of all of humanity, with its vast variety, in which each individual is unique:

> It was for this reason that man was first created as one person…to express the grandeur of the Holy One blessed be He: for a man strikes many coins from the same die, and all the coins are alike. But the King, the King of kings, the Holy One blessed be, He strikes every man from the die of the First Man, and yet no man is quite like his friend. Therefore, every person must say, "For my sake the world was created." (Mishna Sanhedrin 4:5)

The above also applies in relation to the Torah. The Talmud – in commenting on the verse "God has spoken once, twice have I heard this: that strength belongs to God" (Ps. 62:12) – explains: "One biblical verse may convey several teachings" (Sanhedrin 34a). The Lord's strength is apparent in the fact that each person hears something else in each of His utterances. There are a multitude of interpretations for the Torah, and no two are alike.

The truth is that the Torah's multifaceted nature can already be derived from the mishna in Sanhedrin, for it springs from the multifaceted nature of humanity. Because every individual is unique, each of us interprets the Torah differently, thus revealing a novel aspect of it.

Text and Interpretation

New ideas regarding the nature of hermeneutics can help us understand how a multitude of interpretations can all be authentic expressions of the text, and how each can be said to be "the words of the
living God" (Eiruvin 13b). The classic understanding of interpretation sees it as an uncovering of an original meaning intended
by the author. There is one truth that we must strive for, and only
one correct interpretation. The postmodern philosophy of our age
denies the existence of a "text" with a single meaning, and sees the
reader's subjective narrative as the be-all and end-all. Everything is
a commentary, as the intellectual Stanley Fish said.

But there is a third option, and that is that meaning is generated through the encounter between the interpretation and the
text. This idea is delineated by Professor Moshe Halbertal, who
quotes the German philosopher Hans-Georg Gadamer:

> The reaction that the text elicits in the reader is what gen-
> erates the meaning of the text, and it varies from reader
> to reader. That which catches the eye of the reader in one
> epoch will not catch the eye of the reader in a different
> epoch. The attempt to describe the relation within com-
> mentary as a relation between the subjective commentator
> and the object lying before him, waiting to be revealed, is
> incongruous with the phenomenology of commentary....
> The meaning of the text is not dormant within it, waiting
> to be revealed. Rather, it is only created in the encounter
> between the reader and the text.[1]

Halbertal cites Jewish sources to prove that Gadamer's outlook is similar to the manner in which the sages

---

1. Moshe Halbertal, *Interpretative Revolutions in the Making* [Hebrew] (Jerusalem:
Magnes, 1997), 194.

conceptualized the relation between human commentary and the Torah.[2] The Jerusalem Talmud (Sanhedrin 4:2) writes that the Torah was not given "cut and dried," so that its interpretations could yield "forty-nine facets for [declaring] impurity and forty-nine facets for [declaring] purity." Rather, the Torah is written in a purposely ambiguous style, so as to enable a multiplicity of interpretations. God loves the process by which commentary completes the text. In Tractate Makkot (22b), Rabba bemoans the "dull-witted" people who stand in honor of a Torah scroll, but not in honor of the sages who interpret it·

The idea that there are two Torahs – written and oral – derives from the understanding that there is both text and commentary, and that commentary has its own independent status. Rav Kook explains that the uniqueness of the written Torah lies in the fact that it is utterly divine, whereas the special quality of the oral Torah is generated by its human dimension:

> With the oral Torah we descend into life.... We sense that the spirit of the nation, which is bound to the light of the true Torah like a flame to an ember, gave rise, by way of its own special quality, to the oral Torah being created in its unique form. Certainly, this human Torah is part and parcel of the Lord's Torah; it too is the Lord's Torah.... All was conveyed to Moses at Sinai – even the future innovations of a veteran disciple. And these two beacons generate a complete world, in which heaven and earth converge. (*Shemona Kevatzim* 2:57)

On one hand, the oral Torah draws upon the written Torah and is bound to it "like a flame to an ember." On the other, it has a unique shape, formed by the singular characters of its

---

2. Ibid., 199.

commentators. This shape is dynamic and is "being created," as Rav Kook writes, in the present tense.[3] The Torah is an amalgam of the text and the commentator, of the divine and the human.

Uniting the Blessed Holy One and the *Shekhina*

Rav Kook's ideas are informed by the kabbalistic outlook on the Torah, which associates the written Torah with the divine sefira of *Tiferet*, or splendor, and the oral tradition with the sefira of *Malkhut*, or kingship. *Tiferet* represents the aspect of divinity that is outside reality, while *Malkhut* is the *Shekhina*, or divine presence, which lies inside reality. Much of Kabbala is preoccupied with the relation between *Tiferet* and *Malkhut* and the union between them, which is referred to as "*Yihud Kudsha Brikh Hu UShekhinte*," a joining of the blessed Holy One (*Tiferet*) and the *Shekhina* (*Malkhut*). Put more simply, the divine is both transcendent and immanent, with humanity being one of the expressions of immanent divinity. By interpreting the Torah, anyone can participate in the cosmological partnership between humanity and the divine, a process that brings about a union between *Tiferet* and *Malkhut*, heaven and earth.

Torah as Song

In the introduction to the song of *Haazinu*, God commands Moses, "Now therefore write this song for you" (Deut. 31:19). According to the Talmud, that statement refers not only to *Parashat Haazinu*, but also to the rest of the Torah (Nedarim 38a, Sanhedrin 21b). My friend Rabbi David Bigman gives two explanations for why the Torah is called "song." According to the first, the Torah is like song in that it "is not simple and straightforward, but rather multifaceted and allusive. It includes artful gaps that invite the reader

---

3. It bears noting that when this verse was quoted in *Orot HaTorah* (1:2), "being created" was changed to "was created."

to deep investigation of its mysterious words."[4] According to the second explanation, the Torah is like song in that its glory lies in the harmony generated by its many voices. When I contemplate the vast scope of voices that emerge in relation to the Torah, I envision a song that encompasses the entire world, overcoming boundaries between places and people, and between the present and every moment of the past – bringing everything together in one complete symphony that yet retains every single unique voice.

---

4. David Bigman, *The Fire and the Cloud* (Jerusalem: Gefen, 2011), 157. His first interpretation is based on the Netziv in paragraph 3 of his foreword to *Haamek Davar*. The second is based on the *Arukh HaShulḥan*'s foreword to *Ḥoshen Mishpat*.

Vezot Haberakha

Moses Is Not God

The Cult of Man

When I traveled in India I realized that the Torah's concerns regarding idolatry, and its warnings against it, are not as divorced from reality as I had previously thought. I understood that the depth of a given religion is no insurance against it becoming tainted with such practices. I suspect that were it not for our adherence to the prohibition of idolatry, our synagogues, like the temples in present-day India, would be filled with idols as the focal point of Jewish worship.

The great concern regarding idolatry always emanated from a fear that humans would be deified and worshiped. That has indeed been the fate of many spiritual teachers in the East and West. People tend to idolize the personalities they admire. In the film *The Life of Brian*, a satire on the life of Jesus, the protagonist does everything in his power to prevent the people from deifying him, and fails. Thus, rather than sanctify his message, they apotheosize him and his image, something that often has disastrous repercussions.

We do not know much about the historical man Jesus. It is certainly possible that he did not portray himself as divine, but rather as a spiritual teacher who sought to spread to all of humanity the foundational principles of the Torah (charity, faith, and love of God), and that his criticism toward the Jews was in fact directed only at those who did not live by those values. It is possible that, over time, his disciples turned him into a god.

Since the emphasis was placed on the man rather than the message, there were epochs when those who disputed Jesus' divine stature paid with their lives. That absurdity was most pronounced during the Inquisition, when in the name of "love" and a desire to "save" Jews from hell's inferno, they were tortured and burned alive.

From God to the Image of God

But even if deifying a man did not necessarily lead to idolatry, Judaism would still be firmly opposed to it. Counterintuitively, this stems from the very belief that human beings are created in the image of God. If *every* person is cast in the image of the divine, then there is indeed an expression of God in each of us. Yet, the idea that the divine is revealed in the human requires us to believe, as well, that there is an infinite divinity beyond us. A single, transcendent God can be an ever-present constant that unifies all of humanity and the entire universe. When an individual person is deified, it not only diminishes the concept of God; it also debases the very idea of God's revelation in the human – for what is the significance of individuals being created in His image when He is Himself human?

Moses and God

> So Moses the servant of the Lord died there.... And there has not arisen a prophet since in Israel like Moses, whom the Lord knew face to face; in all the signs and the wonders,

which the Lord sent him to do in the land of Egypt, to Pha-raoh, and to all his servants, and to all his land; and in all the mighty hand, and in all the great terror, which Moses wrought in the sight of all Israel. (Deut. 34:5, 10–12)

The Torah ends with Moses and his death. After forty years of dedication to God and His people, Moses is prevented from bringing the Israelites into the Promised Land, all due to a single sin. The passage in which Moses, who had previously refrained from asking for anything for himself, begs God to let him enter the land (Deut. 3:23–25), saying that God "hearkened not to me," is among the saddest in the Torah – and the most puzzling. How could God, who so often forgave the people their sins, refuse Moses, of all people?

It seems that the reason has more to do with Moses than with the people – specifically, with the danger that the people would worship him as a god. Moses performed miracles and ascended to God, and his face emitted beams of light (Ex. 34:30). It does not take much to imagine "Moses the man of God" (Deut. 33:1) turning into "Moses is God." Were that to have happened, we would probably be adherents of the "Mosesist" religion, bowing down to his image and worshiping his visage. That is why Moses has to sin and why he is denied atonement. His sin was etched in the Jewish collective memory as a reminder that even he was ultimately human.

Moses' sin is emblematic of this idea, in that he is com-manded to speak to the rock but strikes it instead, implying that the water gushes from it due to his action, which could lead the people to think that it is his power – not God's – at work (Num. 20:11–12). According to the Midrash, the reason the Torah says the location of Moses' burial remains unknown "to this day" (Deut. 34:6) is the fear that the gravesite would become a place of worship: "Why, then, has his sepulcher remained unknown? To prevent the people of Israel from going and erecting the Temple there, and bringing sacrifices there" (*Midrash Lekaḥ Tov* on *Vezot Haberakha*).

That concern did not abate in subsequent generations, which is why Moses goes almost unmentioned in the Passover Haggada – the one time he is mentioned, it is firmly in the context of God's glory, proving the rule: "And Israel saw the great work which the Lord did upon the Egyptians, and the people feared the Lord; and they believed in the Lord, and in His servant Moses" (Ex. 14:31).[1]

From Perfection to Greatness

The danger inherent in worshiping and deifying human beings is relevant not only to past figures, but also to present-day charismatic personalities. These include, in addition to spiritual teachers and cultural icons, athletes and politicians. Blind adulation divorced of critical thinking idolizes not only what is positive about such figures, but also their shortcomings – and these are easier to imitate. Furthermore, as the *Tao Te Ching*, the foundational text of Chinese philosophy, says, when there is too much adoration for the great people, the regular people lose their significance.

But there is also an opposite danger. When we have appreciation for truly great people, we gain an idea of our own potential, and are motivated to learn from them and grow. But we must acknowledge the greatness of each and every individual. Such awareness can protect us from the pull of narcissism and damaging solipsistic thought patterns.

How are we to strike a balance between deifying humanity, on one hand, and denigrating it, on the other? A famous quote by Mark Twain is helpful in this context: "When I was a boy of fourteen, my father was so ignorant I could hardly stand to have the old man around. But when I got to be twenty-one, I was astonished at how much the old man had learned in seven years." At

---

1. I heard this idea in a lecture delivered by Rabbi Emanuel Gettinger.

first, we think that a great person is utterly flawless. Such idealizations are bound to shatter when the person's shortcomings emerge. But we also have the capacity for a second innocence, in which, having come to grips with life's complexities, we can recognize and understand that even great people are only "people." Though they are imperfect, they are great, and as such they deserve our respect – even our admiration.

The fonts used in this book are from the Arno family

Maggid Books
The best of contemporary Jewish thought from
Koren Publishers Jerusalem Ltd.